Christian Economics for Students

WRITTEN BY GARY NORTH

Marx's Religion of Revolution
An Introduction to Christian Economics
Unconditional Surrender
Successful Investing in an Age of Envy
Government By Emergency
The Last Train Out
Backward, Christian Soldiers?
75 Bible Questions Your Instructors Pray You Won't Ask
Coined Freedom
12 Deadly Negatrends
Conspiracy
Unholy Spirits
Honest Money
Fighting Chance (with Arthur Robinson)
Dominion and Common Grace
Inherit the Earth
The Pirate Economy
Liberating Planet Earth
Healer of the Nations
Is the World Running Down?
Puritan Economic Experiments
When Justice Is Aborted
Political Polytheism
The Hoax of Higher Criticism
Victim's Rights
The Judeo-Christian Tradition
Millennialism and Social Theory
Westminster's Confession
Christian Reconstruction (with Gary DeMar)
The Coase Theorem
Salvation Through Inflation
Rapture Fever
Tithing and the Church
Crossed Fingers
The War on Mel Gibson
The Five Pillars of Biblical Success
The Covenantal Tithe
Gertrude Coogan's Bluff
Mises on Money
Conspiracy in Philadelphia
God's Covenants
Stay of Execution
Christian Economics in One Lesson
The Covenantal Structure of Christian Economics
Christian Economics for Students
Christian Economics for Teachers
Christian Economics for Activists
Christian Economics for Scholars
Protectionism and Poverty
The Five Pillars of Biblical Leadership
The Biblical Structure of History

An Economic Commentary on the Bible (31 vols.)

EDITED BY GARY NORTH

Foundations of Christian Scholarship
Tactics of Christian Resistance
The Theology of Christian Resistance
Theonomy: An Informed Response
The Journal of Christian Reconstruction (1974–1981)

Christian Economics for Students

An Introduction to the Biblical Basis of Economic Theory

Gary North

AXEHEAD
PRESS

First published by Axehead Press in 2025
Version 1.0

Submit typos and corrections to typos@axeheadpress.com.

Published by
Axehead Press
Moulton, Alabama

The NASB's convention of setting New Testament quotations of Old Testament material in all capitals has been changed to normal sentence case for readability purposes. For the same purpose, first lines of poetry have been lowercased when quoted when appropriate.

Paperback ISBN: 978-1-956329-19-3
Library of Congress Control Number: 2023942127

This book is dedicated to

PAX NORTH & BISHOP NORTH

Cousins

Contents

PART II

Fall

PART III

Redemption

Preface

I make the following assumption: you are a Trinitarian Christian. You are in agreement with this ancient confession of faith:

> I believe in God the Father Almighty, Maker of heaven and earth. And in Jesus Christ his only Son our Lord; who was conceived by the Holy Ghost, born of the Virgin Mary, suffered under Pontius Pilate, was crucified, dead, and buried; he descended into hell; the third day he rose again from the dead; he ascended into heaven, and sits at the right hand of God the Father Almighty; from thence he shall come to judge the living and the dead. I believe in the Holy Ghost; the holy catholic [universal] Church; the communion of saints; the forgiveness of sins; the resurrection of the body; and the life everlasting.

This is known as the Apostles' creed. There is an early version from AD 215. This version is from AD 542.

If you are a redeemed covenant-keeper, this book will be of great benefit to you if you read it. It will introduce you to the fundamentals of God's laws of economics. I am sure that you do not want to violate God's laws. This book will help you not to violate them.

This book is the result of my systematic study of every passage in the Bible that relates to economics. In separate books, I have provided commentaries on each passage. I began that project in the spring of 1973. I finished it in early 2012. I devoted over 16,000 hours to this work. No one paid me to do this. I wrote 31 volumes of books on my findings: over 8,500 typeset pages. The title: *An Economic Commentary on the Bible*. I also wrote ten supplementary volumes. No one before me had ever attempted anything like this. I doubt that anyone else will.

There will be critics of this book and the expanded volumes to follow. Most critics will deny that there is any such thing as Christian economics. A few will insist that I have misinterpreted the Bible. A handful will offer a rival version of Christian economics. But before you accept any of these lines of criticism, find out if the critic has written even one volume of exegesis of Bible passages. It is highly unlikely that he has. I can also assure you that he has not read all 31 of my volumes. So, his arguments will rest on prejudice, guesswork, and hostility to my conclusions. These arguments will not be based on detailed exegesis of biblical texts.

A. A Warning

You would be wise to understand this inescapable fact: you do not get something for nothing. This is a fundamental law of economics. Put more personally, with every benefit comes responsibility. Jesus taught this with respect to the final judgment:

> And the Lord said, "Who then is the faithful and sensible steward, whom his master will put in charge of his servants, to give them their rations at the proper time? Blessed is that slave whom his master finds so doing when he comes. Truly I say to you that he will put him in charge of all his possessions. But if that slave says in his heart, 'My master will take a long time to come,' and he begins to beat the other slaves, both men and women, and to eat and drink and get drunk; then the master of that slave will come on a day that he does not expect, and at an hour that he does not know, and will cut him in two, and assign him a place with the unbelievers. And that slave who knew his master's will and did not get ready or act in accordance with his will, will receive many blows, but the one who did not know it, and committed acts deserving of a beating, will receive only a few blows. From everyone who has been given much, much will be demanded; and to whom they entrusted much, of him they will ask all the more." (Luke 12:42–48)

There is something else to consider: *you must finish what you start.*

> But Jesus said to him, "No one, after putting his hand to the plow and looking back, is fit for the kingdom of God." (Luke 9:62)

Therefore, let me offer this warning: do not read this book unless you are prepared to implement what you find in it, assuming that you believe it is true. Do not be a hearer of the word, but not a doer.

> But prove yourselves doers of the word, and not just hearers who deceive themselves. For if anyone is a hearer of the word and not a doer, he is like a man who looks at his natural face in a mirror; for once he has looked at himself and gone away, he has immediately forgotten what kind of person he was. But one who has looked intently at the perfect law, the law of freedom, and has continued in it, not having become a forgetful hearer but an active doer, this person will be blessed in what he does. (James 1:22–25)

What is your primary motivation? Is it to increase your benefits, but minimize your responsibilities? In other words, are you trying to buy benefits from God with a minimal offer? This is the recommended approach of the humanist economist. Pay as little as possible for whatever you buy. Warning: this is not God's way.

B. Responsibility

God wants His people to increase their level of responsibility. Why? Because this is the way we perform more effective service to Him. We are to volunteer for additional responsibility (1) if we think we are competent, and (2) if this does not force us to stop doing something even more important. This has to do with a basic law of society: *power and influence flow to the person who takes responsibility*. Think of Moses. He did not want to go before Pharaoh. Think of Jonah. He did not want to go to Nineveh. In both cases, God forced them to take responsibility that they otherwise would have preferred avoiding.

The best-known example of a person taking responsibility first and benefitting later is the story of David and Goliath. The Philistine army and the Israelite army were stalemated. Goliath challenged the Israelites to send a warrior to fight him. The winner would win the war (I Sam. 17:8–10). This was a great example of the biblical doctrine of representation. Whose god would win? Test this by whose warrior would win. The Israelites were terrified (v. 11).

David had come to the battlefield in order to bring food to his brothers, who were in the army (I Sam. 17:17–20). David was not eligible to serve. He was too young. An Israelite had to be 20 years old to be eligible to serve in God's holy army (Ex. 30:14). So, he was safe. But he heard of the blessings the king would bestow on the man who killed Goliath: his daughter and lifetime exemption from taxes (I Sam. 17:25–27). Now, that's a deal! David volunteered. Why? For the reward and for God's cause. "What will be done for the man who kills this Philistine and rids Israel of the disgrace? For who is this uncircumcised Philistine, that he has dared to defy the armies of the living God?" (v. 26). Saul tried to dissuade him (v. 33). David ignored the warning. He was ready to fight. David did not put on a warrior's armor. He minimized his weapons. He carried five stones. He only needed one. He was relying on God to kill the giant (v. 37). He did not think he was at risk.

Power flowed to David from the moment he killed Goliath. He eventually became king of Israel. But with that high office came many troubles. Here is the biblical pattern: responsibility leads to blessings lead to more responsibility leads to more blessings. This is the pattern of dominion.

The biblical system of cause and effect offers covenant-keepers many benefits for taking on added responsibility. But the quest for responsibility should be primary. The quest for benefits should be secondary. The added benefits make it possible to fulfill the added responsibility and add even more responsibility. This view of responsibility reverses the common view of responsibility as a liability to be avoided if possible.

So, if you are seeking benefits with a minimal increase of responsibility, be prepared to change your mind. This book is going to increase your benefits, but only with a substantial increase in your responsibility. Are you prepared for this? If not, either get prepared or else avoid reading this book.

Introduction

For Christ did not enter a holy place made by hands, a mere copy of the true one, but into heaven itself, now to appear in the presence of God for us; nor was it that He would offer Himself often, as the high priest enters the Holy Place year by year with blood that is not his own. Otherwise, He would have needed to suffer often since the foundation of the world; but now once at the consummation of the ages He has been revealed to put away sin by the sacrifice of Himself. And just as it is destined for people to die once, and after this comes judgment, so Christ also, having been offered once to bear the sins of many, will appear a second time for salvation without reference to sin, to those who eagerly await Him.

Hebrews 9:24–28

Christianity brought a new view of time to the world: linear time. Christianity teaches that there are three periods in history: creation, fall, and redemption. History will end with the final judgment. This view was inherent in Hebrew religion, but the Old Testament only hints at final judgment, mainly in the last three verses of the Book of Daniel. In the New Testament, the doctrine of the final judgment is taught clearly in Matthew 25:31–46 and Revelation 20:14–15.

The rival view of time is cyclical time. It was taught by the ancient Greeks and Romans. It is still taught in Eastern religions. Cyclical time affects the cosmos. There is no doctrine of permanent progress or permanent loss. Individuals are subject to karma: the transmigration of souls. After seemingly endless reincarnations, a truly righteous soul disappears into the cosmic one and loses all individuality. This is the end of its history. But there is no final judgment.

In the Bible, the doctrine of creation occupies just two chapters: Genesis 1 and 2. Genesis 3 tells the story of the fall. The last part of the chapter tell of the beginning of redemption: God separates Adam and Eve from the tree of life. He provides them with animal skins. One or more animals had to die: shed blood. Final judgment occurs after the resurrection of bodies described in Revelation 20:14–15. The final two chapters of Revelation do not refer to history but rather to the post-resurrection, post-final judgment new heavens and new earth. This is not heaven, which is a holding area for souls (Rev. 6:10–11), and it is not hell, which is also a holding area for souls (Luke 16).

The meaning of redemption is tied to the word for redeem: *to buy back*. Christianity teaches that the life, death, resurrection, and ascension of Jesus Christ in history constituted a comprehensive act of redemption. This has paid God for the sins of God's people, who are covenant-keepers by the grace of God. The Apostle Paul wrote: "For there is one God, and one mediator also between God and mankind, the man Christ Jesus, who gave Himself as a ransom for all, the testimony given at the proper time" (I Tim. 2:5–6). Conclusion: "You were bought for a price; do not become slaves of people" (I Cor. 7:23). This has to do with individual salvation.

> For while we were still helpless, at the right time Christ died for the ungodly. For one will hardly die for a righteous person; though perhaps for the good person someone would even dare to die. But God demonstrates His own love toward us, in that while we were still sinners, Christ died for us. Much more then, having now been justified by His blood, we shall be saved from the wrath of God through Him. For if while we were enemies we were reconciled to God through the death of His Son, much more, having been reconciled, we shall be saved by His life. And not only this, but we also celebrate in God through our Lord Jesus Christ, through whom we have now received the reconciliation. (Rom. 5:6–11)

This act of redemption on behalf of individuals in history also applies to institutions in history. Jesus made this clear in what has become known as the Great Commission.

> And Jesus came up and spoke to them, saying, "All authority in heaven and on earth has been given to Me. Go, therefore, and make disciples

> of all the nations, baptizing them in the name of the Father and the Son and the Holy Spirit, teaching them to follow all that I commanded you; and behold, I am with you always, to the end of the age." (Matt. 28:18–20)

Jesus taught His disciples to pray this in what Christians call the Lord's Prayer: "Your kingdom come. Your will be done, on earth as it is in heaven" (Matt. 6:10). This refers to God's kingdom in history. The prayer asks God to make God's kingdom in history more like God's kingdom in heaven, where there is no sin and therefore no disparity between God's ethical standards and people's obedience in every area of life. *This is a request for God's intervention in history in order to redeem society progressively.* This is the meaning of the word "kingdom." It refers to the realm of a king. It is not a call for God to end history or to remove Christians from history. This request is followed by two economic requests: "Give us this day our daily bread. And forgive us our debts, as we also have forgiven our debtors" (Matt. 6:11–12). The historical context is inescapable. So are the economic implications.

A. Creation, Fall, Redemption

I return to where I began, although not cyclically: linear history. There is a beginning, comprehensive development, and a culmination. This applies to individuals. It also applies to institutions.

The Bible teaches that no area of life is exempt from the effects of sin. It teaches that redeemed people are to work to extend the kingdom of God into every area of life. If you do not believe this, please write a list of those areas of life that Jesus did not die to redeem. He supposedly has declared to His people the following: "You do not need to work to improve or reform these areas of life. They are neutral areas that are not in any way cursed by the effects of sin. The gospel of redemption does not apply to them. Leave them alone. Focus your attention elsewhere." My prediction: this will be a short list. My warning: there should be nothing in this list. It should be blank.

When we consider the first two chapters of Genesis, we see how things were supposed to be. This is how things were before sin entered the world. *This is the world we have lost.*

In Genesis 3, we read of the ethical rebellion of man. It is the story of a theft. God had placed a judicial boundary around a single tree: "No trespassing." He had warned of consequences of violating this boundary.

> The LORD God commanded the man, saying, "From any tree of the garden you may freely eat; but from the tree of the knowledge of good and evil you shall not eat, for on the day that you eat from it you will certainly die." (Gen. 2:16–17)

Everything else was allowed, including access to the tree of life. But Eve and then Adam violated the boundary. They committed criminal trespass. They violated God's property rights. This brought initial judgment against the man, the woman, and the serpent. But there was a promise to the serpent: "And I will make enemies of you and the woman, and of your offspring and her Descendant; He shall bruise you on the head, and you shall bruise Him on the heel" (Gen. 3:15). There will be warfare in history between the serpent and mankind. This conflict will represent the historical conflict between the kingdom of God and the kingdom of Satan. This conflict will extend to every area of life, which is an ethical battlefield. There is no escape from this conflict. There is no neutral zone. "The one who is not with Me is against Me; and the one who does not gather with Me scatters" (Matt. 12:30). It will continue until the end of time.

In between the fall of man and the final judgment there is a conflict between bondage and redemption. It is either bondage to sin or bondage to a sovereign God. Men are always in bondage to one or the other. "But thanks be to God that though you were slaves of sin, you became obedient from the heart to that form of teaching to which you were entrusted, and after being freed from sin, you became slaves to righteousness" (Rom. 6:17–18).

There is no zone of neutrality in this conflict. There is no port in the storm. In every area of life, covenant-keepers should ask themselves these three questions:

1. What did we have before the fall?
2. What did we lose because of the fall?
3. How can we get it back?

B. Economics

This book is about a field of study known as economics. It is the study of how people achieve their goals through exchange. Day by day, moment by moment, we exchange one set of conditions for another. We move closer to the day of final judgment, both individually and cosmically. Using the language of a pre-digital era, the clock keeps ticking.

Because of the structure of God's covenant with men as individuals and mankind in general, individuals possess the ability and the legal right in God's eyes to make offers to exchange goods and services with others. This is how we seek to better our conditions without resorting to theft or violence. We offer to buy, which is simultaneously an offer to sell. "I am willing to trade what I own because you own what I want." In the phrase for which Americans are deservedly famous, "Let's make a deal." The intellectual discipline of economics explores the foundations and ramifications of making deals.

Because this is a book on Christian economics, it is the study of deals under three conditions: creation, fall, and redemption. The fall involved a violation of God's property rights. That was the only way that mankind could fall. The boundary around the tree was the only boundary that God told mankind not to violate. Similarly, the concept of redemption is at bottom economic: the purchase of salvation by Jesus Christ on behalf of His people. He paid this price to God. He did not pay Satan. Satan is a thief and a squatter. He owns nothing of his own on his own.

Christian economics begins with the concept of ownership. This is because it begins with the doctrine of creation. This is where the Bible begins: "In the beginning God created the heavens and the earth" (Gen. 1:1). This act of creation established God as the owner of all that exists. "For every animal of the forest is Mine, the cattle on a thousand hills" (Ps. 50:10). To understand what we have lost requires that we understand what we had before the fall, and on what legal basis. Similarly, to understand how we can regain what we have lost, we must understand the process of redemption. At bottom, this is a legal matter. The final judgment will be intensely legal. But because the fall was judicially about theft, which is an economic crime, *redemption affects economics.*

It is about buying back the world we have lost, and then improving it, as originally required by God. "Then the LORD God took the man and put him in the Garden of Eden to cultivate it and tend it" (Gen. 2:15). This was an extension of God's permanent assignment to mankind:

> God blessed them; and God said to them, "Be fruitful and multiply, and fill the earth, and subdue it; and rule over the fish of the sea and over the birds of the sky and over every living thing that moves on the earth." Then God said, "Behold, I have given you every plant yielding seed that is on the surface of all the earth, and every tree which has fruit yielding seed; it shall be food for you; and to every animal of the earth and to every bird of the sky and to everything that moves on the earth which has life, I have given every green plant for food"; and it was so. (Gen. 1:28–31).

With this as background, it is time to begin the inquiry of economics as a manifestation of redemption in history. It asks these three questions.

1. What did we have before the fall?
2. What did we lose because of the fall?
3. How can we get it back?

PART I

Creation

Introduction to Part I

"Know therefore that the Lord *your God, He is God, the faithful God, who keeps His covenant and His faithfulness to a thousand generations for those who love Him and keep His commandments..."*

Deuteronomy 7:9

This book is explicitly biblical. Unless you have read one of my previous books, you have never read a book on economics that is structured in the way that this one is. It is structured in terms of the five points of every biblical covenant. You may be unfamiliar with the five points of the biblical covenant's structure. They are as follows: God's transcendence, a hierarchical system of authority, ethics, sanctions, and time. By time, I also mean the world beyond the final judgment.

My thinking about the biblical covenant was re-structured by a book that my Institute for Christian Economics published. It was written by Ray Sutton, *That You May Prosper: Dominion By Covenant* (1987).[1] It introduces the five points.

This structure governs the structure of God's creation of mankind: God, man, law, sanctions, and time. I have written a detailed book on this: *Unconditional Surrender: God's Program for Victory* (2010). I published the first edition in 1980, but that edition had only the first three points. I added sanctions and time in later editions.

In my 1987 book on economics in the ten-volume Biblical Blueprint Series, I adopted a variation of the structure that I use in this one:

1. Ray R. Sutton, *That You May Prosper: Dominion By Covenant*, 2nd ed. (Tyler, Texas: Institute for Christian Economics, [1987] 1992).

Inherit the Earth: Biblical Blueprints for Economics.[2] I have written a far more detailed book, *The Covenantal Structure of Christian Economics* (2018).[3] I have also written a short book, *God's Covenants* (2014).[4]

I have used a variation of the five points to explain social theory in general: sovereignty, authority, law, sanctions, and time. I have used these five points to structure my two-year high school course in the history of Western literature. I have also used it to structure my one-semester course in government. These courses are available on the Ron Paul Curriculum.

I used the five points to re-write a famous economics book written by my friend Henry Hazlitt. His book was called *Economics in One Lesson* (1946). Mine is called *Christian Economics in One Lesson* (2015).[5]

By adopting the five-point covenant structure, I am attempting to reconstruct all of economic theory. The same categories that govern Christian economics govern all forms of economics. Economists do not recognize this, but that is because they either do not understand the biblical covenant structure (likely) or else they don't think it applies to economics. But it does. The content of economics and social theory in general will differ in terms of the presuppositions regarding sovereignty, authority, law, sanctions, and time, but every comprehensive social theory has to include all five of these points.

Part I applies the five points to the days of creation and the brief period in which man had not sealed a covenant by eating from either the tree of life or the tree of the knowledge of good and evil. That was the age of innocence. I also briefly discuss the fall of man and some of the implications of the fall for economics. In Part II, I discuss the modern secular foundations of economic theory. In Part III, I discuss economics in the age of redemption. This covers the crucial question: "What has God revealed to Christians that will enable them to get back much of the world we have lost?"

---

2. Gary North, *Inherit the Earth: Biblical Blueprints for Economics* (Moulton, Alabama: Axehead Press, [1987] 2025).

3. Gary North, *The Covenantal Structure of Christian Economics* (Moulton, Alabama: Axehead Press, [2015, 2018] 2023).

4. Gary North, *God's Covenants* (Moulton, Alabama: Axehead Press, [2006, 2014] 2023).

5. Gary North, *Christian Economics in One Lesson* (Moulton, Alabama: Axehead Press, [2015] 2023).

I begin my study of economic theory with the biblical doctrine of creation: creation out of nothing. Obviously, this separates my approach from all other approaches by all other economists. Christian economics offers an exclusively and explicitly creationist economics. God spoke the cosmos into existence. The universe is not autonomous. It never was. Man is not autonomous. He never was. The laws of economics are not autonomous. Economic growth is not autonomous. The doctrine of autonomy is the product of the fall of man.

Chapter 1

Ownership

The earth is the Lord's, and all it contains, the world, and those who live in it. For He has founded it upon the seas and established it upon the rivers.

Psalm 24:1–2

Analysis

Point one of the biblical covenant is God's transcendence, yet also His presence. This is the biblical concept of God's sovereignty. It asks: "Who's in charge here?"

The Bible begins with this: "In the beginning God created the heavens and the earth" (Gen. 1:1). This fact conveys a message: all thought must begin with the Bible's account of God's creation of the universe out of nothing. The Bible's unique concept of creation out of nothing categorically denies the validity of all versions of the doctrine of cosmic evolution.

Every area of thought must begin here. This includes every academic discipline. The first chapter of Genesis makes this point clear: *the universe is personal, not impersonal.* It was created by God. Christianity adds this: God is in three Persons. The creation was the work of Jesus, the Second Person of the Trinity. Paul wrote:

> He is the image of the invisible God, the firstborn of all creation: for by Him all things were created, both in the heavens and on earth, visible

> and invisible, whether thrones, or dominions, or rulers, or authorities—all things have been created through Him and for Him. He is before all things, and in Him all things hold together. He is also the head of the body, the church; and He is the beginning, the firstborn from the dead, so that He Himself will come to have first place in everything. For it was the Father's good pleasure for all the fullness to dwell in Him, and through Him to reconcile all things to Himself, whether things on earth or things in heaven, having made peace through the blood of His cross. (Col. 1:15–20).

The intellectual discipline of economics must begin with the biblical doctrine of creation in order to be accurate. How does the doctrine of creation apply to economics? It establishes the doctrine of original ownership. This is asserted explicitly by Psalm 24:1–2. Therefore, every economist should begin his treatise or textbook on economics with the doctrine of God's absolute ownership of the universe. This is where I start.

A. God's Absolute Ownership

Point one of the biblical covenant is God's transcendence, yet also His presence. This is the biblical concept of God's sovereignty. It asks: "Who's in charge here?" How does this apply to God's ownership?

God is the Creator. This brings us to the most important single doctrine of the Bible: *the Creator-creature distinction*. This doctrine establishes that it is God and God alone who is the absolute ruler over the entire creation. God established the laws by which the creation operates, and He continually judges all the creation in terms of His law and His requirements. This is the doctrine of the original creation. God created the world; therefore, He owns it. He is the absolute owner of everything. As we will see later on, He has delegated the ownership of the earth to mankind. The child is made in God's image (Gen. 1:26), and this is why it is so easy for a child to learn the concept "mine."

The first principle of a biblical covenant is the principle of *transcendence*: God's absolute supremacy. God reigns supreme over everything. This means that He is high above the creation, and totally different from it. We deal with a sovereign God. In short, God runs the show.

This principle of transcendence relates to economics because ownership is ultimately theocentric (God-centered). He created all that exists, and He is at the center of the universe as its owner. *This means that ownership is ultimately a theological concept.* It cannot be properly understood without reference to God as the absolute owner of the creation. Similarly, it is impossible to discuss properly the responsibilities of ownership, which is what this book is all about, without also discussing what God specifically requires of men in their capacity as owners of property.

Biblical transcendence is unique. It also involves God's presence. The God of the Bible is not a deistic god who wound up the cosmic clock eons ago and then departed. He is present with the creation. Yet God is not a god of pantheism: immersed in the creation. He possesses absolute sovereignty over it. He is not struggling for control from inside it.

The doctrine of creation leads to a second doctrine, the doctrine of providence, meaning God's full-time maintaining and sustaining of the creation. God watches over and cares for the universe in a personal way. He sees everything. He knows everything: *omniscience.* "And there is no creature hidden from His sight, but all things are open and laid bare to the eyes of Him to whom we must answer" (Heb. 4:13). He has total control over the cosmos: *omnipotence.* "It is He who made the earth by His power, Who established the world by His wisdom; and by His understanding He has stretched out the heavens" (Jer. 10:12). He is everywhere: *omnipresence.* "If I ascend to heaven, You are there; if I make my bed in Sheol, behold, You are there" (Ps. 139:8). It is through the power of God that the earth is sustained. God also sustains the universe. It is not autonomous. In short: no God—no universe.

God created and sustains everything. This is why the Psalmist announced that God is the owner of all the earth. The cattle on the thousand hills are His (Ps. 50:10). So are the hills. There is nothing on earth that God does not absolutely, completely own.

B. Trinitarian Ownership

Point two of the biblical covenant is hierarchical authority. It asks: "To whom do I report?" How does this apply to God's ownership?

This book deals with Christian economics. Christianity preaches the doctrine of the Trinity. It preaches a unified God who exists in three Persons: Father, Son, and Holy Ghost. What about hierarchy? Hierarchy applies to the concept of the economic Trinity. To understand this concept, you should be also aware of the more familiar doctrine of the ontological Trinity, which is not hierarchical.

1. *Ontological Trinity*

What does "ontological" mean? It means "being." The doctrine of the Trinity is a twofold doctrine. The creeds of the church have always insisted that the three Persons of the Trinity are of equal importance, majesty, power, and so forth. In other words, they are one being. There are not three separate gods. In the language of the Nicene Creed, which was formulated in AD 325, speaking of Father and Son:

> I believe in one God, the Father Almighty, Maker of heaven and earth, and of all things visible and invisible. And in one Lord Jesus Christ, the only-begotten Son of God, begotten of the Father before all worlds; God of God, Light of Light, very God of very God; begotten, not made, being of one substance with the Father, by whom all things were made.

This announced the doctrine of creation, and it immediately followed this with an affirmation of the equality of Father and Son: "being of one substance." Theologians call this the ontological Trinity. It has to do with the fundamental being of God.

2. *Economic Trinity*

Theologians have also insisted on hierarchy within the Trinity. Jesus insisted that He was subordinate to the Father. "For I have come down from heaven, not to do My own will, but the will of Him who sent Me" (John 6:38). He also insisted that anyone who had seen Him had seen the Father (John 14:9). That is, He represented the Father. He still does. The doctrine of representation is an aspect of point two of the biblical covenant.

With respect to God's relationship with mankind, there is a *hierarchy of responsibility*. There is a hierarchical relationship within the Trinity insofar as the Trinity interacts with the creation. Jesus represented God to mankind in history, and He represents mankind before the throne of God as the high priest (Heb. 4:14–16). This is basic Christian theology. It has to do with the very nature of God, and then God's relationship with the creation through mankind. The Trinity is a *functional hierarchy*, not an ontological hierarchy. We pray to God the Father in the name of Jesus Christ (John 14:14). Christ represents God to mankind and mankind to God.

History is about the representation of Jesus Christ. Psalm 110:1, which is quoted repeatedly in the New Testament, declares: "The LORD says to my Lord: 'Sit at My right hand until I make Your enemies a footstool for Your feet.'" The apostle Paul wrote about the end of history:

> ...then comes the end, when He hands over the kingdom to our God and Father, when He has abolished all rule and all authority and power. For He must reign until He has put all His enemies under His feet. The last enemy that will be abolished is death. For He has put all things in subjection under His feet. But when He says, "All things are put in subjection," it is clear that this excludes the Father who put all things in subjection to Him. When all things are subjected to Him, then the Son Himself will also be subjected to the One who subjected all things to Him, so that God may be all in all. (I Cor. 15:24–28)

3. *Mankind's Ownership*

God's required system of ownership reflects His Trinitarian being, which reflects both unity (one God) and diversity (three Persons). This is why God sets forth rules of ownership that are at the same time collective (unity) and individualistic (diversity). Some pieces of property are owned by individuals. Some are owned by families. Other pieces of property are owned by associations and corporations. Some are owned by churches, and some are owned by the civil government, meaning the state.

We also find in the Bible a system of overlapping ownership. Certain pieces of property are owned primarily by individuals but only secondarily by the state. In other cases, property is owned by individuals, but families also have rightful claims. In other words, property must never be defined as exclusively and absolutely owned by any single human being or any single human institution. This conclusion is implied by the very statement which begins this chapter: God alone is the absolute owner of all the creation. He, and He alone, possesses absolute rights of ownership. All other ownership claims are subordinate.

When we speak of human ownership, we should speak of God-given ownership. God is the absolute and ultimate ruler over all the creation, and therefore He is the absolute owner of the creation. We are told, however, that God has delegated to man the responsibility of caring for the creation (Gen. 1:28). Man is therefore a steward under the overall supervision of God. This means that man is responsible to God for the proper administration of everything that has been entrusted to him. This relationship is hierarchical.

C. Ethics and Ownership

Point three of the biblical covenant is law. It asks: "What are the rules?" *There is no covenant without law.* How does this apply to God's ownership?

God issued the command to Adam and Eve to be fruitful and multiply, and to exercise dominion across the face of the earth. This was not an option. The very definition of mankind rests upon this original command, which I call *the dominion covenant.* Built into every individual is the desire to extend his reign over the creation.

The second phase of the dominion covenant was God's transfer of ownership of the garden to Adam. He was to keep it and defend it. "Then the LORD God took the man and put him in the Garden of Eden to cultivate it and tend it" (Gen. 2:15). Third came the negative command and the negative sanction. "From any tree of the garden you may freely eat; but from the tree of the knowledge of good and evil you shall not eat, for on the day that you eat from it you will certainly die" (Gen. 2:16b–17). Fourth, Adam now faced a covenantal decision. Would he formally affirm this covenant or formally reject it?

The dominion covenant before the fall had a boundary: the forbidden tree. It has far more boundaries today. These boundaries are primarily ethical: right versus wrong. They are also judicial: legal versus illegal. They are also economic: profitable versus unprofitable. When individuals and institutions violate these boundaries, God brings negative sanctions against them. Some of these sanctions are from within the creation itself, such as venereal diseases. Some are imposed by other societies: war. Some are imposed by civil magistrates. Some are imposed by the marketplace itself. *Without sanctions, there are no laws. There are only suggestions.*

D. Profit and Loss

Point four of the biblical covenant is sanctions. It asks: "What do I get if I obey? Disobey?" How does this apply to God's ownership?

These sanctions have to do with covenantal oaths: oaths of allegiance. A lawful covenantal oath invokes God's judgments in the form of sanctions, positive and negative, on the person who takes the oath. The oath ratifies the covenant. Without it, there is no covenant. How does this apply to the doctrine of God's ownership?

The dominion covenant was established before the creation of Adam. It was announced by God to God. Mankind must subdue the earth. But there was no ratifying oath from Adam. There was an implicit ratification by God in Adam's name as God's son. This was a representative oath. It had to be formally confirmed or rejected by Adam at some point in time. Adam lived briefly in a unique period of time: *a church covenant without sacramental ratification.* That was the test period of his obedience.

A church covenant requires oath-signs as ratifications. In the Old Testament, the oath-signs were circumcision (Abraham) and later passover (Moses). In the New Testament, they are baptism and the Lord's Supper. There were two covenantal trees in the garden: the forbidden tree and the tree of life (Gen. 2:9). Adam could eat from the tree of life. The benefit was eternal life. That was a crucial positive sanction. That would have affirmed the dominion covenant on God's terms: obedience. Alternatively, he could eat of the forbidden tree. That would have denied the dominion covenant on God's terms. It would have been affirmation of the dominion covenant on man's terms: autonomy (self-law). Adam at some point would have to affirm or reject God's covenantal authority. The means of either affirmation or rejection was a communion meal at a tree. Which tree would Adam choose?

He faced a choice: profit or loss, life or death. These remain men's choices. But in the garden prior to the fall, Adam initially deferred making a decision. He could postpone this by avoiding both trees. But it is clear from Genesis 3 that he and Eve did not consider eating from the tree of life. The forbidden tree was at the center of their attention.

It was judicially mandatory that Adam seal the dominion covenant or reject it by means of a communion meal. There had to be an oath-sign. He postponed making the decision. He let his wife decide which tree to approach first. He deferred leadership to her.

Economists acknowledge the existence of economic patterns. Free-market economists believe that most of these patterns are imposed by the market itself. They are imposed in a specific form: *accounting profits and losses*. Economists generally do not believe in the existence of economic laws that are outside the institutional sanctions of profit and loss. They do not speak of economic laws as the equivalent of gravity. They also do not speak of economic laws as the equivalent of a moral code. They speak only of market sanctions and their effects on behavior. They do not believe in an institutional order created by God, governed by His laws, and restrained by economic sanctions. They see the market's sanctions as autonomous, not imposed by God. When Adam Smith coined the phrase "the invisible hand," he was not talking about the hand of God. The deistic morality that he proclaimed in his 1759 book, *The Theory of Moral Sentiments*, was completely absent in *The Wealth of Nations* in 1776. Yet the same phrase appears in both volumes.

The twin sanctions of profit and loss remain in force. They are the heart of the market order. Christian economics teaches that these sanctions are still governed by biblical law, not by self-proclaimed autonomous man's law, whether market law or state law. *This makes Christian economics a matter of ethics primarily, not ethically neutral techniques.* This sets Christian economics apart from humanist economics.

E. Inheritance

Point five of the biblical covenant is succession. It asks: "Does this outfit have a future?" How does this apply to God's ownership?

Adam and Eve were told to have children. Their adult children were then to have children. Through time, compound growth of the population would have achieved a rapid filling of the earth. No deaths, when coupled with a high birth rate, would have produced a large population within a half a millennium. A 5% per year birth rate for 450 years produces 6.5 billion people from the initial pair. The higher the rate, the shorter the time period required to do this.

Mankind is required to serve as God's steward. Prior to the advent of compound population growth and compound economic growth, which began approximately in 1800 in North America and the British Isles, the world seemed to be a very large place for mankind to occupy. Today, we hear cries of alarm about population growth and an unsustainable economy in a world of limited natural resources. World population is over seven times what it was in 1800. The economist Robert Malthus in 1798 anonymously warned against the belief that population growth could continue for long, because resources were too scarce. Most people who read his book believed him. He was wrong.

The Bible clearly teaches the doctrine of long-term economic growth. It not only teaches that this is possible; it mandates it. It is an ethical responsibility for each individual to work to extend man's dominion, under God, across the face of the earth. This is the explicit message of Genesis 1:26–28. Each generation is expected to leave an inheritance for the next. "A good person leaves an inheritance to his grandchildren" (Prov. 13:22a). This would have compounded capital to match or exceed the growth of the population. Per capita wealth would have increased.

Conclusion

The biblical concept of ownership is centered in God. "For every animal of the forest is Mine, the cattle on a thousand hills" (Ps. 50:10). God is the absolute owner of all the creation, and He sustains it by means of His supreme ruling power. He established man as a manager over His property, and He has laid down laws for the administration and transfer of property that must be obeyed if this work is to be profitable. They are to be faithful stewards to God.

Economic theory must begin with the doctrine of the creation. It therefore must begin with the doctrine of original ownership. It does not begin with the doctrine of self-ownership by man.

This leads us to a more detailed discussion of what I call the dominion covenant: the legal relationship between God and mankind regarding the extension of the kingdom of God in history.

CHAPTER 2

STEWARDSHIP

Then God said, "Let Us make mankind in Our image, according to Our likeness; and let them rule over the fish of the sea and over the birds of the sky and over the livestock and over all the earth, and over every crawling thing that crawls on the earth." So God created man in His own image, in the image of God He created him; male and female He created them. God blessed them; and God said to them, "Be fruitful and multiply, and fill the earth, and subdue it; and rule over the fish of the sea and over the birds of the sky and over every living thing that moves on the earth."

GENESIS 1:26–28

ANALYSIS

The first principle of a biblical covenant is the sovereignty of God. This means the absolute transcendence of God. In the field of economic theory, this principle is revealed in the doctrine of God's original ownership of all the creation, including mankind.

The second principle of a biblical covenant identifies the principle of hierarchical authority. This is also the law of *judicial representation*. God directly and personally controls His creation (principle one: transcendence). Nevertheless, God has delegated to mankind the full responsibility of caring for the earth as a whole. God doesn't directly control the earth apart from those He has chosen to manage His property. He directly controlled all of it during the first week of creation, but He no longer does. In His providential control and mercy, He has decided to delegate control over His property to mankind throughout history.

This raises a whole series of very difficult questions. The most important question is: What or who is the primary manager of God's property?

A. Image of God

Point one of the biblical covenant is God's transcendence, yet also His presence. This is the biblical concept of God's sovereignty. It asks: "Who's in charge here?" How does this apply to stewardship under God?

God is present with mankind. He is not a distant deistic god. He is the God of the covenant. He has made a covenant with redeemed men. It is the same covenant that He established on day six of the creation week. Covenant-keepers are enabled by grace to ratify that original covenant, unlike Adam, who ratified his own version of the dominion covenant: a man-centered version.

The passage begins: "Let Us make mankind in Our image, according to Our likeness" (Gen. 1:26). This is fundamental to our understanding of point two of the biblical covenant: hierarchy. *Because man is made in God's image, he has a legitimate claim on authority.* God is both one and many: "Our image." So, this hierarchy involves grants of authority to individuals and collectives.

God did not turn over the administration of the world to angels. Angels have greater power than men do in history, but they do not possess greater authority. This is why redeemed men will judge the angels at the final judgment (I Cor. 6:2).

Because man is made in the image of God, he possesses similar characteristics, although on a creaturely basis. First, he has been delegated ownership. Second, he has been delegated authority. Third, he has been given the law, and it is his task in life to apply the law to specific circumstances. He is to protect God's property. Fourth, he has the ability to impute value and make judgments in terms of this law. In other words, he applies the general laws of God to specific cases. Fifth, he extends dominion in history by means of children. This is what God does in his extension of authority in history. God acts through mankind, and mankind is the family of God. There have been two branches of this family after the fall: the eternally disinherited heirs of Adam and the eternally inheriting heirs through adoption by means of Christ's substitutionary atonement on their behalf.

A heresy that has continually afflicted the church and the world in general is the idea that nature and man are in some way equal. The idea of the equality of nature and man is a mirage. People who argue for the symbiotic equality of man and nature usually come to the conclusion that nature is superior to man. They assume that nature has rights, just as man does. They usually do not say exactly who granted such rights to nature, other than autonomous nature. This is the concept of mother nature. It is the concept of Gaia: Mother Earth. It is the idea that man is basically subordinate to nature, and therefore any attempt by individuals or organizations to extend dominion over nature is perverse. This idea became widespread in the 1960s as an outgrowth of a popular book by an amateur ecologist, Rachel Carson: *Silent Spring*. It was a book against the use of DDT, a chemical which saved more lives in the twentieth century than any other invention of mankind. Her book launched the modern ecology movement. In the case of the deep ecology movement, mankind is identified as a cancer in nature: a malign, uncontrolled growth.

This view of mankind has been common in Eastern mysticism and in all forms of animism. Mankind is supposed to placate the gods of nature. He is not to violate the domains of the gods of nature. Biblical religion broke with all forms of animism.

Nature is subordinate to man. Certain aspects of nature have rights protecting them from men's interference, but this is only because God owns nature, and the terms of His lease to man specify the protection of His property. As with all property rights, these restrictions on men's use of property are rights of God as the original owner.

B. Delegated Ownership

Point two of the biblical covenant is hierarchical authority. It asks: "To whom do I report?" How does this apply to stewardship under God?

God is supreme. Man is subordinate. *Delegated ownership is the heart of the relationship between God and man.* God has delegated authority to mankind to administer nature on behalf of God. As soon as we use the phrase, "on behalf of," we are talking about the doctrine of representation. A similar phrase is this: "in the name of." This is a judicial relationship, having to do with law enforcement. It is also an economic relationship, having to do with the allocation of assets.

1. *Family Ownership*

Analogous to the Trinity, mankind is both one and many. The Bible teaches that property is primarily owned by families. God made His covenant with Adam and Eve. It specified biological multiplication. Mankind reproduces and extends dominion over the creation through the most universal institutional unit, the family. God placed Adam and Eve under the terms of the dominion covenant as a family. He told them to be fruitful and multiply. This is a biological task to be performed within the bounds of the family covenant.

When we are speaking of the world prior to the rebellion of mankind, we are speaking of a world in which there was voluntary cooperation. Clearly, there was no theft until the fall of man, which was the first act of rebellion. Prior to this act of theft, people did not steal from each other, nor would they have stolen from each other apart from sin. Because of the nature of the prohibition against eating from the tree of knowledge of good and evil, sin could only be committed against God. It had to do with a hierarchical relationship between God and mankind. The subordinates rebelled against their superior.

There was a hierarchical relationship between God and mankind. There was a hierarchical relationship between mankind and the earth. There was a hierarchical relationship within the family unit itself. The man was not to be alone. The woman's task was to assist him in his assignment to dress the garden and care for it. She was an assistant to him.

There would have been children. Again, there would be a hierarchical relationship within the family unit itself until such time as the children grew to maturity, married, and moved out of their parents' family. This pattern of family authority was established by God before the fall. "For this reason a man shall leave his father and his mother, and be joined to his wife; and they shall become one flesh" (Gen. 2:24).

So, with respect to the structure of ownership after the creation of man, it was a hierarchical relationship based on mankind's covenantal position as a subordinate under God but also as a ruler over the creation. *Ownership was inherently hierarchical from the beginning.* Before man was created, God was solely in charge. After the creation of man, God was still in charge, but He was no longer alone. Ownership became hierarchical. This was because God delegated authority over the earth to mankind.

2. *Individual Ownership*

Does this mean that individuals who are not married and who have never been married are not entitled to own property? No, because they are still heads of households: their own.

The biblical pattern is that children grow to maturity, and as they do, they take on greater responsibility. *Childhood is an exercise in the development of responsibility.* Because God delegated responsibility to mankind for overseeing the earth, individuals must develop responsibility associated with this task.

Each individual is different. People have different talents, goals, interests, hobbies, and everything else associated with economic production. Each person is held responsible for whatever skills or advantages that he has been given in life. This is a fundamental principle of responsibility: *to whom much is given, much is expected.* Jesus taught this explicitly:

> "And that slave who knew his master's will and did not get ready or act in accordance with his will, will receive many blows, but the one who did not know it, and committed acts deserving of a beating, will receive only a few blows. From everyone who has been given much, much will be demanded; and to whom they entrusted much, of him they will ask all the more." (Luke 12:47–48)

Therefore, God holds individuals responsible for the use of whatever gifts and benefits He has provided them. They are responsible to Him as stewards. This was built into the creation from day six.

This system of stewardship began in the garden. There would have been rewards to all producers. But some producers would have been more productive than others. Their rewards would not have been equal. There was no equality prior to the fall. *Inequality was basic to creation.* It still is.

C. Property Rights

Point three of the biblical covenant is law. It asks: "What are the rules?" How does this apply to stewardship under God?

Property rights are grounded in ethics. Christian economics teaches that the laws defending property rights are ethical. They are matters of right and wrong. They are not ethically neutral laws whose primary function is to promote efficiency.

The economist's concept of property rights rests on the idea of a *bundle of legal rights* associated with a particular piece of property. These rights are not inherent in the property. They are not natural rights. They are not intrinsic rights. They are *imputed rights, i.e., judicially declared rights.* They are initially declared by God as the original owner and then enforced by Him as the sovereign judge. Then they are declared and enforced by human courts. They create a legal boundary around the property. The owner can legally restrict access to this property.

1. *Boundaries*

Basic to God's relationship with mankind prior to the fall of man was the tree of the knowledge of good and evil. In the midst of the garden, God placed a tree which He declared to be off-limits for mankind. He allowed men to eat of any other tree, but access to this one tree was prohibited.

Similarly, property rights are basic to the development of a program of dominion in history. Analogous to the legal boundary around the tree of the knowledge of good and evil, there are boundaries around specific units of property. *The mark of legitimate authority is the legal authority to place boundaries around property.* The most fundamental of all property boundaries is the boundary around the oath of marriage. Husbands and wives have exclusive access to each other's bodies, and both have rights of exclusion. *This right of exclusion is the essence of every property right.* It is the right not to be interfered with in the use of property.

The tree of the knowledge of good and evil was representative of property rights in general. Men and women were to honor the designated boundary that excluded mankind from access to the tree, and then they were to use this as a model for the covenantal bond of marriage. They were also to use this exclusion as a model for establishing legal claims over specific pieces of property in the garden and beyond. They were supposed to become responsible for the administration of this property. They were responsible to God, a fact that had to do with delegated ownership of property. They were also responsible to each other, for they were to honor each other's claims of ownership. This enabled them to specialize in production. This led in turn to the division of labor.

2. *The Division of Labor*

From the beginning, there was an inherent division of labor. Christian theology rests on a twofold definition of the Trinity. Each of these definitions has to be acknowledged if the individual wants to maintain orthodoxy. The New Testament teaches the *equality in eternity* of the Persons in the Godhead: Father, Son, and Holy Ghost. Yet, with respect to God's *relation to humanity*, the Persons of the Godhead have different functions.

Equality and inequality also exist in humanity. There is *judicial equality*. Every individual is subject to the final judgment. This means there is an essential unity of humanity. Everyone is made in the image of God. Everyone is held accountable by God. There has to be a fundamental unity here. It is a unity of our basic being, and it is a *judicial unity*. Yet at the same time, different people have different talents (skills, not units of money). In order to extend their personal dominion in history, men and women must seek to improve their skills, accumulate more property, gain more authority, and accept greater responsibility. This leads to *economic inequality*.

There is a division of labor in society, and it affects every institutional relationship. This division of labor is based on the fact that different people have different skills. It also is based on the fact that each piece of land is different from the next piece. People live in different geographical areas, and therefore they specialize in production. Then they voluntarily trade with each other in order to increase their individual wealth and their family wealth. This is why there is voluntary cooperation among individuals. Individuals specialize in production. This is not the result of the fall of man. It was built into the very structure of the creation.

God intended that families would move out of the garden and into the rest of the world. He wanted them to subdue the whole earth. This is why He told Adam and Eve to be fruitful and multiply. More people meant more productivity. More people meant more wealth. More people meant a greater development of the earth, meaning the raw materials God had provided to mankind. *Grace precedes law.* Life is a manifestation of the grace of God. So is the earth itself. Had there been no rebellion, there still would have been extensive development of the earth's resources, as families spread across the face of the earth.

Individuals and families are responsible to God for increasing the capital value of the earth. God owns it. God expects mankind to increase it on His behalf. Individuals and organizations act as stewards, meaning legal representatives of God and also as economic representatives of God. This is a major economic aspect of hierarchy. It is an economic hierarchy pointing to God as Owner. It is also a judicial hierarchy over which God reigns: the kingdom of God.

To extend their dominion, individuals specialize in production. This increases their output. It increases their responsibility before God. They are responsible for increasing the value of their God-delegated zone of responsibility. They cooperate with each other, and they do so in the hopes that they as individuals will be better off after the cooperation. The primary area of cooperation is the family, but outside the family, it is the marketplace.

Again, this is not the result of the fall of man. This was built into the structure of humanity from the beginning. This is why God held Adam and Eve responsible individually, but this is also why He held them responsible as a family unit. God kept the family together when He expelled them from the garden of Eden. He showed grace to them as individuals, and He showed grace to them as family members. They were responsible to God as individuals, and they were responsible to God as family members. This delegation of ownership and responsibility is neither pure individualism nor pure collectivism. It is a mixture. It reflects the Trinity: one and many.

D. Accountability

Point four of the biblical covenant is sanctions. It asks: "What do I get if I obey? Disobey?" How does this apply to stewardship under God?

The archetype model is God's final judgment at the end of history, where all people will be held legally accountable (Matt. 25). God holds each person responsible for all of his actions. This is true in every area of life, not simply economics. Individuals are held eternally liable for their actions unless Christ's death, resurrection, and ascension have judicially erased their sins. Negative or positive sanctions are associated with disobedience or obedience to God. Negative sanctions fall heavily on covenant-breakers in eternity. The New Testament's doctrine of the final judgment makes it clear just how responsible individuals are (Luke 16; Rev. 20:14–15). But it was also clear in the rebellion in the garden. God cross-examined Adam first. Adam blamed Eve. God cross-examined Eve second. Eve blamed the serpent. God didn't bother to cross-examine the serpent. He simply cursed the serpent. My point is this: in the garden, the two individuals who made up the family of man, Adam and Eve, were quick to try to shift responsibility away from themselves as individuals, despite the fact that this blame-shifting would undermine the unity of their family. Adam after the fall had no loyalty to his family above his loyalty to himself. He had no loyalty to Eve above his loyalty to himself. This is a characteristic feature of sinful man in every society and in every time period. This is because individuals are responsible to God as individuals.

Everyone in history has received his life as a gift of God. *Grace precedes law.* Individuals are responsible to God from the moment of their conception. But if this is true, then there is individual ownership of property. Some people like to say that ownership begins with self-ownership, but this is incorrect except with respect to God. It begins, not with self-ownership, but with a lease from God for whatever property they possess. Everything they own comes from God. *Delegated ownership is the foundation of ownership by mankind.* Original ownership is God's, but He delegates ownership to individuals, families, and other covenantal and non-covenantal institutions. *Ownership is both individual and collective.* That is because no one is ultimately autonomous. At the same time, no one can escape personal responsibility for his administration of whatever God has given to him. This is clear in Jesus' parable of the talents. A talent was a unit of weight: gold or silver.

> "For it is just like a man about to go on a journey, who called his own slaves and entrusted his possessions to them. To one he gave five talents, to another, two, and to another, one, each according to his own ability; and he went on his journey. The one who had received the five talents immediately went and did business with them, and earned five more talents. In the same way the one who had received the two talents earned two more. But he who received the one talent went away and dug a hole in the ground, and hid his master's money. Now after a long time the master of those slaves came and settled accounts with them. The one who had received the five talents came up and brought five more talents, saying, 'Master, you entrusted five talents to me. See, I have earned five more talents.' His master said to him, 'Well done, good and faithful slave. You were faithful with a few things, I will put you in charge of many things; enter the joy of your master.' Also the one who had received the two talents came up and said, 'Master, you entrusted two talents to me. See, I have earned two more talents.' His master said to him, 'Well done, good and faithful slave. You were faithful with a few things, I will put you in charge of many things; enter the joy of your master.' Now the one who had received the one talent also came up and said, 'Master, I knew you to be a hard man, reaping where you did not sow, and gathering where you did not scatter seed. And I was afraid, so I went away and hid your talent in the ground. See, you still have what is yours.' But his master answered and said to him, 'You worthless, lazy slave! Did you know that I reap where I did not sow, and gather where I did not scatter seed? Then you ought to have put my money in the bank, and on my arrival I would have received my money back with interest. Therefore: take the talent away from him, and give it to the one who has the ten talents.' For to everyone who has, more shall be given, and

> he will have an abundance; but from the one who does not have, even what he does have shall be taken away. And throw the worthless slave into the outer darkness; in that place there will be weeping and gnashing of teeth." (Matt. 25:14–30)

Immediately following this passage is Jesus' description of the final judgment (Matt. 25:31–46).

E. Dominion Through Multiplication

Point five of the biblical covenant is succession. It asks: "Does this outfit have a future?" How does this apply to the doctrine of stewardship under God?

Genesis 1:28 reads as follows:

> God blessed them; and God said to them, "Be fruitful and multiply, and fill the earth, and subdue it; and rule over the fish of the sea and over the birds of the sky and over every living thing that moves on the earth."

This made it clear to Adam and Eve that biological reproduction is basic to the extension of mankind's authority across the face of the earth. God began testing them in the garden, but the garden was not to be their permanent place of residence. They were to use the garden as a training ground of dominion, but then they were to reproduce biologically, train up their children, and send their children out to replicate the process. They might have gone themselves, leaving the garden as a sanctuary. It was the place where the tree of life was planted, where they had eaten their first communion meal, thereby sealing the covenant by an oath-sign.

The economic idea here is the idea of economic growth. It has to do with biological expansion over nature. It has to do with increased productivity of individuals and families. It has to do with extending knowledge in history, which means also applying that knowledge to nature and society.

Despite the fact that God repeatedly announced to Himself regarding His work that it was good, there was more to be done. There was no flaw in the creation. It was not in some way inherently evil. But it was undeveloped. In this sense, the creation is a means of grace. *Grace precedes law.* God gave mankind a grant of capital. Mankind is to increase the value of this capital. It is God's capital, and it is mankind's responsibility to increase the value of this grant of capital. Everything is geared to growth. Everything is geared to expansion, meaning most importantly, the expansion of men's authority under God across the face of the earth. With each increase of the value of their capital, individuals and families increase the responsibility to continue to expand the value of their capital. This is the foundation of the concept of economic growth: an increase in personal responsibility.

At this point, I must make it clear that I have broken fundamentally with Adam Smith and virtually all modern economic theory. Here is Smith's formulation of the primary goal of production. He stated categorically that the goal of production is consumption.

> Consumption is the sole end and purpose of all production; and the interest of the producer ought to be attended to only so far as it may be necessary for promoting that of the consumer. The maxim is so perfectly self-evident that it would be absurd to attempt to prove it. But in the mercantile system the interest of the consumer is almost constantly sacrificed to that of the producer; and it seems to consider production, and not consumption, as the ultimate end and object of all industry and commerce.[1]

In stark contrast with this, the Bible teaches that consumption is a reward for production. The Bible makes it clear that God owns the world, and mankind administers the world for the benefit of God. God is originally productive; mankind is derivatively productive. The assigned goal of mankind is to extend mankind's dominion across the face of the earth, but only on behalf of God. This requires thrift: consuming less than we receive as income. It also requires wise investing, i.e., entrepreneurship: allocating capital in the present in order to meet customer demand in the future. *Dominion is the primary purpose of all production.* Consumption is a gracious reward and a means of motivation that God offers to those whom He determines have served him most faithfully, which means most efficiently. He does this through the profit-

1. Adam Smith, *The Wealth of Nations* (1776), bk. IV, ch. 8, par. 49

and-loss system. *The profit-and-loss system is representative of the final judgment.* It is a warning of things to come. But in the garden, there was only one way to experience a loss: by eating from the forbidden tree. Everything else that man could do would have been ethically and judicially acceptable to God, even 100% consumption. But this would not have produced greater wealth. This would have delayed dominion.

There are people who love their work so much that they say that they would do it, even if they were paid nothing. But they have to be paid something, or else they would starve to death. Still, the attitude of those who say this is correct. If somebody asked me if I write for a living, I would tell the person that I live for my writing. It happens that I earn money for some of my writing, which I call my job. But the most important writing that I do is in the field of Christian economics, for which I have never been paid. I did this from the beginning. I made sure that I would take no money from my writing in the field of Christian economics. I wanted to make it clear that any money that I raised to print books and market my materials was to be used exclusively for this, not to provide a source of income for me. I distinguish between my job and my calling. My job is what puts food on the table. My calling is the most important work that I can do in which I would be most difficult to replace. That is my work to develop Christian economic theory.

Conclusion

God is the absolute owner of the entire creation. In His grace, He created man to represent Him in the subduing of the earth. God announced to Adam and Eve that they were His stewards, and they were responsible to Him. This is why they were not allowed to eat from the forbidden tree. There would be negative sanctions against them if they did.

With respect to everything else in the garden of the world, they had full authority. They could do whatever they wanted with it. They and their children and their grandchildren were to spread across the face of the earth, bringing the whole world under their authority. But their authority was not autonomous. Their authority was representative. It was representative judicially, and they would be held accountable. But it was also representative economically, and they would prosper to the extent that they were effective in subduing the earth.

None of this has changed as a result of the fall of man. Man is still defined as a representative agent of God, both judicially and economically. Man is still defined in terms of the assignment given by God at the time of their creation. In fact, God announced this even before Adam and Eve were created. The announcement began: "Let us." Adam and Eve were not present to hear that announcement. It was made on their behalf covenantally, but they had no part in accepting it at the time of the announcement was made. Grace precedes law, but there is always law in a covenant. There are always sanctions, both positive and negative.

Christian economics teaches explicitly that ownership is delegated from God, and is therefore representative, not autonomous. Any attempt to say that man's ownership is autonomous, including his self-ownership, is a denial of the biblical doctrine of ownership. I will deal with this in greater detail in chapter 7.

Chapter 3

Property

Then the Lord God took the man and put him in the Garden of Eden to cultivate it and tend it. The Lord God commanded the man, saying, "From any tree of the garden you may freely eat; but from the tree of the knowledge of good and evil you shall not eat, for on the day that you eat from it you will certainly die."

Genesis 2:15–17

Analysis

Point three of the biblical covenant is law. It asks: "What are the rules?" How does this relate to property?

God placed a judicial/covenantal boundary around this tree. The theological issue of boundaries is always the issue of ethics. Ethics is a series of boundaries: "Do not do this." There are no covenants without boundaries.

The issue of boundaries in the field of economics centers on the issue of property rights. The issue of property rights is inextricably connected to the issue of ownership. They are, as Americans like to say, a package deal.

The issue of ownership is also connected to the issue of responsibility. The owner of an asset is responsible for the use of the asset, including the effects on other people of whatever use the owner adopts for the particular piece of property.

Another important aspect of property rights is the definition of what constitutes a right. A right is legal immunity from interference by others, including interference by the civil government. In other words, there is a legal boundary around a particular piece of property. But the property is owned by somebody, so *the issue of property rights is inescapably an issue of human rights.*

Then there is the issue of specialization. When somebody owns a piece of property, including the property right associated with his own labor, he allocates it to a particular use. If he allocates it to one use, he cannot allocate it to a competing use at the same time. By allocating a piece of property to a particular use, he specializes in this use of the property. Specialization is an aspect of economic efficiency. People are more productive when they concentrate their time and effort and money on a particular production process. They get better at what they do over time. They buy tools that enable them to increase their output. In other words, they specialize. The civil government's guarantee of property, whether raw materials, tools of production, or the output of this production, increases the willingness of people to specialize.

In order to understand how these important issues are connected to each other, you must understand the biblical concept of boundaries. At bottom, these are ethical boundaries.

A. Holiness

Point one of the biblical covenant is God's transcendence, yet also His presence. This is the concept of God's sovereignty. It asks: "Who's in charge here?" How does this apply to property?

The biblical concept of holiness has to do with ethics. It is a matter of ethical purity. Grammatically, holiness is based on the Hebrew word, *qadash*. It means to set apart or to consecrate. The English word used in the King James Version of the Bible, "hallowed," refers to this consecration. Theologically, to be holy is to be set apart by God in terms of ethical purity.

The original setting apart was God's setting apart of Himself. He is different from the creation. There is a fundamental distinction between the Creator and the creature. This has to do with the very being of God, but it also has to do with the ethical purity of God. He is the ethical standard. His commitment to purity is absolute. Jesus said: "Therefore you shall be perfect, as your heavenly Father is perfect" (Matt. 5:48).

Another word related to purity is "sanctification." It also means to be set apart. We speak of someone or something as being sanctified. This is related to the English word "saint." We speak of someone as a saint because of the person's ethical purity. We regard that person as being different from the rest of us. We set apart that person in our own minds. We think to ourselves: "This person is special." Theologically, we are to begin with God as our model. God is uniquely holy. His holiness makes Him special. There is an English word, "sacrosanct." It is a combination of "sacred" and "sanctification." God is uniquely sacrosanct.

The biblical doctrine of creation leads to a conclusion: the universe is personal. We can call this *cosmic personalism*. The God of creation providentially upholds the entire universe. But because this God is uniquely holy, the universe itself is governed by the ethical standards that God has identified as required for personal holiness. The universe is both personal and ethical.

We do not think of the supposed two trillion galaxies, each with its hundred billion stars, as being related to ethics, but they are. They were created by God and are at all times providentially administered by God. This God is transcendent. He is above the creation. He is fundamentally different from the creation. He is the source of the creation. He has delegated to mankind the administration of the earth and any other place in the universe where men may eventually travel, either before or after the final judgment. God's dominion is inherently and inescapably ethical.

Every social science is at bottom ethical. Secular scientists usually deny this. They believe that the scientific principles that govern their area of study are ethically neutral. They search for causes and effects in history, and they insist that these causes and effects are governed by impersonal laws that have no connection to ethics. In other words, they deny the existence of ethical cause and effect that is transcendent to man in his institutions. Social scientists and historians acknowledge that particular views of ethical cause and effect do have effects in history. But they insist that these views were invented by individuals, and these theories have no connection to any transcendent source of social order. This is the atheists' view of society. It is dominant in academia. It is at war with the biblical worldview.

B. Service

Point two of the biblical covenant is hierarchical authority. It has to do with God's delegation of limited sovereignty to man: the dominion covenant. How does this apply to property?

God's covenant with mankind, which was made before either man or woman was created, is a *covenant of service*. Mankind is dependent on God. God upholds mankind and man's environment by means of providence. God created mankind in order to serve Him as His corporate agent in extending the kingdom of God across the face of the earth. Man is a legal agent. Man is also an economic agent. God holds individuals and institutions responsible for the administration of the assets He has delegated to them, including their own lives.

This system of service to God mandates service to the creation. Men represent God to the creation, and they also represent the creation to God. What mankind does as God's agent influences what happens in the general creation. When men rebelled against God in the garden, the world came under negative sanctions. This was taught explicitly by the apostle Paul in the eighth chapter of the epistle to the Romans.

> For I consider that the sufferings of this present time are not worthy to be compared with the glory that is to be revealed to us. For the eagerly awaiting creation waits for the revealing of the sons and daughters of God. For the creation was subjected to futility, not willingly, but because of Him who subjected it, in hope that the creation itself also will be set free from its slavery to corruption into the freedom of the glory of the children of God. For we know that the whole creation groans and suffers the pains of childbirth together until now. (Rom. 8:18–22)

Men are to serve as stewards over the creation. But this is only part of the story. Covenant-keeping people are also to serve as stewards in their relationship with others in God's church. Jesus was explicit about this.

> "You know that the rulers of the Gentiles domineer over them, and those in high position exercise authority over them. It is not this way among you, but whoever wants to become prominent among you shall be your servant, and whoever desires to be first among you shall be your slave; just as the Son of Man did not come to be served, but to serve, and to give His life as a ransom for many." (Matt. 20:25–28)

This principle of service is fundamental to a correct Christian understanding of the free market economy. In order to prosper in a free market, producers must serve the desires of customers. Producers dare not lord it over customers. *Customers, because they have money, lord it over producers.* Money is the most marketable commodity. Everybody would like more money, but at zero additional cost, of course. This is the basis of *consumer authority* in the free market.

If someone wants success, he must learn to serve. This is fundamental to the free market social order, and it is fundamental in nonprofit institutions. This is a matter of ethics. God built this into the social order from the beginning. There is an ethical cause-and-effect system that is inherent in the human condition. It did not come from man. It came from God.

C. Test

Point three of the biblical covenant is law. It asks: "What are the rules?" How does this apply to property?

God gave Adam and Eve unrestricted authority over the entire creation, with only one exception: the tree of the knowledge of good and evil. That alone was closed to them. As we learn in Genesis 3, that was the exclusive focus of their attention. What they were not allowed to have, they soon wanted. They were tempted by a serpent to violate this law, and they succumbed to the temptation.

God placed a judicial boundary around that tree. This was an assertion of ownership. The tree belonged exclusively to God. The human race, meaning Adam and Eve, was not allowed to violate this judicial boundary. The tree was sacrosanct. It was sacred. It was set apart. It was part of God's covenant with mankind. This tree was representative of mankind's relationship to God. Would mankind remain loyal to God, or would mankind become disloyal? This tree was a representative token of mankind's loyalty to God.

Yet there was another covenantal token in the garden: the tree of life. We first hear of this tree in Genesis 2:9. It is mentioned along with the forbidden tree. It was a covenantal tree. Why do I say this? Because there was a positive sanction associated with it: eternal life. This is why God placed a flaming sword at the entrance of the garden after the fall: so that Adam and Eve could not get back to it to gain its positive sanction (Gen. 3:22). Had they taken their first communion meal at that tree, the tree of the knowledge of good and evil would no longer have posed a threat to them, either because they would not be tempted to eat from it or else because the test would have ended. Adam and Eve had three choices, not two: (1) avoid eating from the forbidden tree, (2) eating from the tree of life, or (3) eating from the forbidden tree. Yet with two righteous options available, they chose the third.

God established the dominion covenant before He created mankind. Then He placed Adam in the garden. There was a negative sanction associated with one tree, and a positive sanction with the other. These two trees were oath-signs. They had covenantal importance. Man could seal the dominion covenant by eating from the tree of life: loyalty. He could also break the dominion covenant by eating from the forbidden tree: disloyalty. At some point, they would have eaten from one or the other. Mankind could not have lived in an oathless world for long. This was a world without an implicit "yes" or "no" to God's covenant. This was a *covenantally provisional* world. It was open-ended. This was the only time in history when such a world existed. It was a world left incomplete by God until they decided whether to affirm the covenant of God or else attempt to establish their own autonomous covenant, in which they would test the accuracy of God's promise of death. They failed the test. We failed with them. They were our covenantal representatives.

Because of man's rebellion, Christians and Jews focus on that forbidden tree. So did Adam and Eve. But what we should never forget is the other aspect of the covenant, namely, God's grant of the unrestricted use of every other asset in the garden and anywhere else, including the tree of life. *God in his grace transferred the whole earth to mankind as an undeveloped capital asset.* Individuals and institutions were allowed to produce whatever they wanted. In order to fund economic growth, which was required by God in the original covenantal document, which appears in Genesis 1:26–28, they also would have to be thrifty. They would have to become entrepreneurs, looking into the future as a guide to allocating capital assets in the present. But they could consume anything they wanted. This was a spectacular grant of wealth to mankind.

Their right to enjoy the fruits of the entire creation was a grant of liberty. They had liberty of action. They also had the liberty to accumulate wealth. This was part of the dominion covenant. Wealth is a capital resource. It necessarily involves responsibility, because wealth can be allocated in so many different ways. *Liberty of action was crucial to the responsible accumulation of wealth.* Again, this was a package deal: a grant of capital, a grant of liberty of action, the right to accumulate wealth, and the responsibility associated with ownership. It all rested on the judicial and ethical concept of private property rights.

Mankind paid no attention to this grant of capital, liberty, and the potential for building up an inheritance. Adam and Eve, as judicial representatives of the entire human race, went to the forbidden tree in order to enjoy the fruits thereof. The fruits thereof were deadly, just as God had promised.

The test of mankind's loyalty was the judicial boundary around the tree. The explicit test was based on the concept of private property. The tree was exclusively God's tree, and Adam and Eve were not to violate this boundary. It was an ethical boundary as well as a judicial boundary. Because it was sacrosanct, it was also an ecclesiastical boundary. Another tree could be appropriated by Adam and Eve as priests. They could lawfully participate in another communion meal. They could have gone right to the tree of life and gained eternal life through their participation in a communion meal at that tree, but they chose not to do this. They chose instead to participate in a communion meal of guaranteed death. That was the legacy, the inheritance, that they passed on to their heirs, including you.

The original test of mankind's loyalty to God was a test of their willingness to honor God's property rights. Their violation was inherently an act of theft. This should remind us of just how important ethically, judicially, and ecclesiastically the concept of private property is. The doctrine of property rights is an extension of the doctrine of God's original ownership, and therefore it is an extension of the doctrine of God-delegated ownership. It is manifested in the commandment: "You shall not steal" (Ex. 20:15).

Until that first act of theft, mankind had no need to allocate resources to defend individual property against thieves. There was only one thing that they could steal: the fruit of the tree of the knowledge of good and evil. There was no need to steal anything else. There was plenty to go around. Adam and Eve did not eat from the tree because they were hungry. They ate from the tree because they were sinners. They had already made the decision to violate the boundary. As a result, they came under the promised sanction. There was plenty of death to go around. Furthermore, there was not a lot of demand for it. The supply of death is always much greater than the demand.

God is holy. This holiness was manifested by the forbidden tree. It was set apart. That is the meaning of holiness. *Mankind's act of theft was the supreme unholy act.* But until the rebellion, mankind had free use of the creation. I use the word "free" in both senses: legally free and economically free. They did not have to buy the cornucopia from God. It was His gift to them.

D. Sanctions

Point four of the biblical covenant is sanctions. It asks: "What do I get if I obey? Disobey?" How does this apply to property?

There are always positive and negative sanctions in life. There are also positive and negative sanctions in eternity. There are heaven and hell (Luke 16). There are the lake of fire (Rev. 20:14–15) and the new heavens and the new earth (Rev. 21–22).

God warned Adam of the negative sanction of death (Gen. 2:17). Adam later warned Eve. We know this because Eve knew about the threatened negative sanction when the serpent tempted her (Gen. 3:2). Other than the sanctions associated with death, there were no other negative sanctions in the garden. *The whole world was a gigantic treasure chest of positive sanctions.* Adam and Eve made a self-conscious decision to grab the robes of authority instead of dipping their hands deep into the cornucopia of wealth. When you read commentaries on the forbidden fruit and the fall of man, you will find very little about the positive sanctions that were all around them. The commentators don't talk about the grant of capital and the grant of liberty to put this capital to use. It was a grant of the right to consume anything in the general creation. This was the potential available to them for building the kingdom of God. The focus of the commentators is on the rebellion. This is consistent with the nature of the rebellion, because Adam and Eve also ignored the cornucopia. The negative sanctions were at the heart of the argument between Eve and the serpent. The loss of the positive sanctions did not come up in the record of their discussion.

When we discuss the world we have lost, we should focus on the positive sanctions. That is because we lost them. Only through the grace of God, which was shown in the slaying of the animals in order for God to provide Adam and Eve with animal skins (Gen. 3:21), were some of the positive sanctions restored. *The animal skins were covenantal tokens of God's continuing grace to mankind.*

The post-fall appeal of great riches is based on the loss of great riches in Genesis 3. Men want riches, but on their own terms. They want a restoration of what mankind once had. We should never forget that people really did possess great riches, and they also possessed the liberty to accumulate even greater riches. They owned these riches. More important, they owned the liberty to accumulate even greater riches. *Their liberty was a property right.* But it could be lost through the violation of God's property right. What mankind possessed, Adam and Eve could forfeit. And they did.

God did not warn them about the forfeited wealth. He simply said that the penalty for violating his property rights was death. He did not say that He would take away their property. He said that He would take away their lives. That threat was greater than the threat of taking away their property, which included their liberty. If someone is not overly impressed by the threat of being executed, he is not going to be impressed by the threat of having his property taken away.

There is something else to consider. In building wealth, the most important thing you can do is to avoid losses. If you could just avoid the losses of life, your investments would compound over your lifetime. In the case of Adam and Eve, there was no limit on their lifetime, as long as they did not eat from the forbidden tree. There were no negative sanctions in the world prior to their theft of God's property. There could be various rates of profit, but there could not be losses, which are negative sanctions. When it came to capital, there was always more where that came from. *There were no setbacks in life; there were only varying rates of success.* This was the world we have lost.

E. Inheritance

Point five of the biblical covenant is succession. It asks: "Does this outfit have a future?" How does this apply to property?

God told Adam and Eve to be fruitful and multiply. Therefore, from the beginning, there was to be an inheritance. The sons and daughters of each generation would inherit capital assets from their parents. Their parents would not do this in order to be supported in their old age. There would be no setbacks as a result of aging. People would get wiser over time. They would specialize over time. They would increase their rate of productivity over time.

Nevertheless, parents would have provided their children with capital. They provided the capital associated with child-rearing. It would make no sense to send them into the world without capital. They would be provided with capital in the same way that God had provided Adam and Eve with capital. God had set the pattern.

By turning over capital to children, parents contributed to the extension of the kingdom of God in history. Their children would have specific skills and interests. They would specialize in the production process. This specialization would lead to greater output per capita. This would lead to more rapid economic growth and a more rapid extension of mankind across the face of the earth: the fulfillment of the dominion covenant. Mankind would multiply and subdue the earth for the glory of God. This would have been done within a few centuries. Then the preliminary arena of the administration of capital in the extension of the kingdom of God would be changed. The new heavens and a new earth would have come into existence, as described in Revelation 21 and 22.

There would have been a final judgment. We could call this a final accounting. The concept of accounting is appropriate in describing the final judgment. But the final judgment would not have involved the threat of what Revelation 20:14 calls the second death. There would have been different rates of positive return, but no one would have declared bankruptcy. *Bankruptcy ultimately is spiritual and ethical.* Without the fall of man, this would have been avoided.

Conclusion

The fall of man took place as a result of mankind's violation of God's private property rights. Adam and Eve violated the judicial and ethical boundaries that God placed around the tree of the knowledge of good and evil. God had warned Adam of the penalty for such a violation: death. Adam had warned Eve. Eve quoted this warning to the serpent. But the serpent's temptation prevailed. They decided to test the accuracy of God's warning. In running this experiment, Adam asserted his own autonomy. He would test God's word. God would no longer test Adam's loyalty.

This act of theft had enormous consequences historically. But Christians rarely think about the world that their covenantal parents forfeited as a result of that act of theft. The centrality of theft in the story of the fall of man should remind Christians of the magnitude of God's hostility toward theft. God's announcement of the sanction against such theft should have been sufficient to persuade Adam and Eve not to indulge themselves in violating the judicial and ethical boundaries that God placed around the tree of the knowledge of good and evil. But it did not suffice. Neither does the commandment against theft in the Ten Commandments.

Chapter 4

Imputation

And God saw all that He had made, and behold, it was very good. And there was evening and there was morning, the sixth day.

Genesis 1:31

Analysis

Point four of the biblical covenant is sanctions. It asks: "What do I get if I obey? Disobey?" How does this relate to imputation?

"Imputation" is not a familiar word these days. In Christian theology, it refers to God's sovereign judicial declaration as the cosmic judge: "guilty" or "not guilty." It refers specifically to God's imputation of Jesus Christ's perfect righteousness to the objects of God's special or saving grace, who are then reckoned by God as covenant-keepers. Christ's judicial payment to God is the legal basis of redemption, which means "to buy back." It is a substitute payment on behalf of the redeemed.

In the field of economics, imputation means "to attribute value to." An individual evaluates the value of some good or service in terms of his personal scale of economic values at the moment. This scale of values is ordinal: first, second, third, etc. This is a subjective action. *Economic value is subjective.* But, after making this evaluation, a person then decides what he is willing and able to pay to gain either the ownership or the temporary use of this desired item. He makes a bid to purchase or rent. Others also make bids. The result of these competing bids is an objective price. So, *imputation is subjective, but the final price is objective.* This is how value and price are related in the free market. This is a conclusion on Jesus' parable of the pearl of great price. "Again, the kingdom of heaven is like a merchant seeking fine pearls, and upon finding one pearl of great value, he went and sold everything that he had and bought it" (Matt. 13:45–46). The great subjective value of the pearl resulted in a high price. Others saw the value of the pearl and were also bidding.

How do we know that something is good? When I say "we," I mean each individual, but I also mean groups. We make evaluations as individuals. Next, we take specific actions in light of these evaluations. We must then bear the consequences of our actions. We also are members of groups that make evaluate situations and then make collective decisions. The members must individually bear the consequences of their collective actions. After the final judgment, we must bear the these consequences individually. So, each person's primary focus should be on how we as individuals decide what is good and what is bad—morally, but also technically. We must individually decide what is *right to do*, and then decide how to *do it right*.

We are not autonomous. We are subordinate to God. We are stewards. So, we are required to make our evaluations and decisions in terms of our covenantal roles as stewards. We should ask: "What is best for God?" Our evaluations and decisions should be theocentric.

The fourth point of the biblical covenant has to do with covenantal oaths: the judicially binding vows that we take in the special judicial presence of God. We take formal oaths individually, as family members, as church members, and as citizens. These vows possess greater authority than other promises. They are covenantal, not merely contractual. The eternal stakes are much higher with covenants than with contracts. Three of these vows involve corporate membership. Individual vows to God and vows made in church carry into eternity.

To understand how we can evaluate the way God does, we should consider the week of creation.

A. God's Original Imputation

Point one of the biblical covenant is God's transcendence, yet also His presence. This is the biblical concept of God's sovereignty. It asks: "Who's in charge here?" How does this apply to economic imputation?

The creation week was sequential: start to finish. It was linear.

At the end of every day except day two, God announced His evaluation: good. This was a public declaration. Only God heard it, but that was sufficient.

On what basis did He make these evaluations? I offer this explanation, which is structured in terms of the five points of the biblical covenant. First, God had a goal: the kingdom of God. The week's creation produced the future arena of this kingdom. Second, He had a plan. But because God is both omniscient and omnipotent, it was more than a plan. It was a decree. Third, there was a blueprint: standards. These were subjective, because God had established them, but they were also objective, also because God had established them. God's sovereign subjective judgments are declarations of what is objectively true. Fourth, He evaluated His daily work in terms of all three: goal, decree, and standards. He made these evaluations both individually and corporately, for God is the Trinity. Fifth, there was a sequence to the week. The week ended with rest, which was the culmination of the work.

B. Subordinate Imputation

Point two of the biblical covenant is hierarchical authority. It has to do with God's delegation of limited sovereignty to man: the dominion covenant. How does this apply to economic imputation?

God holds all people responsible for imputing value in terms of His standards. Is this just? Yes. Why? Because they are made in the image of God. But sin has made this task impossible for covenant-breakers. To assist covenant-keepers in this task, God has given them the mind of Christ. "For who has known the mind of the Lord, that he will instruct Him? But we have the mind of Christ" (I Cor. 2:16).

Adam and Eve faced a decision. Should they delay eating from the forbidden tree and also from the tree of life? Or should they eat immediately? If so, from which tree? If we accept the Bible's account, we might be tempted to call this a no-brainer. "Eat from the tree of life. Now!" But this test was not about testing their intelligence. It was about testing their loyalty. *This test was about evaluating the locus of sovereignty.* Adam and Eve imputed high value to the forbidden tree and low value to God's word. They thought the serpent might be correct; they would not die, and they would become wise in the ways of ethics, knowing good and evil. They decided to test the word of God versus the word of the serpent. *Only people who thought they were sovereign would have done this.* The stakes were too high otherwise.

They imputed value to the forbidden fruit. "When the woman saw that the tree was good for food, and that it was a delight to the eyes, and that the tree was desirable to make one wise, she took some of its fruit and ate; and she also gave some to her husband with her, and he ate" (Gen. 3:6). It was a joint decision. It was a team effort.

They imitated the procedure of God in the creation week. First, they had goals: to become wise. Second, they had a plan: to violate God's law by eating. Third, they had standards: man's test. Fourth, they imputed high value to the fruit, some value to the serpent's word, and little value to God's word. Fifth, their program had a sequence. Eve listened to the serpent. She ate. She gave fruit to Adam. He ate.

C. Standards

Point three of the biblical covenant is law. It asks: "What are the rules?" How does this apply to the idea of economic imputation?

God had set forth a simple ethical standard: do not eat. He had announced a negative sanction: if you eat, you will die. This was a law. It had a negative sanction. This was a test based on ethical cause and effect.

The serpent had also set forth ethical standards: go ahead and eat. He had announced a positive sanction: to know good and evil. He had denied the promised negative sanction. They would not surely die.

Adam and Eve decided to run their own test. God was testing them.

They would now test God. They would test the two ethical systems: God's and the serpent's. They had to make an assumption to run this test: they were sovereign. They also made this assumption: *their test was authoritative*. God's test of them was not.

They imputed high value to the serpent's interpretation of God's law. They imputed low value to the explicit words of God. Like a chemistry experiment gone wrong, their test of God's law blew up in their faces.

D. Profit

Point four of the biblical covenant is sanctions. It asks: "What do I get if I obey? Disobey?" How does this apply to economic imputation?

We come now to the heart of the matter: *judgment*. This is the art of applying fixed laws to specific circumstances. We do this in every area of life.

For economic theory, the following issues are involved: imputing economic value (subjective) to goods and services, deciding how much to bid (objective) in order to buy or control these assets, estimating the future income and the costs of owning capital assets (objective), and discounting this expected future net income by the rate of interest in order to arrive at the maximum price to pay for capital (objective). What do I mean by costs? A *cost is whatever I must forfeit in order to purchase some asset*. If it costs money (objective), what is the most valuable (subjective) thing that I could otherwise do with the money that I will have to give up in order to own the asset?

1. *Limited Knowledge of the Future*

Unlike God, men are not omniscient. Therefore, everyone must deal with uncertainty. There are specialists who deal with economic uncertainty. They are called *entrepreneurs*. Sometimes they are called speculators. They perform the important economic service of bearing the costs of uncertainty. They try to buy low and sell high. But how can they buy low if they are competing with other entrepreneurs? Only because rival entrepreneurs do not see the opportunity. They do not see that future customers will pay as much as they eventually do, or buy as many products. Rival entrepreneurs therefore do not enter the capital markets and bid on the raw materials, labor, and other production goods and services. This keeps prices lower. This makes available an entrepreneurial opportunity. However, if the entrepreneur buys production goods, but customers do not buy the output at a price that will produce a profit, he will lose money.

It is legitimate for people to seek opportunities to buy low and sell high. It is therefore legitimate to make a profit. No one has a moral obligation to tell a potential buyer what he paid for the item he is selling.

Is this analysis biblical? Are there biblical examples? Yes. Consider Jesus' parable of the hidden treasure. "The kingdom of heaven is like a treasure hidden in the field, which a man found and hid again; and from joy over it he goes and sells everything that he has, and buys that field" (Matt. 13:44). A man finds a hidden treasure. He does not steal it. He wants to own it. If anyone else knew it was there, that person might bid a lot of money to buy the field and thereby become the owner of the treasure. The man who found the treasure does not want to face competition from anyone else in purchasing the field. He buries the treasure, making it less likely that anyone else will discover it. Then he buys the field. The seller does not know about the treasure. If he did, he would not sell the field for the price of the field. He would sell it for the price of the field plus the expected price of the treasure. This is the entrepreneur's goal: "Buy low. Sell high." The man who found the treasure benefits from hidden knowledge. The treasure can be bought for a low price only because of the ignorance of other potential buyers, who also want to buy low and sell high. The discoverer wants to profit from the difference between the present price of the field and the future price of the treasure and the field. Most of the profit will come from the sale of the treasure.

The discoverer seeks a profit. The potential to make a profit comes from others' ignorance regarding the presence of a treasure. The treasure can be had for a minimal payment, but only because of widespread ignorance regarding its whereabouts. This is the conceptual model for all profit. It stems from *widespread ignorance regarding the present value of something,* which in the case of the parable is the field. If other investors recognized the presence of a profit opportunity, they would enter the market and bid up the price of the field. The price of the field would soon exceed the expected value of the treasure: field plus treasure. The field has minimal value in comparison with the treasure.

If the field had been located in downtown Jerusalem in Jesus' day, or downtown Rome, the market price of the field might have been greater than the price of the treasure. There would have been some profit opportunity, since the treasure was worth something, but not so great proportionally than if the field had been located in some distant village.

There was always the possibility that the owner of the field had put together a fake treasure. It looked real, but it wasn't. The discoverer would not have been able to get the treasure examined by an expert. That would have involved sharing the information with the expert. The expert might have had more money than the discoverer to buy the field. He might have grown inquisitive. So, the discoverer pays more than he should to buy the field. This strategy was common in the American West in the days of the gold rush in California after 1848. The owner of an abandoned mine would put bits of gold ore in the mine. This was called "salting the mine." Then he would wait for some profit-seeking amateur to discover the gold. He would sell the mine at a large profit over what it was worth without veins of gold. The buyer would suffer a loss. *There is always a possibility of a loss in any entrepreneurial venture.* That was not true before the fall.

2. *Before the Fall*

There was no possibility of a loss in the world before the fall of man. There was only one negative sanction, death, and it was covenanal. The rest of creation was a large field that was filled with treasures.

> Now a river flowed out of Eden to water the garden; and from there it divided and became four rivers. The name of the first is Pishon; it flows around the whole land of Havilah, where there is gold. The gold of that land is good; the bdellium and the onyx stone are there as well. (Gen. 2:10–12)

The whole earth was filled with buried treasures: valuable metals of all kinds. The land itself was productive: a farmer's treasure. The land was there for the taking. But Adam and Eve were too busy eating from the forbidden tree to be concerned about the treasures they were not digging up or not planting.

They made the greatest entrepreneurial error in history. It began with misleading information.

> The serpent said to the woman, "You certainly will not die! "For God knows that on the day you eat from it your eyes will be opened, and you will become like God, knowing good and evil." (Gen. 3:4–5).

Eve was deceived. She took the serpent's words seriously. She decided that the information that her husband had given her was incorrect. *She imputed greater value to the serpent's word than her husband's.* "When the woman saw that the tree was good for food, and that it was a delight to the eyes, and that the tree was desirable to make one wise, she took some of its fruit and ate; and she also gave some to her husband with her, and he ate" (Gen. 3:6). Adam imputed greater value to the serpent's word than to God's word, but only after his wife ate. She became his experimental test case. She did not immediately die. So, he ate.

Neither of them accurately forecasted the future impact of the promised negative sanction or its inevitability. They discounted the odds of the probability of being discovered by God as thieves. They discounted the probability of God's imposition of the penalty. *They brought the possibility of loss into a world without negative rates of return.* That was the world we have lost.

E. Inheritance

Point five of the biblical covenant is succession. It asks: "Does this outfit have a future?" How does this apply to economic imputation?

Inheritance began with God's transfer of the earth to Adam and Eve. They were the children of God. They received their inheritance at the beginning of their marriage. They were supposed to continue the practice of endowing their children with an inheritance when they married.

Death would end all inheritance. But God showed grace to them. He gave them a stay of execution. He allowed them to extend their lives and their family. This was an act of grace, meaning unmerited favor. But God had another motive: to fulfill His original goal. He would extend His kingdom in history under the new conditions. He would not give Satan and his subordinates the satisfaction of having lured mankind into rebellion and certain death. Death was still certain, but not immediately. He also gave the serpent a promise. This promise was representative of how He would deal with all of the representatives of Satan. "And I will make enemies of you and the woman, and of your offspring and her Descendant; He shall bruise you on the head, and you shall bruise Him on the heel" (Gen. 3:15). It involved inheritance: offspring. This meant time.

If Adam and Eve trusted God, they would have hope. Their heirs would impose negative sanctions against their deadly enemy. God cursed the serpent physically, making it crawl on its belly and swallow dust. That curse was a token of the deadly future sanction of death by head-crushing. *Despite God's promise of death for individual heirs, there was a promise of victory to mankind.* Their heirs would impose justice on Satan's minions. The covenant-keeping children of Adam and Eve would extend the kingdom of God through time and across borders: boundaries. But there would be conflict. There would be pain: bruised heels. Covenant-keepers and covenant-breakers would battle for control until the end of time. At the heart of this battle is ethics: the law-order of God versus the law-orders of men.

Conclusion

Adam and Eve failed in their work of imputation. They did not impute high value to God's word. They did not impute high value to the tree of life. They did not impute high value to the other trees and capital assets in the creation. They imputed high value to the word of the serpent. They imputed high value to the forbidden tree and the promised wisdom that eating its fruit would provide. But they did impute value. *Imputation is an inescapable concept.* It is never a question of imputation versus no imputation. It is always a question of imputing value in terms of a specific law-order: God's or self-proclaimed autonomous man's.

The key to dominion in the garden was obedience to God. He had given them only one prohibition. They had disobeyed it. Now God would multiply His laws, for the whole earth had become an ethical battlefield between the kingdom of God and the kingdom of self-proclaimed autonomous man. This warfare was revealed in Cain's murder of Abel (Gen. 4). There would be no permanent peace treaty in history between these kingdoms. There would only be temporary truces or cease-fires. Each side would then use the truce to plan a new campaign. There could be no ethical neutrality between the two kingdoms. Jesus said: "The one who is not with Me is against Me; and the one who does not gather with Me scatters" (Matt. 12:30).

In the garden there was only one battlefield: inside the boundary around the forbidden tree. The war between the two kingdoms would begin there. The tree was off-limits. The rest of creation was on-limits. The task of applying God's law to specific circumstances was easy. There was only one law: avoid the tree. There was no threat of negative sanctions outside that boundary. There were no weeds. There was no sweat. That was the world we have lost.

Chapter 5

Inheritance

> *Who is the person who fears the* Lord*? He will instruct him in the way he should choose. His soul will dwell in prosperity, and his descendants will inherit the land.*
>
> Psalm 25:12–13

Analysis

Point five of the biblical covenant is succession. It asks: "Does this outfit have a future?" How does this relate to inheritance?

The Bible teaches the concept of linear time. This was not believed in the ancient world, including classical Greece and classical Rome. The ancient world believed in cyclical time: no end of time's cycles. *This was a major reason why biblical religion was a radical break with the ancient world.* The Bible teaches that there was a beginning, a period of history, and a final judgment, both for individuals and for the existing cosmos. After time ends, hell will be deposited into the lake of fire (Rev. 20:14–15), and the new heaven and new earth will replace the sin-cursed earth. It will also replace heaven as a holding place for the bodyless souls of the redeemed (Rev. 21–22). Eternity will replace history. There will be eternal development for covenant-keepers. There will be neither development nor mercy for covenant-breakers.

Not only is this outlook linear, it is progressive. It is progressive because of the concept of dominion. God mandated that the human race extend across the face of the earth in order to make it flourish (Gen. 1:26–28). This is a religious responsibility that is inherent in humanity.

Dominion is through inheritance. Inheritance is established through growth, especially economic growth. The Bible teaches this: "A good person leaves an inheritance to his grandchildren, and the wealth of a sinner is stored up for the righteous" (Prov. 13:22). Over time, covenant-keepers will inherit. Covenant-breakers will be disinherited. By what means? By purchase and conversion. Covenant-keepers will buy the assets of covenant-breakers. They will also preach the gospel of redemption through faith in the substitutionary atonement of Jesus Christ at Calvary. If the hearer accepts this, he becomes a covenant-keeper. This new man inherits the wealth of the old man. "Therefore if anyone is in Christ, this person is a new creation; the old things passed away; behold, new things have come" (II Cor. 5:17). His wealth is transferred by covenant oath from the kingdom of man to the kingdom of God.

A. Capital Creation

Point one of the biblical covenant is God's transcendence, yet also His presence. This is the biblical concept of God's sovereignty. It asks: "Who's in charge here?" How does this apply to inheritance?

The model is the creation week. God created everything. He began with nothing. He spoke the light into existence. He continued to add to the creation over the next five days. Each day was a separate act of creation. Each day was cumulative. God expanded the capital base in a linear fashion: from beginning to end. God ended the process of creation with the creation of Adam and Eve, who were His designated heirs.

The original goal of capital creation was inheritance. God created the universe, but it had a purpose. Purpose was built into the creation. He made the sun, moon, and stars for the purpose of giving mankind a way to measure time. He began with the stars.

> Then God said, "Let there be lights in the expanse of the heavens to separate the day from the night, and they shall serve as signs and for sea-

> sons, and for days and years; and they shall serve as lights in the expanse of the heavens to give light on the earth"; and it was so. (Gen. 1:14–15)

This was astronomical in more than one sense. God created at least two hundred billion galaxies with a hundred billion stars each. Why? To produce the astronomical basis of a calendar. Yet it was not until the twentieth century that men could perceive the magnitude of the heavenly creation: multiple galaxies. All of this is for man's sake? Yes. There is purpose in the universe. The enormous size of the universe testifies to the magnitude of the sovereign God who created it as a tool for calendar design. Yet calendars today are based on the rate of deterioration of cesium atoms. What this means is that God created an extra hundred billion galaxies or so for an unstated reason. Amusement? Showing off? To lure evolutionists into greater rebellion? I don't know. I do know this. What men do on earth is cosmically far more significant than the silent, slow rotation of two hundred billion galaxies, or maybe two trillion. The galaxies are a kind of afterthought for God: a backdrop to history. *The significant action in cosmic history takes place on earth.* What you do with your life is far more important to God than your per capita share of galaxies. It is also far more important to you. God did not send His son to die primarily in order to redeem the galaxies. The galaxies do not change in response to the gospel. People do.

God mandated capital accumulation from the beginning. This is a matter of ethics. Again, "A good person leaves an inheritance to his grandchildren, and the wealth of a sinner is stored up for the righteous" (Prov. 13:22). This is what a good man does. Of course, too much capital can be a curse. Too much of any blessing can be a curse. *With capital comes responsibility.* There is no escape from this unbreakable connection. Some children are not ready for excessive responsibility. It can destroy them. The multi-billionaire Warren Buffett put it this way: "I will leave my children enough money so that they can do anything, but not so much that they can do nothing." Buffett is famous for sage observations. This is one of his best.

It takes thrift to accumulate capital: less spending than income. It also takes skilled entrepreneurship: the wisdom to imagine enough about future economic conditions so as to invest wisely. The owner of capital must buy low and sell high. This is what two of the three men in Jesus' parable of the talents did. The third man buried his talent, and he was condemned for this (Matt. 25:14–30).

The inheritance is supposed to be mostly productive capital: *marketable tools of production*. This includes the training necessary for the heir to manage the inherited capital. The first kind of tools can be capitalized: sold for a price that factors in expected future output. The second kind cannot be sold for cash wherever slavery is illegal. But it can be rented: wages. If the two kinds of tools of production do not match well, the heir should sell the capitalized tools of production in order to buy different tools that are more suitable to his skills.

B. Preliminary Inheritance

Point two of the biblical covenant is hierarchical authority. It asks: "To whom do I report?" How does this apply to inheritance?

God gave the garden to Adam and Eve. Before God created Eve, He assigned Adam a preliminary task: to name the animals of the garden. God tested Adam's skills of classification. God had built these skills into Adam's nature, but He nevertheless imposed an objective test. Only when Adam passed this test was his given a specially designed assistant. The two were a team from then on.

Had they not sinned, they would have extended their dominion beyond the garden. The garden was the origin of four rivers (Gen. 2:10–14). These were sources of cheap transportation downstream in all directions.

The farther away they moved from the forbidden tree, the less immediate and intense the temptation would have been. But this also applied to the tree of life. The preliminary inheritance would be followed by the general inheritance after a communion meal: either the forbidden tree or the tree of life. The dominion covenant had to be sealed judicially. The oath-sign had to be a meal.

After they sinned, God cast them out of the garden into the world. He placed a boundary around the garden to keep them away from the tree of life and its positive sanction. Their preliminary test was over. They had failed it. The whole world was cursed by God in response to this failure (Gen. 3:17–19). The task of dominion would be more difficult. But it was not revoked.

C. Terms of the Inheritance

Point three of the biblical covenant is law. It asks: "What are the rules?" How does this apply to inheritance?

It is common for large inheritances to be governed by written rules contained in the will or the trust document. The person who accumulated the capital had the testament drawn up so that the heirs have to meet certain requirements for their continued ownership of the inheritance.

God's initial transfer of property to Adam had requirements. The first was positive: subdue the earth on behalf of God. This was the general requirement. It preceded the creation of man. The second was positive and specific: defend the garden and care for it. "Then the LORD God took the man and put him in the Garden of Eden to cultivate it and tend it" (Gen. 2:15). This was the initial transfer. The third was negative: do not eat from the forbidden tree (Gen. 2:17).

There was no escape from the general requirement: the dominion covenant. There was one escape from the second requirement. They had to exercise dominion over the garden, but this would end if they sinned. God would remove them from the garden. He did not tell them about the procedure he adopted: physical exclusion. The promise of death was supposed to persuade them that they would be removed. Finally, the third requirement regarding the forbidden tree would have been revoked at the time that they ate from the tree of life. The sanction of death would have ended; therefore, the prohibition would have ended. Because they did not eat from the tree of life, God expelled them from their initial inheritance after they violated the terms of the covenant.

> Then the LORD God said, "Behold, the man has become like one of Us, knowing good and evil; and now, he might reach out with his hand, and take fruit also from the tree of life, and eat, and live forever"—therefore the LORD God sent him out of the Garden of Eden, to cultivate the ground from which he was taken. So He drove the man out; and

> at the east of the Garden of Eden He stationed the cherubim and the flaming sword which turned every direction to guard the way to the tree of life. (Gen. 3:22–24)

D. Imputation

Point four of the biblical covenant is sanctions. It asks: "What do I get if I obey? Disobey?" How does this apply to inheritance?

This is a matter of judgment: declaring God's law in specific circumstances and then imposing the law's mandated sanctions. Adam named the animals of the garden. This involved judgment. How did each species differ from the others? Which difference was the key one in each case? The names had to have meaning. Adam had to assess the meaning of the differences within the framework of the garden's principles of action. The garden was representative of the world.

Adam had to impute both meaning and purpose based on his knowledge of God's laws. As a creature, he was required by God to think God's thoughts after Him. He was not authorized to impute meaning or purpose in terms of any rival standard. Adam passed this test. His reward was Eve. But with every blessing comes responsibility. He would now have to warn her of the prohibition regarding the tree. If she misunderstood, she might lead him into rebellion. This is what happened.

Eating from either tree was a covenantal act. Covenants are established by an oath. This is a two-way loyalty oath. The two trees represented rival responses. The meals were oath-signs. They were tokens of loyalty. But because these were rival oaths, each tree represented disloyalty to one or the other source of law. *Covenantal loyalty or disloyalty are the judicial foundations of either inheritance or disinheritance.* God rewards covenantal loyalty with inheritance. He punishes covenantal disloyalty with disinheritance.

The curse of the ground was a blessing in disguise. Man was now a covenant-breaking species. Sin was now endemic, meaning original. It would be transferred to the biological heirs. The heirs would at times have murder in their hearts, as we learn from the act of Cain. So, in order to reduce the extent of sin, God cursed the ground. This reduced mankind's productivity. To regain control over a now less productive nature, men would have to cooperate. *The division of labor would be necessary to offset the curse.* The benefits of cooperation would hold in check the innate evil of men. There would be a payoff for cooperation: greater output and therefore greater individual wealth.

E. Transfer

Point five of the biblical covenant is succession. It asks: "Does this outfit have a future?" How does this apply to inheritance?

From the beginning, God planned to transfer ownership of the world to Adam and Eve. This was the basis of the dominion covenant, which He announced on day six. Mankind was to fill the earth through biological multiplication. God assigned the task of dressing the garden and defending it from any unauthorized invader (Gen. 1:26–28). This was an aspect of delegated ownership. They were to imitate God. They were to train their children in the tasks of trusteeship: guardianship (legal) and stewardship (economic).

Before God created Eve, He assigned Adam a preliminary task: naming the animals of the garden. He remained with Adam in the garden. He watched Adam do his task. This was a kind of apprenticeship. God was there in case Adam needed guidance. Adam did the job without fault. In response, God gave Eve to Adam to serve Adam as a lifetime partner. Adam would have to train her, which he did. Eve knew about the prohibition on the tree of the knowledge of good and evil, because she responded to the serpent with God's word (Gen. 3:2–3). There is no indication in Genesis 2 that God spoke directly to her. Adam must have.

There was mandatory training involved in the process of inheritance. God was the original owner of the capital that He created on days one through five. Then He gave it to Adam and Eve. This was an unmerited gift to mankind. *Grace precedes law.* But God did not intend to transfer this inheritance to Adam and Eve free of charge. They needed to understand how to use it productively on His behalf (economic stewardship) and in His name (legal guardianship). This meant that God would have to provide initial guidance to Adam, who would in turn provide initial guidance to Eve. There was a technical aspect to this training: naming the animals. Naming required Adam first to understand God's categories for the various roles of each species, which would be followed by his imputation of names consistent with God's standards.

There was a reward for completing this task: a wife. Adam had seen how God had guided him. Now he would be in a position to provide guidance for Eve. There would be a transfer of information. Shared information regarding cause and effect, which means a shared worldview, was fundamental for mankind's cooperation. This was made clear at the tower of Babel, when all cooperation was undermined by God's destruction of mankind's single language (Gen. 11).

A transfer of information preceded God's transfer of ownership of the creation to mankind. This was a multi-step process. It began with the transfer of authority over the garden. The garden was representative of the whole earth. They would learn to administer this preliminary grant of capital before they and their heirs moved out of the garden to extend mankind's dominion across the earth. This preliminary grant of capital was what the Bible calls an *earnest*: a down payment that reveals good faith on the past of the grantor. This also revealed the progressive aspect of inheritance. The inheritance was initially perfect, but it was not developed. Adam and Eve had to dress the garden in stages. There is therefore a pattern to inheritance: an original representative transfer that is followed by administration. Then there is another transfer, also followed by administration. This is the mandated biblical process of capital accumulation. It is inter-generational: father to son.

Before the fall, the son was ethically untested. He might squander the inheritance by disobedience. That was why God conducted a test. He left as soon as He had made the transfer. He would see how well His children would administer the garden. This process of observation remains in force. Parents have about two decades to train each child in the responsibilities of ownership. Then, if the children appear to be responsible stewards, the parents transfer a portion of their capital to them. This is how covenant-keeping families are supposed to extend the dominion covenant.

Conclusion

Christianity offers hope to those redeemed by His special grace. Their eternal futures are secure covenantally. This is a doctrine of personal optimism. But this optimism is not confined to the world beyond the grave. It also applies to history. *Righteousness will progressively replace evil in history.* God's promise to the serpent will take place in history: "And I will make enemies of you and the woman, and of your offspring and her Descendant; He shall bruise you on the head, and you shall bruise Him on the heel" (Gen. 3:15). This was a messianic prophecy. The power of Christ is greater than the power of Satan. God's kingdom has greater authority than man's kingdom. Jesus said: "upon this rock I will build My church; and the gates of Hades will not overpower it" (Matt. 16:18b). The message is clear: Satan's kingdom, which is the kingdom of self-proclaimed autonomous man, is on the defensive in history.

Dominion is inter-generational. This is why the doctrine of inheritance is so important. God made it clear that each generation must look to the next generation for greater fulfilment of the dominion covenant. Wherever and whenever Christians have believed this, they have been future-oriented. They have been willing to sacrifice income and comforts in the present for the sake of capital accumulation. *Capital accumulation has a purpose: to provide tools of dominion for the next generation.* Future-orientation is the basis of low interest rates. Future-oriented people save for the future even when interest rates are low. Present-oriented people do not. Present-oriented people prefer to borrow money when rates are low, with the borrowed money to be used for present consumption. Future-oriented people lend to them. This increases the authority and wealth of future-oriented people. *Through voluntary exchange, future-oriented people increase their supply of capital at the expense of present-oriented people.* No coercion is involved. This is an aspect of dominion. Thus, God told covenantally faithful Israelites: "and you will lend to many nations, but you will not borrow" (Deut. 28:12b).

With each increase of wealth comes a necessary increase of responsibility. This is basic to capital accumulation. Covenantally faithful stewards act on behalf of the owner, who is God. They must train their children to have this attitude of responsibility: forward into the future, and upward toward God. As humanity's numbers increase, this is supposed to lead to widespread property ownership and therefore widespread responsibility. Ownership should be decentralized among individuals, families, and businesses. This outlook was basic to inheritance before the fall of man.

Conclusion to Part I

You have just read five brief chapters. I am now going to ask you a few questions.

First, if you were asked to teach a class in Sunday school on the first three chapters of the book of Genesis, would you review the five chapters you have just read? If you did review them, do you think that you could teach the class? Do you think that you could teach five sessions? If not, why not?

Second, if you were asked to teach a class session in Sunday school on Christian economics, would you review the five chapters you have just read? If you did review them, do you think that you could teach the class? Do you think that you could teach five sessions? If not, why not?

Third, if you were asked to teach a class session in Sunday school on covenant theology, would you review the five chapters you have just read? If you did review them, do you think that you could teach the class? Do you think that you could teach five sessions? If not, why not?

Have you ever been taught anything like these chapters from the pulpit? Have you ever been taught anything like these chapters in Sunday school? I think I can safely answer for you: "No."

This leads to my next question: Why do you think no one has taught you this? With respect to the topics of Christian economics and covenant theology, I think the answer is simple: *your pastor and your Sunday school teachers have never heard of any of this.* With respect to the first three chapters of Genesis, the answer is less clear. You have probably been taught about the first three chapters of Genesis. You have probably not been taught about the implications of these three chapters for economic theory. Yet what I wrote in the five chapters dealt with a good deal more than just economic theory. Again, why have you never been taught these things?

Here is the correct answer: *there is abysmal understanding of the Bible in Bible-believing churches.* This is especially true whenever the Bible speaks to important issues of the day. Economics is surely an important issue of the day, and it will be an important issue tomorrow, next week, and a century from now. Yet most pastors do not focus on these practical issues when they preach most of the time. This is not a new phenomenon.

You now have greater knowledge about the covenantal structure of economics than the overwhelming majority of Christians have ever understood, yet it only took five short chapters to impart this knowledge to you. That is not much. You also have greater knowledge about the structure of the biblical covenant than the vast majority of preachers who have ever called themselves covenant theologians. They have been completely unaware of the five-point structure of the biblical covenant. This may sound unbelievable, but it is true. Yet it only took five chapters to impart this knowledge to you.

What you have learned so far is not that difficult. You should be able to teach this in a Sunday school. You might have to review the chapters, but so what?

This raises the issue of your personal responsibility. If you are capable of doing it, should you be doing it? Should you be helping other people learn these fundamental principles? If not, why not?

Now you are going to read Part II. Anyway, I hope you are. Your knowledge after you read Part II will be substantially greater than it is now. You will therefore have even greater responsibility for teaching this material to others. That is because you will have even greater capability of doing so. *With greater capability comes greater responsibility.* I hope you understand this covenantal principle.

You have learned a great deal about what economics was before the fall of man. You learned a little about what it was after the fall, especially with respect to the curse of Adam and the ground. You have learned about the world we have lost.

In Part II, I analyze the effects of the fall of man on economic thought. In the fall, Adam adopted a rival worldview to the one that God had revealed to him. Ever since the fall, covenant-breakers have developed the implications of this rival worldview. Some of these implications apply to economic theory. Covenant-breaking economists have adopted the outline of the biblical covenant's five-point structure as it applies to the economic order, but they have substituted a rival confession of faith. Self-professed autonomous man, not the God of the Bible, is central to this confession. The logical structure of economic theory is the same; the confessional content is not. There is no escape from the five points of the covenant. They are inherent in men's thinking.

PART II

Fall

Introduction to Part II

> *"Otherwise, you may say in your heart, 'My power and the strength of my hand made me this wealth.' But you are to remember the* Lord *your God, for it is He who is giving you power to make wealth, in order to confirm His covenant which He swore to your fathers, as it is this day."*
>
> Deuteronomy 8:17–18

This passage makes it clear that positive economic sanctions confirm God's covenant with covenant-keepers. This was announced to the nation of Israel by Moses just prior to the invasion of Canaan. Moses warned against the assumption of man's autonomous productivity as a confirmation of a rival confession of faith. There are rival confessions that reflect rival religions: the worship of God and the worship of mammon. What is mammon? A statement of faith: "More for me in history." Jesus warned: "No one can serve two masters; for either he will hate the one and love the other, or else he will be loyal to the one and despise the other. You cannot serve God and mammon" (Matt. 6:24, NKJV).

The five points of the dominion covenant are these: God, man, law, sanctions, and time. I have presented this in my book, *Unconditional Surrender* (2010). Before the fall of man in the garden, the five economic points mirrored the five points of the dominion covenant: ownership, stewardship, property, imputation, and inheritance. I have covered this in Part I.

The fall of man did not change the structure of the dominion covenant. This structure is universal. Man cannot abandon any of the five points. These categories define the human condition. But covenant-breaking man immediately substituted new content for the original dominion covenant's content: polytheism, the divine state, salvation by ritual, magical invocation, and cyclical history. Christianity steadily replaced this worldview through evangelism for its first thousand years. Humanistic man ever since Darwin has changed his confession of faith again: cosmic impersonalism, autonomous man, situation ethics, state sanctions, and social evolution. He also restructured economic theory to reflect and then implement his new confession of faith: chance, autonomy, theft, bureaucratization, and the disinheritance of covenant-keepers. I explore some of the implications of the new economics in Part II.

CHAPTER 6

CHANCE

The lot is cast into the lap, but its every decision is from the LORD.

PROVERBS 16:33

ANALYSIS

Point one of the biblical covenant is God's transcendence, yet also His presence. This is the biblical concept of God's sovereignty. It asks: "Who's in charge here?"

Proverbs 16:33 is clear: *there is no such thing as chance.* But men do not believe this. This is why they gamble. They cast lots. They roll the dice. They play cards for money. They bet on horse races. These are what economists call *zero-sum games.* Winners win at the expense of losers. There is no net increase of wealth. Men's ability to predict the outcomes of zero-sum games is limited to statistical probability. The outcomes may seem to be part of a statistical pattern, or they may seem to be statistically random. This is an illusion that is due to men's lack of omniscience. No event is ever based on chance. "The king's heart is like channels of water in the hand of the LORD; He turns it wherever He pleases" (Prov. 21:1). Any theory of causality that denies this also necessarily denies the clear teaching of the Bible.

This denial began early, when Eve listened to the words of the serpent.

> Now the serpent was more cunning than any animal of the field which the LORD God had made. And he said to the woman, "Has God really said, 'You shall not eat from any tree of the garden'?" The woman said to the serpent, "From the fruit of the trees of the garden we may eat; but from the fruit of the tree which is in the middle of the garden, God has said, 'You shall not eat from it or touch it, or you will die.'" The serpent said to the woman, "You certainly will not die!" (Gen. 3:1–4)

Eve began with her own view of God's word. She and Adam were not to eat from this tree. She added this: "or touch it." The serpent countered: she would not die. He lied. She was deceived, Paul said (I Tim. 2:14). She ran an experiment to see who was right.

Adam was not deceived. He was self-conscious. He saw that nothing bad happened to her after she ate. So, he ate. In short, he decided that the outcome of eating was not predictable. He decided to run an additional test. The outcome would be either life or death. Either God had told him the truth or else He was a liar—or at least very badly misinformed. The serpent was either a liar or well-informed. Adam decided to test who was right: God or the serpent. But, from his preliminary assessment of Eve's condition, he favored the serpent. He had no coin to flip, but he would not have flipped it if he had owned one. Who would risk death for the sake of better knowledge about outcomes if he thought the odds were 50-50? Only a fool.

A fool says in his heart that there is no God (Ps. 14:1). Adam did not say there was no God. He did say in his heart that the being who had given the command regarding the outcome of eating from the tree was no more a sovereign God than the serpent. Actually, He was less sovereign. We know this was Adam's view, because Adam decided to test the two predictions. If Adam was in a position to test God's word, then he was in charge of evaluating the accuracy of God's word. He decided to run an empirical test. This test was based on Adam's assumption that God's word in this case was more like 30-70. Or maybe 20-80. In fact, given the enormously high stakes, the accuracy of God's word was so low in probability that the outcome probably was what the serpent said. God's word was wrong. Humans would not die.

Adam appears to have been an early polytheist. There was God's word. There was the serpent's word. Which one was the true god with the true word? Were they both merely potential divinities? Adam would run a test to find out. There was the tree. There was a probable outcome of the test. The outcome was not random, i.e., indeterminate. But it was certainly not 100% predictable, he believed. He concluded that *the reliability of God's word was dependent on Adam's test.* The test involved covenantal disobedience. But if God's word was not 100% reliable, then God was not sovereign. If he was not sovereign over the creation, then He was not the Creator described in Genesis 1. He was a big, fat fibber. Adam concluded that the universe needed Adam to provide an objective assessment of God's lack of reliability. How? By running an experiment.

The experiment blew up in his face. It therefore blew up in our faces.

The issue of *cosmic origins* is inescapably connected to the issue of sovereignty. This is why the Book of Genesis is all about sovereignty. It is about origins. It says that God created the universe out of nothing. This is why He is sovereign. He is the original owner.

The modern world of academic humanism denies this story of origins. The humanist is not polytheistic in the way that Adam was. He is far more consistent. He does not run tests of God's word versus the serpent's word. He denies both the existence of God or a serpent that represents Satan. He teaches that the universe was not created. It arose out of the Big Bang approximately 13.7 billion years ago.

A child asks: "But who set off the Big Bang?" The cosmic evolutionist says: "You are a child. I choose not to answer this. That is like asking who created God." But it really isn't. The substance that blew up/out 13.7 billion years ago is not said to be of infinite duration by cosmologists. Then how did it get there to blow up/out? What blew up/out? We are back to the journalist's big five questions: who, what, when, where, and why? To which is added: how?

Neither of these rival systems of origins explains how something came out of nothing. But biblical religion teaches that there was someone creative before there was something created. There was purpose before there was creation. The humanist denies that there was purpose prior to the appearance of man. There was no cosmic purpose 13.7 billion years ago. Cosmic purpose arrived with homo sapiens, unless there is some smarter alien race out there somewhere. If there is, then there will have to be either a showdown or a working agreement over which race's concept of purpose is correct. This is the survival of the fittest.

In the long run, there is no purpose, says the cosmic evolutionist. There is only the heat death of the universe. I will get to this in Section E.

A. No Cosmic Purpose

Point one of the biblical covenant is God's transcendence, yet also His presence. This is the biblical concept of God's sovereignty. It asks: "Who's in charge here?" How does this apply to the humanists' theory of the chance origins of the universe?

There was no cosmic purpose before man evolved. This was Darwinism's most important confession of faith. There was no intelligent design. There was no unintelligent design. There was only the Big Bang. It led to the creation of timeless, unbreakable laws of nature, coupled with random developments in nature. Nature is a mixed amalgam of law and chance. Humanists do not agree on the answer to this question: "Which is more fundamental, law or chance?"

They really do not care about the answer with respect to evolution prior to man. What they care about is this: "There was no purpose prior to man." This is a denial of the Bible's account of creation. The Bible declares that God had purposes before the creation. "Blessed be the God and Father of our Lord Jesus Christ, who has blessed us with every spiritual blessing in the heavenly places in Christ, just as He chose us in Him before the foundation of the world, that we would be holy and blameless before Him" (Eph. 1:3–4). This doctrine is anathema to the Darwinist.

Christian economics begins with the doctrine of God's creation of the universe out of nothing. Non-Christian economics begins with the doctrine of Darwinian evolution. Christian economics begins with the doctrine of God as cosmic owner. Humanist economics may begin with the autonomous individual, or the autonomous state, or a mixture. But it categorically rejects God's original ownership as the foundation of economic theory.

Humanist economics teaches that randomness or chance is the test of any theory. A theory proposes cause and effect. It is tested by statistical techniques that rest on the doctrine of randomness. The only rival theories of coherence rest on coherence that is outside of time and which proposes human omniscience as an ideal measure of coherence. This means a world without profit or loss. It is called *equilibrium*. This means that a hypothetical mental world which can never exist is the measure of the relevance of every economic policy or theory of causation. Modern economics is an unstable mixture of randomness, meaning 100% incoherence, and omniscience, meaning 100% understanding by humans.

While Austrian School economics as developed by Mises and Hayek rests on the doctrine of man's evolution, it begins with purposeful human action as the foundation of economic science. Mises titled his magnum opus *Human Action* (1949). This is why Austrian School economics is closer to Christian economics than its rivals are. It focuses on what individuals think and do. It does not focus on aggregates determining economic events.

The only source of economic coherence is mankind, humanists believe. A few economists say that the pure free market can provide all of the coherence required. Most free market economists say that there must be some civil government. Most economists are Keynesians. They say there must be government regulation. There must be some central planning, mainly by central bankers. There are few socialists remaining, and virtually no Marxists. But all are agreed: there is neither cosmic nor social providence. Men and their institutions provide the coherence. Everything else is ruled by chance.

B. No Cosmic Policeman

Point two of the biblical covenant is hierarchical authority. It asks: "To whom do I report?" How does this apply to the humanists' theory of the chance origins of the universe?

The humanist denies that there is a chain of responsibility outside of time's limits. Hierarchies begin and end with mankind. This means only two economic hierarchies: the state and the free market. They are cosmically autonomous. They influence each other. The state provides courts and enforcers, which rest on violence. It provides military defense. But there is no appeal above the state. Nothing threatens the state with negative sanctions, other than another state or armed revolutionaries.

There is no guarantor of ethics other than state officials. The supposedly impersonal market cannot enforce morals. There is no free market court that can settle issues finally. Any market-derived system of law enforcement turns into a state. The bully starts a gang. Successful gang leaders become regional warlords. These warlords invade the free market. *There is no market-derived ethics that can be enforced predictably.*

Economists deny that their theory of market operations is in any sense dependent on a theory of morality. Markets are impersonal, economists insist. So, they insist that their theory of how markets operate is equally impersonal, equally value-free.

Most people find it hard to believe that the theoretically autonomous free market can produce righteous outcomes. The masses will not grant legitimacy to such an idea. They will not obey such a system of law. Self-government is close to non-existent apart from legitimacy. Without self-government, men face either anarchy or tyranny. Anarchy never lasts long.

Men appeal to power to settle disputes. They seek stability. They seek legal predictability. They want a hierarchical court of appeals that is grounded in unchanging ethics: right versus wrong. But humanist economics as a science offers no theory of ethics, only efficiency. Men want to know that there is some trustworthy agency of law enforcement that will rule justly. Humanistic economic theory cannot provide either the philosophical or institutional basis of such a system within the framework of economic profit and loss.

C. No Cosmic Ethics

Point three of the biblical covenant is law. It asks: "What are the rules?" How does this apply to the humanists' theory of the chance origins of the universe?

Men want to know that they live in a world that is at bottom grounded by ethics. They want to believe that honesty is the best policy. They want to believe that righteous behavior produces profits, and that criminal behavior produces losses. *They want to believe that economic causation is ultimately ethical.* They teach their children that this is the case. But humanistic free market economists cannot affirm this. They say that economic analysis is value-free, having no connection with ethics.

Socialists for two centuries came to readers and voters with this message: "The free market produces evil results. It allows wealthy people exploit the poor and defenseless. We need to place limits on the free market. Production should be in terms of use, not profits. Economic inequality is unjust. The state must rectify these evils." These arguments persuaded millions of voters. Most voters did not become socialists, but they voted for the construction of welfare states in the West. Intellectual defenders of the free market have been unable to persuade most voters to vote the welfare state out of existence. The economic interventionists claim to occupy the moral high ground. Free market economists let them occupy this rhetorical high ground. They say this in response: "Economic science is value-free." They invoke the myth of neutrality. They have continued to lose the argument against the welfare state. Welfare implies a system of morality.

Is there a God-revealed, God-enforced ethical system? If so, does it speak plainly to economic issues? Hundreds of millions of Christians want to believe in yes answers, but their religious leaders do not know much about economic science as taught in universities. Those few economists who oppose the welfare state do not understand the Bible, nor do they cite it as an authoritative source of ethical information. So, Christian laymen do not know where to turn for guidance on economic issues, whether personal or political.

D. No Cosmic Meaning

Point four of the biblical covenant is sanctions. It asks: "What happens if I obey? Disobey?" How does this apply to the humanists' theory of the chance origins of the universe?

Men want to believe that there is meaning governing their lives. They impute meaning to the world around them. They want to believe that their subjective evaluation of the world is connected to its actual operations. When they pursue some goal, they want to believe they are not fooling themselves.

There is cause and effect in economic affairs. Why is this the case? People make accurate predictions about the outcomes of certain policies. But how is this possible in a world governed by chance? What meaning does chance offer to mankind or to individuals? No God lies behind the seeming chance events of the world, the humanist believes. The economist teaches that economic theory is meaningful only if it allows an economist to make better predictions. Better predictions than what? Flipping a coin? In this case, the meaningfulness of economic theory is defined only in terms of chance. Meaning is a predictable deviation from chance.

Then the question arises: Is this pattern good or bad? Is it right or wrong? Is it something that the government should encourage with positive sanctions or discourage through negative sanctions? The economist may have an opinion, but it is not a scientific opinion, he says. He cannot evaluate the outcome in terms of ethics. Economic theory is value-free, he says. But, he insists, so is all other social theory. Social scientists are in the same theoretical boat, he says. They cannot make interpersonal comparisons of subjective utility.

Humanists insist that the operations of the world around us are a mixture of absolutely fixed impersonal laws and absolutely unpredictable random events, also impersonal. There is no God who evaluates the meaning of all events in terms of His plan and His providence. Individual decisions are based on human freedom. This is the basis of personal responsibility. But to evaluate the rightness or wrongness of any action or outcome, a person needs a fixed ethical system of cause and effect. The economist denies that such a system has any relevance for economic theory. He denies that it even exists. Then how can someone accurately assess the outcome of his economic decisions? By means of his personal system of ethics, he is told. But how can the decision-maker know if there is any connection between his system of ethics, economic causation, and its effects on society? The economist says that economic theory cannot answer this question.

What is the role of personal ethics, personal evaluation, and objective outcomes in an evolving universe that is governed by the interplay of fixed impersonal law and meaningless random events? The humanist cannot say. Man is personal, he says. Man imputes meaning, he says. An intelligent non-economist responds: "Yes, as you say, I do this. But how do I know if the meaning that I impute to events and outcomes has any meaningful relationship with impersonal natural law and impersonal natural randomness?" The economist, like the ethicist, says that he just cannot say, either scientifically or logically.

E. No Cosmic Future

Point five of the biblical covenant is succession. It asks: "Does this outfit have a future?" How does this apply to the humanists' theory of the chance origins of the universe?

Every Western theory of the cosmos offers a theory of the future of the cosmos. But the Darwinian future is exceedingly bad news. The world is dying. There is a steady, irreversible movement from stored-up kinetic energy to dissipation. This is the second law of thermodynamics at work. The process is called entropy: the movement from order to disorder. This is modern man's definition of time: the dissipation of order, including heat. Especially heat. The end of this process is called the *heat death* of the universe. Wikipedia's entry for "Heat death of the universe" says this:

> The heat death of the universe... is a hypothesis on the ultimate fate of the universe, which suggests the universe will evolve to a state of no thermodynamic free energy and will, therefore, be unable to sustain processes that increase entropy. Heat death does not imply any particular absolute temperature; it only requires that temperature differences or other processes may no longer be exploited to perform work. In the language of physics, this is when the universe reaches thermodynamic equilibrium.[1]

This is the most widely shared cosmology among humanistic scientists in the West. It points to universal death, in which electrons whirl

1. "Heat death of the universe." *Wikipedia*, Wikimedia Foundation, August 28, 2022.

around protons, or not, depending on your theory of electrons. But there is no progress. There is no now and later, no here to there. *There is no meaningful change because there is no one and no thing to impute meaning.* Cosmic impersonalism without man returns to cosmic impersonalism without man. There is no one to ask: "What was that all about?"

How long will all this take? Wikipedia says this:

> From the Big Bang through the present day, matter and dark matter in the universe are thought to have been concentrated in stars, galaxies, and galaxy clusters, and are presumed to continue to be so well into the future. Therefore, the universe is not in thermodynamic equilibrium and objects can do physical work. The decay time for a supermassive black hole of roughly 1 galaxy-mass (10^{11} solar masses) due to Hawking radiation is on the order of 10^{100} years, so entropy can be produced until at least that time.... After that time, the universe enters the so-called Dark Era, and is expected to consist chiefly of a dilute gas of photons and leptons. With only very diffuse matter remaining, activity in the universe will have tailed off dramatically, with extremely low energy levels and extremely long time scales. Speculatively, it is possible that the universe may enter a second inflationary epoch, or assuming that the current vacuum state is a false vacuum, the vacuum may decay into a lower-energy state. It is also possible that entropy production will cease and the universe will reach heat death.
>
> It is suggested that, over vast periods of time, a spontaneous entropy decrease would eventually occur via the Poincaré recurrence theorem, thermal fluctuations, and fluctuation theorem. Through this, another universe could possibly be created by random quantum fluctuations or quantum tunnelling in roughly $10^{10^{10^{56}}}$ years.[2]

This is humanism's latest alternative to this scenario:

> "But when the Son of Man comes in His glory, and all the angels with Him, then He will sit on His glorious throne. And all the nations will be gathered before Him; and He will separate them from one another, just as the shepherd separates the sheep from the goats; and He will put the sheep on His right, but the goats on the left. Then the King will say to those on His right, 'Come, you who are blessed of My Father, inherit the kingdom prepared for you from the foundation of the world.'" (Matt. 25:31–34)

2. Ibid.

Which sounds more plausible to you?

It does not matter how long the heat death of the universe takes to arrive. The universe was 100% meaningless at the beginning, 13.7 billion years ago. It is relentlessly heading back toward 100% meaninglessness. "Meaninglessness giveth, and meaninglessness taketh away. Blessed be the name of meaninglessness." This, we are told, will be the final resting place of chance. It is the final triumph of chance. The cosmic impersonal laws of the universe will be swallowed up by chance. The laws will rule over nothing; chance will be all in all. When whirl is king, it brings forth only randomness.

Conclusion

When Adam substituted his judgment for God's, he picked up a much heavier philosophical burden than he had calculated. Then he died.

When Adam imputed meaning to the serpent's word, he downgraded the meaning of God's word. He ate. Then he died. It took time, but he died—just as humanists say the universe is dying. This was God's curse on Adam. It was also His curse on the universe.

A Darwinian economist cannot extract more meaning out of the Darwinian cosmos than any other Darwinian scientist can. There is no meaning, other than man's, as far as we know, he says. God does not impute meaning, he says—no meaningful meaning, anyway, i.e., no authoritative meaning. There is no God, he says. Or if there is, He does not speak a meaningful word to economists.

It is on this philosophical foundation that modern economic theory rests.

Chapter 7

Autonomy

Now he was very angry with the people of Tyre and Sidon; and with one mind they came to him, and having won over Blastus the king's chamberlain, they were asking for peace, because their country was supported with grain from the king's country. On an appointed day, after putting on his royal apparel, Herod took his seat on the rostrum and began delivering an address to them. The people repeatedly cried out, "The voice of a god and not of a man!" And immediately an angel of the Lord struck him because he did not give God the glory, and he was eaten by worms and died. But the word of the Lord continued to grow and to be multiplied.

Acts 12:20–24

Analysis

Point two of the biblical covenant is hierarchical authority. It has to do with God's delegation of limited sovereignty to man: the dominion covenant. Mankind represents God judicially. Each individual also represents God in his temporary sphere of authority, which is a legal jurisdiction. He speaks in the name of God. He is responsible to God. This is a judicial hierarchy.

The English word "hierarchy" comes from the Greek word for priest, *hieros*, and the Greek word for ruler, *archon*.

Herod was in a position to impose authoritative law in the name of God. Instead, he spoke an authoritative word in his own name. He died a non-authoritative death. This is the arrogance of autonomy in action. King Nebuchadnezzar learned this lesson, and he testified to it in Daniel 4, which he wrote. Herod did not learn this lesson.

The English word "autonomy" in a transliteration of the Greek word for self, *autos*, and the Greek word for law, *nomos*. Autonomy means self-law.

The first person to declare judicial autonomy was Eve. She was deceived (I Tim. 2:14). The first person to declare his judicial autonomy self-consciously was Adam. He refused to submit himself to God's law. He could have eaten from the tree of life at any time. This would have been a covenant meal. God had offered him access to this tree. Adam refused to take advantage of this opportunity to secure eternal life for himself. Instead, he ran a test on God's word versus the serpent's word. He took a chance on death, when he could have had life for certain. But to accept life on these terms was unacceptable to him. He would have had to submit to God's word in preference to the serpent's. If he was present when Eve was verbally tempted, he could have taken her to the tree of life immediately. If she did it alone, he could have led her in a prayer of forgiveness. Then he could have led her in a communion meal from the tree of life. But then there would have been no test of God's law. After that, the forbidden tree would have been no threat. The positive sanction of life would have removed the threat of death. But that would have meant judicial subordination to God. It would have ruined Adam's test of God's word. It would have placed him in a judicial hierarchy in which he possessed limited sovereignty, but not absolute sovereignty. He wanted absolute sovereignty. He wanted autonomy.

Adam decided that he would be in charge of the test. He substituted his own concept of ethical cause and effect for God's. He decided that God's law is not self-attesting. It needed verification. Adam decided that he was the self-appointed agent of verification in history. Eve was not self-conscious about this. She had been deceived. Adam was not deceived. He substituted his empirical law for God's authoritative law.

He did not accept the fact that God had laid down the law to him. He would now lay down the law to God. He would run the test of God's word on his own authority.

Covenant-breaking men believe that they either lay down the law or else autonomously interpret it and apply it to historical circumstances. A humanistic scientist does not believe that mankind has established the laws of nature. He believes that no one established laws of the universe. Nature is autonomous, he declares. Its laws are independent of everything except nature. They arose out of nature. He also believes that scientists can discover nature's laws and put them to use for mankind, either for good or evil. The law-order of nature is therefore separate from ethics. *Mankind, not nature, is the source of ethics for humanists.* With respect to using nature, man is in charge of some aspects of nature. The realm of man's control over nature is expanding, we are told. The supreme example is nuclear fission and nuclear fusion. Scientists, we are told, have "unlocked the secrets of the atom." Then politicians made decisions as to how these secrets should be used: for weapons or for healing.

This concept of man's hierarchical relationship to nature raises a series of problems. These problems are at bottom philosophical, but they are also practical. These are questions of sovereignty. Is man sovereign over nature, or is nature sovereign over man? Who speaks on behalf of whom? Who speaks the final authoritative word?

Here is a practical question that comes out of this larger question of sovereignty versus authority. "If some innovative people have found ways to use nature to work productively for themselves as individuals, and also for others, who is in charge: man or nature?" It seems that man is. But this conclusion is called into question by the technological issue of robotics and algorithms. Question: "Will scientists produce robots or computer programs that will enable impersonal nature to become conscious and therefore personal, thereby enabling nature to take control of man because of its now vastly superior computational power?" This has been a familiar theme in science fiction for over a century. This practical question was first asked by Samuel Butler in 1863 in a letter to a New Zealand newspaper: "Darwin Among the Machines." He wrote a Utopian novel about this, *Erewhon*, which is "nowhere" spelled backwards, published in 1872. It contains three chapters, "The Book of the Machines." The novel is about a closed-off society that forbade all mechanical inventions. The problem with the novel is this: only technology and science have enabled societies to overcome grinding poverty since 1800. Always before, population growth had consumed available resources, mainly food. Mankind used nature briefly, but was then starved into submission. This changed with the industrial revolution. Man definitively took control over nature. The symbol of this was the steam engine. But now there are new symbols: the computer and the robot.

This dualism in philosophy came shortly after the steam engine was perfected by James Watt. The German philosopher Immanuel Kant came up with a new theory of man's relation to nature. Nature operates autonomously. Men know nothing of these laws. The laws that men use to interpret nature come from men's minds. Men are free to subjugate nature because their minds grasp nature's regularities. Nature does not control man. Man has freedom. He has morals. These are independent of nature. If they were not, men would not be free to choose. But this raises a problem. If men's hopes, dreams, and plans are independent of nature's control, how can they become tools in man's toolkit of controls over nature? If men's decisions are not under nature, how can men be over nature? What is the basis of the seeming coherence of men's minds and nature? Why is cause and effect only one way: from man to nature? What protects man from an invasion across the drawbridge into men's internal castles of mind, emotion, and ethics? (As a side note, Kant was also the first major Western philosopher to propose a theory of cosmic evolution.)

Kant's dualism between the realm of nature (scientific phenomenal realm) and the realm of freedom (contingent noumenal realm) is called the *nature/freedom dualism.* It is also called the *science/personality dualism.* This is no longer some rarified speculation of philosophers. If algorithms can think the way that men do, what is to prevent them from taking control of mankind, or even eliminating mankind? How can men program humanistic ethics into computer programs and robots? No one knows. Even if this is possible, who is to say who the programmer will be? What will his ethics be? What if he thinks that Adolf Hitler was a softie?

These are economic problems. Will computers and robotics eliminate the jobs of millions of people? It is economically efficient for specific employers to substitute computer programs and smart machines for humans. How can we be sure that what is good for specific employers is also good for the masses of workers who may lose their jobs?

Microeconomic decisions of employers have macroeconomic effects on the economy. What theory of economics provides accurate guidance for policy-makers? Should the government intervene? To do what? How? With what system of sanctions? These are significant macroeconomic questions in the second decade of the twenty-first century.

Humanistic economics has no theory of a sovereign God who providentially brings all things to pass. It also has no concept of economic causation as inherently ethical. Economists insist that economic theory is value-free, and must remain value-free. But if economic analysis is value-free, how can it provide accurate insights into a world that is governed by men? Men are inherently ethical, for good or evil. Causation in human institutions is ethical. The Bible makes this clear (Deut. 28). The vast majority of parents have taught this to their children. Humanistic economists tell us that we have it all wrong. They insist that what matters economically is efficiency, not ethics. They expect people to believe them. Then they sneak ethics into their analyses through the back door of policy recommendations, which they claim will produce good results, meaning ethically good, i.e., not evil. In short, they cheat. They don't convince anyone except other economists about their supposedly value-free theory. Yet they cannot figure out why their arguments fall on deaf ears. *Their arguments are clearly inefficient.* So, they shout louder: "Economic theory is value-free!" No, it isn't.

I ask: "How can humanistic economic analysis deal accurately with the realm of economics as a covenantal system of cause and effect that is imposed by God, which economists deny?" They want people to believe that a coherent, predictable, ethically decent social system autonomously developed out of voluntary economic exchanges, whether these exchanges were ethical or not. No one believes this except economists. No one should—not even economists.

A. Polytheism

Point one of the biblical covenant is God's transcendence, yet also His presence. This is the biblical concept of God's original sovereignty. It asks: "Who's in charge here?" How does this apply to autonomy?

If God does not rule the world as the Creator and Providential Sustainer of the world, then what does?

The Darwinist argues that nothing did until man evolved out of non-man. Man now imputes purpose. He plans. He executes plans. The formerly purposeless universe now has purpose.

Hardly anyone has ever believed this. Anyone who argues in this fashion is doomed to a life of frustration. No religion teaches it. No ethical system teaches it. Only a handful of university graduates teach it to their children. It is the argument of a fool. "The fool has said in his heart, 'There is no God' " (Ps. 14:1a).

In contrast, polytheism has had lots of supporters in history. This is the product of their rebellion.

> For the wrath of God is revealed from heaven against all ungodliness and unrighteousness of people who suppress the truth in unrighteousness, because that which is known about God is evident within them; for God made it evident to them. For since the creation of the world His invisible attributes, that is, His eternal power and divine nature, have been clearly perceived, being understood by what has been made, so that they are without excuse. For even though they knew God, they did not honor Him as God or give thanks, but they became futile in their reasonings, and their senseless hearts were darkened. Claiming to be wise, they became fools, and they exchanged the glory of the incorruptible God for an image in the form of corruptible mankind, of birds, four-footed animals, and crawling creatures. (Rom. 1:18–23)

Atheists are operational polytheists. If God is not God, then man is. But man is plural, not just a single species. One person's opinions are as good as any other person's views, defenders of democracy insist. Each person imputes meaning and coherence to the world around him. Who is to say any of these imputed realities is incorrect? Problem: there is no way to use logic and persuasion to shape these rival imputations into a coherent unity. The competing worldviews of men have proven to be irreconcilable. So, he who wants to attain unity must use coercive force. Every political system operates on the basis of a book and guns to enforce it. There is no agreement on which book possesses autonomous authority.

With many gods there are many hierarchies, many legal systems, many sanctions, and many predicted futures. Systems come, but most of them fade away. A few persist. Christianity, Judaism, and Islam deny polytheism. Hinduism affirms it. Buddhism is either polytheistic or atheistic, depending on the variety. Confucianism doesn't care. Marxism is atheistic. That experiment went belly-up in 1991. Darwinism is atheistic. Few people believe it. But most economists do.

If the universe is autonomous but without purpose apart from mankind, then man must impose order. But there is a problem. Man evolved out of autonomous nature, Darwinists tell us. Mankind is therefore under the laws of nature. Some scientists say that they understand these laws. Conclusion: these elite planners must be the ones to bring social order and scientific progress. They shout: "Man must take control of man!" That means that a few men must take control of all the others, a point made by a power-seeking atheist in a 1946 novel by Christian theologian C. S. Lewis, *That Hideous Strength*. This is operational polytheism: lots of competing scientific gods, each seeking to impose his order on the rest of humanity. Sometimes the gods cooperate, as the Olympian gods did occasionally. Usually, the gods of Olympus were at war with each other, by way of men and women in history.

B. Irresponsibility

Point two of the biblical covenant is hierarchical authority. It asks: "To whom do I report?" How does this apply to autonomy?

In a world of competing sovereignties, different people will report to different sovereigns. This is the problem of polytheism. A person may seek to remain faithful to one sovereign, but he will be regarded as irresponsible by participants in rival hierarchies.

Some systems of belief produce centralized, top-down social systems. Marxism did. Fascism did. These do not last for long. They create great resistance. They run out of resources to fund the control system. They break apart or else are defeated in a war.

Socialism is a top-down system of state ownership and central planning. All socialist systems of state ownership of the means of production are inherently irrational, a point made by Ludwig von Mises in his classic 1920 essay, "Economic Calculation in the Socialist Commonwealth." Without capital markets based on private ownership, open entry, and competition, no socialist planning board can gain access to prices within its borders. Without prices, central planners are blind. Socialism is therefore self-defeating.

The free market is a bottom-up system of private economic planning. It is based on private property, open entry, and competition. Its problem is its institutional polytheism. How can confrontations be settled peacefully? To whom do all participants report? Who imposes negative sanctions on criminals? If the state can impose sanctions on evil-doers, who defines evil? On what basis? What factors limit the domain of each state? A state powerful enough to settle disputes by force is powerful enough to interfere with the operations of the market. The market is not autonomous.

C. Lawlessness

Point three of the biblical covenant is law. It asks: "What are the rules?" How does this apply to autonomy?

If man is autonomous in an autonomous universe, and mankind is also plural, then which god's laws are authoritative? On what basis?

There are theories of natural law. They have these problems in common: hardly anyone believes in them, and among the few who do, there is no agreement on what they are or how they are discovered. Natural law theory was a product of the Roman Empire. Stoic philosophers attempted to provide a philosophical foundation to hold the empire's many gods together. The Jews never accepted this. The Christians didn't, either. Christianity adopted natural law theory in the late Middle Ages. Aquinas was the model. Luther also accepted it. Today, a few Christian ethical theorists accept it, but in the age of Kant, it is obsolete. Austrian School economist Murray Rothbard accepted it, but his mentor Mises was a Kantian. Mises rejected natural law theory. So did Mises' other major disciple, F. A. Hayek. Both of them were Darwinists.

So, on what ethical basis can economists defend economic theory? None. Most of the major economists have acknowledged this openly. They deny that economic theory has anything to do with ethics. They say that economics is value-free. Rothbard held this position, following Mises.

This assertion is undermined by the policy recommendations of economists.

D. Self-Deception

Point four of the biblical covenant is sanctions. It asks: "What do I get if I obey? Disobey?" How does this apply to autonomy?

Governments rely on economists for recommendations. No other group of social scientists has this degree of authority. The high priests of social science are economists.

Economists claim to be able to apply economic theory to real-world situations. This is the art of *casuistry*: applying general laws to specific situations. It was a major area of Christian theology prior to 1700. It has faded since then. It barely exists today. Similarly, Jews have had private courts that have handed down decisions for 1700 years. These decisions are called *responsa*. No other religion has anything like these collections of court cases: hundreds of thousands.

There is no escape from casuistry, but it can be concealed. Consider this. Free market economists officially hold to methodological individualism. They do not think about these issues often. They may acknowledge that there is no way to tabulate economic value, which is imputed subjectively. This acknowledgment has been common ever since 1932, with the publication of Lionel Robbins' book, *An Inquiry into the Nature and Significance of Economic Science*. Chapter VI argued that there is no way scienticально to make interpersonal comparisons of subjective utility. There is no common scale of values. But he surrendered on this point in 1938 when Keynesian economist Roy Harrod pointed out that if Robbins were correct, then there would be no legitimate way for economists to make policy recommendations of any kind. Conclusion: there is no way that a methodological individualist can know scientifically whether any policy would produce results consistent with increased collective social value. *There can be no such thing as collective social value if methodological individualism is correct.* Robbins admitted that Harrod was correct, and he retracted his position. He did not explain why he had been wrong in 1932. This academic debate is long forgotten. Yet it took place in the influential scholarly journal that Harrod edited, *The Economic Journal*. (Note: this was an old debate in 1938. It began with the medieval debates between realists and nominalists. Robbins in 1932 was a pure nominalist.)

So, if men are autonomous, then there can be no way for them to come to policy decisions that can satisfy all of the mini-gods. The state must impose policies on protesting citizens. If it outlaws sticking pins in people, it will reduce the liberty of many sadists and even some masochists. Will this reduce aggregate social value? There is no way for a consistent methodological individualist economist to determine this scientifically.

If economic science is value-free, and if all value is subjective, then economists are engaged in a self-interested deception. They claim to be able to do what their own principles say is impossible: offer advice based on science.

E. Noise

Point five of the biblical covenant is succession. It asks: "Does this outfit have a future?" How does this apply to autonomy?

In economics, succession is the issue of economic growth. Most economists agree on this: the benefits of economic growth. They advocate policies they believe will produce economic growth. They always include limiting factors, such as non-polluting growth or growth that promotes greater economic equality. But they favor economic growth in general.

The problem is this: there is no agreement about how to achieve economic growth. Keynesians favor government deficits, at least in recessions. Austrians favor stable money, preferably gold coins, and low taxes. Monetarists favor a slow but steady expansion of the central bank's monetary base. Rational expectations economists favor changing nothing. Behavioral economists don't have any theory of economic growth. In short, there is a lot of noise. The realm of policy-making has a low signal-to-noise ratio. There are lots of conflicting signals and too much noise.

If there were agreement among economists, there would be less noise. But these aphorisms are common. "Where there are five economists, there will be six opinions." "If you laid all the economists end to end, they would never reach a conclusion." President Harry Truman's comment was appropriate sometime around 1948: "Give me a one-handed economist. All my economists say 'on the one hand…', then 'but on the other…'" The autonomy of man has produced an army of economists. There is no unity within the camp of the economists. This has led to conflicting advice.

There has been economic growth, but economists are not agreed on why. There are at least two dozen different explanations about how, sometime around 1800, economic growth began to compound at about 2% per capita per annum in Great Britain and North America's British colonies. Prof. D. McCloskey devoted chapters 16 to 40 of *Bourgeois Dignity* (2010) to a refutation of all of them. But McCloskey's book, *Bourgeois Equality* (2016), does not offer an explanation that I find persuasive. There is no historical or theological explanation of how and why Dutch theologians adopted a new casuistry favoring wealth. There is also no explanation of how and why they adopted a new view of the future, one in which compound long-term economic growth is possible. There is no discussion of postmillennialism versus amillennialism in Dutch theology in the seventeenth century, or Scottish theology, or Puritan theology. McCloskey says that rhetoric changed. Fair enough. But whose rhetoric? Pastors? Theologians? Calvinists? Arminians? On what theological basis did they change? Rhetoric is persuasion, but persuasion needs ethical content. The book offers no evidence from primary sources of any shift in ethical content regarding the legitimacy of riches. What was it that changed in Dutch, Scottish, and Puritan theology—a break from Calvin's theology? This is the crucial historical issue in McCloskey's theory of what changed rhetorically. But there is not a paragraph in these books that answers this question, or even asks it.

If economists cannot specify what caused this change, which was the most profound change in man's economic history since Noah's flood, then on what basis will compound growth continue? Is it autonomous? If so, then this is incorrect:

> "Otherwise, you may say in your heart, 'My power and the strength of my hand made me this wealth.' But you are to remember the LORD

> your God, for it is He who is giving you power to make wealth, in order to confirm His covenant which He swore to your fathers, as it is this day." (Deut. 8:17–18)

If economic growth is autonomous, then advice from economists is irrelevant. If it is autonomous, then there is no science of economics that connects with the real world.

Conclusion

Covenant-breaking man began with an assumption: "God is not sovereign." This was followed by another assumption: "There are many gods." This was followed by a third assumption: "Man must test which self-professed god is sovereign." This led to a conclusion: "Man is sovereign, since his tests are authoritative." This led to the final conclusion: "Man is autonomous."

This created an immediate problem: there are many men and many views of truth. Cain and Abel divided over this issue (Gen. 4). How can men come to agreed-upon solutions to this problem, which is the problem of noise? There has been no solution offered so far that has begun to bring theoretical unity out of theoretical diversity in any area of life.

The assumption of man's autonomy has shattered theoretical unity. This has affected the science of economics as profoundly as it has affected every other social science. There is no agreement regarding economic theory. There has been no agreement on economic policy. If methodological individualism is true, there can never be any agreement on policy. This is because it is impossible to make scientific interpersonal comparisons of subjective utility. It is impossible to add up gains and losses. Value is subjective. It cannot be measured. Humanistic economic theory has reached a dead end.

Chapter 8

Theft

Then the Lord God took the man and put him in the Garden of Eden to cultivate it and tend it. The Lord God commanded the man, saying, "From any tree of the garden you may freely eat; but from the tree of the knowledge of good and evil you shall not eat, for on the day that you eat from it you will certainly die."

Genesis 2:15–17

Analysis

Point three of the biblical covenant is law. It asks: "What are the rules?"

God gave a garden to Adam. Adam was to care for it. He was allowed to eat from any tree except one. He had almost universal access. There was only one piece of property that God set apart. He placed a judicial boundary around it. This made it holy. The meaning of the word "holiness" means *set apart by God*. When Adam violated the tree's boundary, he committed an act of theft. But he also committed a profane act. The biblical meaning of "profane" is this: *the violation of a holy boundary.* This was an act of sacrilege.

The tree of life was also holy, but God gave Adam access to it before the fall. This changed after the fall.

> Then the Lord God said, "Behold, the man has become like one of Us, knowing good and evil; and now, he might reach out with his hand,

> and take fruit also from the tree of life, and eat, and live forever"—therefore the LORD God sent him out of the Garden of Eden, to cultivate the ground from which he was taken. So He drove the man out; and at the east of the Garden of Eden He stationed the cherubim and the flaming sword which turned every direction to guard the way to the tree of life. (Gen. 3:22–24)

This turned the entire garden into a holy place: set apart by God. God placed a boundary around it. This boundary was not merely judicial. A judicial boundary around the tree had failed to protect it. God made sure this time that Adam could not again commit another profane act. This was an act in defense of private property.

This event teaches clearly that the original sin was an act of theft. Adam had already mentally calculated that God was not who He said He was, i.e., a sovereign God who possessed the power of life and death. So, Adam had mentally rebelled. But God had not announced that mental rebellion against Him was a prohibited act. There had to be a physical violation of a property boundary in order for God to impose the negative sanction of death.

The original sin of man placed economics at the center of ethics. God had made this so. He placed the forbidden tree at the center of His covenantal relationship between God and man. It was the test of man's loyalty. Adam did the same with respect to God. He decided to run a test to see if God was who He said He was. The test would produce specific outcomes. Either Adam would get away with this, proving that God was not sovereign, or else God would impose negative sanctions on the two violators.

The negative sanctions on Adam included sweat through his labor, an economic sanction, and weeds in the ground, an economic sanction (Gen. 3:17–18). His work would be more difficult. His costs of production would rise. This would decrease Adam's desire to work. *When costs rise, less is demanded.* This in turn would increase his desire to trade. Specialization increases output per unit of input.

From this time on, men stole. This seemed easier than making a living through serving customers. But the act of theft remained a violation of boundaries established by God. God continued to allocate wealth, skills, and opportunities according to His priorities, just as He had with

Adam. He placed people in specific positions of authority, just as He had with Adam. This is the meaning of Jesus' parable of the talents. Jesus used it to describe the kingdom of God. A rich man prepares to go on a long journey. He transfers coins to his stewards. He later returns for an accounting. He hands out further rewards in terms of his personal economic gain as a result of their management of his money (Matt. 25:14–30). He condemns a poor money-manager.

This being the case, every act of theft is a violation of God's property rights. The victims of theft are agents of God, both from a legal standpoint and an economic standpoint. They are His representatives. The thief is saying that he has better uses for other people's wealth than they do. He prefers to benefit from their loss. The alternative is to serve customers through production. He finds it easier to steal. Theft is not productive. It does not create wealth. It reduces wealth. The gains of the thief come from the loss to the victim. But the theft increases other people's insecurity. They may decide to spend money on theft prevention. This removes money from their budgets for consumption, making them poorer.

Theft is a system of coercive wealth distribution from owners to thieves. It moves wealth from those who deserve it to those who do not. When this becomes widespread in society, it interferes with economic growth. The prophet Isaiah brought a covenant lawsuit against Israel. The moral corruption of the nation was manifested in acts of theft. "Your rulers are rebels and companions of thieves; everyone loves a bribe and chases after gifts. They do not obtain justice for the orphan, nor does the widow's case come before them" (Isa. 1:23).

The thief says to himself: "The present distribution of wealth does not suit me. I will intervene in the economy and take what in principle is mine. I have been dealt with unfairly. I deserve better." This is an accusation against God that His present distribution of wealth is mistaken. The thief makes plans to place ownership on a better foundation. He places himself above God. Or, if he does not believe in God, he places him above the decisions of consumers in allocating a portion of their own wealth to those entrepreneurs who serve them best, according to their individual assessments of value. *Theft is a revolt against God's social order and economic order.*

God prohibits theft. "You shall not steal" (Ex. 20:15). He prohibits ideas that might lead to theft. "You shall not covet your neighbor's house; you shall not covet your neighbor's wife, or his male slave, or his female slave, or his ox, or his donkey, or anything that belongs to your neighbor" (Ex. 20:17). He places boundaries around the property of everyone who has gained his wealth legally. This is an affront to thieves. They see this as an illegitimate intrusion into their activities and plans. They do not accept the legitimacy of wealth distribution performed in competitive markets.

Men seek to protect their property. They spend a portion of their wealth on strategies to secure their property from thieves. Money that they would otherwise have spent on consumer goods and services goes for the purchase of locks and electronic security systems. Money that would have been invested to increase output is spent on private guards and vaults. Because it costs money to defend property, this reduces the net return from owning it. This forces down prices. Owners suffer economic losses. A good example is the price of real estate in high-crime neighborhoods.

The most serious crimes against property are committed by civil governments, especially national civil governments. Politicians raise taxes far above the 10% rate identified by God as tyrannical (I Sam. 8:15, 17). Bureaucrats intrude into every area of the economy with detailed rules and regulations that were never approved by any legislature. They set up central banks that inflate away people's investments as a result of falling currency value. This undermines trust in the civil government. People lose respect. They hide wealth. They do what they can to escape the tax man. Big businesses hire teams of lawyers and accountants to find loopholes in the tax laws. These firms build wealth by legal but costly tax avoidance schemes rather than by increasing output to satisfy consumers.

When the covenantal institution that God has established to be a scourge to criminals (Rom. 13:1–7) itself becomes criminal, the public seeks deliverance. The public senses that injustice is dominant in society.

It is much worse when the public decides to join in the looting process. They vote for politicians who promise to "soak the rich" by getting the rich to pay "their fair share." This is theft, pure and simple. It is theft by the ballot box. It is the re-writing of the commandment against theft. "Thou shalt not steal except by majority vote." This is the sale of votes for the purpose of looting the wealth of others. Blocs of voters vote for politicians who promise to use the coercive power of the state to extract wealth from political enemies and give it to the voters who won the last election. It is done in the name of social justice. It is not social justice. It is social injustice. It is the politics of plunder.

What is most appalling is that these policies of political plunder are endorsed by Christian leaders. This is based on a theology called the social gospel or liberation theology. It is baptized theft by the state. There is nothing in the Bible that justifies it. These theologians can point to no Mosaic law or New Testament principle that authorizes the state to take money from one group to give to another group.

Modern man accepts the politics of plunder. This is the economics of authorized theft.

A. Squatter

Point one of the biblical covenant is God's transcendence, yet also His presence. This is the biblical concept of God's sovereignty. It asks: "Who's in charge here?" How does this apply to theft?

Satan was the original squatter. He did not purchase property from Adam, let alone from God. He had the serpent lure Eve into a revolt. Then she served as spokesman for the serpent. Adam broke covenant with God on behalf of the serpent, who in turn acted on behalf of Satan. This was a case of creatures who were lower in God's hierarchy asserting both sovereignty and autonomy for themselves.

Satan did not require that Adam and Eve worship him. That was not necessary. It was sufficient that they broke covenant with God. Ultimately, however, Satan does demand man's worship. We see this in his temptation of Jesus in the wilderness.

> Again, the devil took Him along to a very high mountain and showed Him all the kingdoms of the world and their glory; and he said to Him, "All these things I will give You, if You fall down and worship me." Then Jesus said to him, "Go away, Satan! For it is written: 'You shall worship the Lord your God, and serve Him only.'" (Matt. 4:8–10)

The devil offered Jesus the kingdoms of the world in exchange for worship. On what judicial basis could he make this offer? He was not the owner of these kingdoms. He was a squatter. He was dealing with Jesus, the incarnation of the son of God, the Second Person of the Trinity. He was the Creator. Paul wrote of Jesus:

> He is the image of the invisible God, the firstborn of all creation: for by Him all things were created, both in the heavens and on earth, visible and invisible, whether thrones, or dominions, or rulers, or authorities—all things have been created through Him and for Him. He is before all things, and in Him all things hold together. (Col. 1:15–17)

Satan was offering to Jesus what Jesus already owned as the incarnate Son of God. Jesus was the lawful heir of God. He collected His inheritance immediately after the resurrection (Matt. 28:18–20). Satan's theory of ownership was this: squatter's rights. He hoped that Jesus would accept his claim. If Jesus worshipped him, this would be Jesus' transfer of allegiance from God the Father to Satan. This would transfer ownership of the world in the name of God the Father to Satan. *This was the ultimate temptation.* This was why it was the third and final temptation of Jesus. This was the essence of the original temptation of Adam. Satan could not secure ownership from Adam, for Adam was only a temporary trustee in God's name. He was being tested by God. Would he respect God's property rights to the forbidden tree? Adam chose to test God's word by eating. But Adam could not legally transfer to Satan what the Second Person of the Trinity held in trust for God the Father.

The modern welfare state asserts original ownership when it is in fact a squatter. It has violated the limits of taxation, as God announced to Samuel. It has proven itself to be tyrannical.

B. Rebellion

Point two of the biblical covenant is hierarchical authority. It asks: "To whom do I report?" How does this apply to theft?

Jesus related this parable. It is the parable of the thieving stewards.

> "Listen to another parable. There was a landowner who planted a vineyard and put a fence around it, and dug a wine press in it, and built a tower, and he leased it to vine-growers and went on a journey. And

> when the harvest time approached, he sent his slaves to the vine-growers to receive his fruit. And the vine-growers took his slaves and beat one, killed another, and stoned another. Again, he sent other slaves, more than the first; and they did the same things to them. But afterward he sent his son to them, saying, 'They will respect my son.' But when the vine-growers saw the son, they said among themselves, 'This is the heir; come, let's kill him and take possession of his inheritance!' And they took him and threw him out of the vineyard, and killed him. Therefore, when the owner of the vineyard comes, what will he do to those vine-growers?" They said to Him, "He will bring those wretches to a wretched end and lease the vineyard to other vine-growers, who will pay him the fruit in the proper seasons." (Matt. 21:33–41)

Jesus used a pocketbook parable to drive home a point: the Jews were in revolt against God. They would lose the kingdom because of this. "Therefore I say to you, the kingdom of God will be taken away from you and given to a people producing its fruit" (Matt. 21:43). He presented this warning by means of a parable of a revolt against an owner by his servants.

It should take no leap of faith to see that the modern welfare state is the equivalent of this conspiracy of servants. It extracts four or five times the tax rate that God identified as tyrannical (I Sam. 8:10, 14). It does so in the name of the poor. This is a false claim. The poor have no Bible-based legal claim on the wealth of the middle class or the rich. The Bible proclaims a law-order which does not discriminate against rich or poor. "You shall not do injustice in judgment; you shall not show partiality to the poor nor give preference to the great, but you are to judge your neighbor fairly" (Lev. 19:15).

C. Invasion

Point three of the biblical covenant is law. It asks: "What are the rules?" How does this apply to theft?

Adam invaded God's property when he ate from the forbidden tree. He violated a legal boundary. This is the essence of all moral and legal transgression: a boundary violation. The archetype of such a boundary violation is theft.

The Mosaic law placed a boundary around a family's home.

> If the thief is caught while breaking in and is struck so that he dies, there will be no guilt for bloodshed on his account. If the sun has risen on him, there will be guilt for bloodshed on his account—a thief shall certainly make restitution; if he owns nothing, then he shall be sold for his theft. (Ex. 22:2–3)

A man has the right to protect his property against invasion. He has the right to kill the invader at night. The owner does not know who this invader is. It is dark. He may lawfully kill him, according to God's law.

But what if a tax collector invades during the day? The home owner must submit. But this is theft. The person with the badge and the gun is coming to steal in the name of the People. The People is the new god of society. It is the self-appointed squatter that claims original ownership of everything. Individuals and organizations are allowed by the state to act as trustees of the state's property, but the state reserves the right to revoke this trusteeship. This is the politics of plunder. It is based upon a revision of Exodus 20:15: "You shall not steal, except by majority vote." It argues that individuals and organizations do not posses the right (legal immunity) to use their property.

This is the only theory of property rights that is legally consistent with the level of taxation imposed by the modern welfare state. What the Old Testament regarded as tyranny, voters today regard as ethical taxation.

D. Taxation

Point four of the biblical covenant is sanctions. It asks: "What do I get if I obey? Disobey?" How does this apply to theft?

The modern welfare state imposes income taxes. These taxes are imposed at higher rates on the rich than on the poor. There are usually loopholes, but in the statutes, the pre-loophole rates are always higher for people with greater income. This is a violation of biblical justice. "You shall not do injustice in judgment; you shall not show partiality to the poor nor give preference to the great, but you are to judge your neighbor fairly" (Lev. 19:15). Voters are not familiar with God's law, including Christian voters. They have been told that the graduated income tax is moral. They have been told this by advocates of the welfare state, who preach the doctrine of getting even with the rich through politics. This is the so-called politics of the fair share.

The welfare state imposes negative sanctions on economically successful people: high marginal tax rates. It transfers wealth to members of favored voting blocs: positive sanctions. The welfare state sees the state as a healing agency in society. It provides healing through government funding of medical services. There is nothing in the Bible authorizing state funding of medical care. Jesus' parable of the good Samaritan is based on the willingness of an individual to bear the costs of healing a victim of thieves (Luke 10:25–37).

Modern politics is the story of who wins and who loses. Winners impose economic losses on successful people in the name of the poor. But the poor remain poor. The big winners are the bureaucrats who administer the welfare state's compulsory wealth-transfer programs at salaries above what they could earn in the private sector.

E. Disinheritance

Point five of the biblical covenant is succession. It asks: "Does this outfit have a future?" How does this apply to theft?

The most famous biblical story of inheritance and disinheritance is the story of Jacob and Esau. Esau was a covenant-breaker. God had told his pregnant mother that Esau was under a permanent curse.

> For this is the word of promise: "At this time I will come, and Sarah will have a son." And not only that, but there was also Rebekah, when she had conceived twins by one man, our father Isaac; for though the twins were not yet born and had not done anything good or bad, so that God's purpose according to His choice would stand, not because of works but because of Him who calls, it was said to her, "The older will serve the younger." Just as it is written: "Jacob I have loved, but Esau I have hated." (Rom. 9:9–13)

Jacob did not steal Esau's inheritance. Esau had sold it to him for a plate of stew and some bread: the most ludicrous voluntary economic exchange in the Bible (Gen. 25:29–34). Then, after Jacob and Rebekah had tricked the blind, stubborn Isaac into giving the blessing to Jacob, Esau was outraged.

> When Esau heard the words of his father, he cried out with an exceedingly great and bitter cry, and said to his father, "Bless me, me as well, my father!" And he said, "Your brother came deceitfully and has taken away your blessing." Then Esau said, "Is he not rightly named Jacob, for he has betrayed me these two times? He took away my birthright, and behold, now he has taken away my blessing." And he said, "Have you not reserved a blessing for me?" (Gen. 27:34–36)

Esau was a cheat and a liar. He expected the blessing he had sold for a plate of stew. He got more than he deserved from Isaac. He wanted revenge. "So Esau held a grudge against Jacob because of the blessing with which his father had blessed him; and Esau said to himself, 'The days of mourning for my father are near; then I will kill my brother Jacob'" (Gen. 27:41). He was an evil, present-oriented man.

Esau is the archetype of today's present-oriented sons who have long since surrendered their inheritances for the economic equivalent of plates of stew. They want to get even with those who lawfully bought the inheritances by means of greater productivity. *The Esaus of the world want to disinherit the lawful heirs.* They want to reverse God's allocation of property. They are thieves. They use the state to serve as the agent of their theft. They want the state to veto the decisions of customers to reward some producers and not others. Yet most of these thieves never get ahead. The wealth that the state steals in their name dribbles away.

Conclusion

With Adam's theft of forbidden fruit, theft was unleashed on the world. Theft is the archetypal crime in the Bible, the representative sin against God. By means of the politics of plunder, theft remains the representative sin against God. How? Through stealing from successful people. God has raised them up. The welfare state seeks to tear them down.

This does not apply to the super-rich. They have enough money to buy off the politicians. They get loopholes built into the tax code. They escape. But those who are lower down the wealth hierarchy fund the welfare state at high tax rates. Meanwhile, the state taxes all workers through non-regulated retirement taxes and sales taxes.

Theft before modern times was mostly individual. Kings and lords and the aristocracy plundered those under them, but never at the high tax rates of the modern welfare state. *We live in the consummate age of theft.* It is done in the name of the poor. It is done in the name of morality. There are thousands of academic economists who place their seal of approval on the welfare state and its taxes. They are paid above-market salaries in tax-funded universities to do this.

Chapter 9

Bureaucratization

It pleased Darius to appoint 120 satraps over the kingdom, to be in charge of the whole kingdom, and over them, three commissioners (of whom Daniel was one), so that these satraps would be accountable to them, and that the king would not suffer loss. Then this Daniel began distinguishing himself among the commissioners and satraps because he possessed an extraordinary spirit, and the king intended to appoint him over the entire kingdom. Then the commissioners and satraps began trying to find a ground of accusation against Daniel regarding government affairs; but they could find no ground of accusation or evidence of corruption, because he was trustworthy, and no negligence or corruption was to be found in him. Then these men said, "We will not find any ground of accusation against this Daniel unless we find it against him regarding the law of his God."

Daniel 6:1–5

Analysis

Point four of the biblical covenant is sanctions. It asks: "What do I get if I obey? Disobey?"

The ancient kingdoms were massive bureaucracies. The larger the geographical territory brought into the kingdom, the more extensive the bureaucracy had to be. These were centralized, top-down bureaucracies. Ancient Egypt was the most comprehensive of these bureaucracies. It was based on the control over water: the Nile River. The Medo-Persian empire, which replaced the Babylonian empire, was extensive. The king had to appoint regional bureaucrats to maintain order.

Bureaucracies have universal characteristics. One of them is resentment of the hierarchy's senior officials against outstanding performers. Senior managers think along these lines. "This person is making the rest of us look bad. We are competent, but this person is extraordinary. We must get rid of him. Of course, we don't want to replace him with someone who is incompetent. If the politicians discover an incompetent person, it will look as though we are unable to screen out incompetents. They may order an investigation. This is always bad. We should be autonomous. Worse, they may cut our budget for next year. That would be catastrophic. So, we must find a way to get rid of the super-achiever, and replace him with someone merely competent." This is what happened to Daniel for a time.

How can senior bureaucrats get rid of someone who is above average? The same way they do everything else: *by the book*. The Medo-Persian bureaucrats needed to persuade the king to change the book. They did exactly this.

> Then these commissioners and satraps came by agreement to the king and spoke to him as follows: "King Darius, live forever! All the commissioners of the kingdom, the prefects and the satraps, the counselors and the governors, have consulted together that the king should establish a statute and enforce an injunction that anyone who offers a prayer to any god or person besides you, O king, for thirty days, shall be thrown into the lions' den. Now, O king, establish the injunction and sign the document so that it will not be changed, according to the law of the Medes and Persians, which may not be revoked." Thereupon, King Darius signed the document, that is, the injunction. (Dan. 6:6–9)

The bureaucrats had a hidden agenda. The king was naive. He did not predict the chain of events that would follow. Daniel refused to obey the new law, just as they knew he would. He went out of his way to disobey. He worshipped God. He opened the windows to reveal what he was doing (Dan. 6:10). The king was trapped.

> Then, as soon as the king heard this statement, he was deeply distressed, and set his mind on rescuing Daniel; and until sunset he kept exerting

> himself to save him. Then these men came by agreement to the king and said to the king, "Recognize, O king, that it is a law of the Medes and Persians that no injunction or statute which the king establishes may be changed." Then the king gave orders, and Daniel was brought in and thrown into the lions' den. The king said to Daniel, "Your God whom you continually serve will Himself rescue you." (Dan. 6:14–16)

The lions did not eat Daniel. An angel shut their mouths. This was a minor miracle compared to what happened next. "The king then gave orders, and they brought those men who had maliciously accused Daniel, and they threw them, their children, and their wives into the lions' den; and they had not reached the bottom of the den before the lions overpowered them and crushed all their bones" (Dan. 6:24). Why was this a miracle? Because the king fired them all... permanently.

This never happens in modern times. In extensively bureaucratic civil governments, a major failure of any bureaucracy usually leads to an increased budget the next year. "We failed because the legislature did not allocate enough money." The politicians fall for this every time. In bureaucracies, nothing succeeds like failure.

The bureaucrats were initially consumed with envy against Daniel. They wanted to destroy him. They preferred living under a less efficient, less wise man than Daniel. *This is the essence of envy: the desire to pull down a successful person, even when it costs the perpetrators economically.*

These men were in positions of authority. They advised the sovereign. They advised him so as to achieve their goals, not to benefit either the king or the kingdom. This is common under bureaucracies. Bureaucrats act on the basis of self-interest, just as everyone else does. This is an ancient insight. But it was long ignored by economists. It led in the final third of the twentieth century to a specialized field of economics: public choice theory.

The rise of the modern administrative state is the most important single judicial development of modern civil government. This is a system of law in which administrative agencies, which are close to immune from intervention by the elected legislature and the senior executive, interpret the laws. In the United States, a law may be 2,000 pages. The administrative interpretations of this law may be five times as long within two years. The number will continue to grow. In the

United States, over 65,000 pages of three-column fine-print administrative rules are published each year in the *Federal Register.*

It gets worse. These agencies hire their own judges. Then the agencies bring legal accusations against businesses and individuals. These individuals must then hire lawyers at huge fees per hour to defend themselves. They are not allowed initially to go into civil courts. They must first be tried by the administrative law courts of the regulatory agencies. Only after a final decision is reached by the agency's judge may a convicted business appeal to a civil court. Then the legal process starts over. Only the richest firms can afford to pay for all this unless a non-profit public law firm takes the case. Public law firms do this only where a major legal issue is at stake. This rarely happens.

Ludwig von Mises wrote his little book, *Bureaucracy,* in 1944. He described the differences between bureaucratic management and profit management. The profit-seeking entrepreneur seeks profits from accurately forecasting the uncertain economic future. Customers reward successful entrepreneurs by purchasing their goods and services. Customers possess final authority. In contrast, the bureaucrat has an assured budget. The legislature has authorized it. This money must be used according to the book. So, the bureaucrat is constrained by a rule book. This book may be huge. This gives autonomy to bureaucrats who interpret the arcane, complex, and self-contradictory rules.

There is no escape from bureaucracy, Mises said. It continues to extend its power into the economy whenever politicians extend the jurisdiction of the state into the profit-seeking private sector. *This substitutes bureaucratic management for profit management.* It substitutes complex rules written in the past for flexible responses to new conditions.

The modern mixed economy is partly government by central planning through the central bank. Multiple executive bureaucracies impose regulations on a business. But these regulations can conflict with each other. They are issued by dozens of agencies. These agencies do not coordinate their regulations. In short, *bureaucratic regulation presumes an omniscience comparable to God's.* Unlike common law courts, where judgments build up over time, administrative laws are announced by lawyers inside regulatory agencies. Then the agencies' army of investigators enter businesses to enforce these rules by imposing fines. Seeking greater efficiency by reducing the costs of establishing precedents, agencies prosecute small, underfunded companies that cannot afford a long fight in two sets of courts: administrative and civil.

Harvard University's legal scholar Harold Berman wrote in 1983 that this system of administrative law was undermining the Western legal tradition, which stretches back to the Papal Revolution of 1076, when the church's courts gained autonomy from the emperor's courts. He presented his case in the Introduction to *Law and Revolution* (1983).

A. Blindness

Point one of the biblical covenant is God's transcendence, yet also His presence. This is the biblical concept of God's sovereignty. It asks: "Who's in charge here?" How does this apply to bureaucratization?

When an organization limits its planning to those things that may affect the organization, decision-makers are able to focus on specifics. If they attempt to consider events that could affect the organization, but probably will not, then they are more likely to make major mistakes. No one, and no committee, possesses the information or wisdom to plan beyond his area of expertise. The planners focus on the industry and its market footprint. Only those events from the outside that may affect the industry, such as possible central bank policies, should be considered. The planners must specialize.

In contrast is all central planning. The planners must consider their decisions' effects across an entire economy. The failure of central planners was predicted by Mises in 1920 in his essay, "Economic Calculation in the Socialist Commonwealth." The accuracy of his prediction became clear in the transition of mainland China's economy, beginning in 1979, and the public suicide of the Soviet Union on December 25, 1991.

In between market planning and central planning is the administrative state. This state is not centralized. Its agencies regulate the broad mass of large-scale production, but they do not attempt to produce a coherent outcome. Instead, new regulations by the thousands are released annually by these agencies in large nations. There is no attempt to coordinate these regulations across the agencies. There is also no attempt to coordinate them within an agency. Each regulation is issued on an ad hoc basis in response to a perceived problem in an industry. There is no master plan into which each regulation is carefully fitted by senior planners. In almost all instances, the people who write the regulations are lawyers with no training in economics. These lawyers are focused on the outcomes of each regulation on specific practices in a industry. There is no attempt to analyze the secondary effects of each regulation outside of a specific practice in the industry or sector of the economy.

The authority to regulate presumes the ability to coordinate. But the nearly autonomous civil government agencies do not coordinate. They do not presume to coordinate. They defend their own administrative turf. If they are forced to share a particular jurisdiction, they cooperate only under pressure. The most obvious example in early twenty-first century American history was the unwillingness of the FBI, which is in charge of monitoring domestic subversion, to share information with the CIA, which is in charge of monitoring international subversion. On September 11, 2001, three hijacked airliners crashed into their targets. A fourth crashed in rural Pennsylvania. This unwillingness to share relevant intelligence information has a name: stovepiping.

The regulations create judicial noise: a confusing lack of coherence. They create havoc for some companies. They bankrupt small companies that protest.

B. Autonomy

Point two of the biblical covenant is hierarchical authority. It asks: "To whom do I report?" How does this apply to bureaucratization?

Administrative agencies are judicially separate from the civil courts. The civil courts have the final say, but the number of regulations is huge, and the number of administrative law rulings that get overturned by a nation's Supreme Court is small. Administrative agencies are close to autonomous. This was Harold Berman's argument in *Law and Revolution*.

A government agency is funded by the central government. Its decisions are complex and expensive to reverse in the courts. The legislature can change a law, but it rarely does. The legislature can force a bureaucracy to change a rule, but almost never does. There are too many rules. No one monitors them. Voters do not pressure the legislature to change obscure rules that affect only a narrow sector of the world. The money provided annually by the legislature flows into each agency. This flow of funds usually increases annually. If the funds keep coming, the legislature has little control over what any agency does in the name of the law. The legislature can revise a statute, but the agency and its courts will still decide on what terms the revised law will be enforced, if at all. The agency may drag its feet in enforcing any law. It is selective. That is to say, it is arbitrary.

Autonomous decisions are arbitrary decisions. Arbitrary laws undermine liberty by strengthening the state and its agents. Citizens do not know which statutes will be enforced, or in what ways, or with what consequences.

In all bureaucracies, there are laws protecting employees' jobs. Workers may be fired only when the agency can prove malfeasance. This rarely happens. When anyone outside the agency complains, the agency defends the employee. To do otherwise would be to admit that the agency did not screen out an incompetent. It dares not admit this.

The bureaucrats represent the government. They enforce this representation in their own courts. Anyone who resists gets fined. He must spend money to defend himself. If he wins in the agency's court, he is not compensated by the agency.

As long as the funds keep flowing into any agency, it will continue to seek to expand its jurisdiction. This is a fundamental law of bureaucracy. Why? First, because bureaucrats are promoted when the number of bureaucrats under their authority rises to a specific promotion point. Second, because it pays every bureaucrat to delegate work. He receives no pay cut. He may even receive a salary increase, since there are more people working under him.

C. Discoordination

Point three of the biblical covenant is law. It asks: "What are the rules?" How does this apply to bureaucratization?

There is little inter-agency coordination except during national emergencies. In national emergencies, no agency's budget is at risk. It would look bad if an agency refused to cooperate. The national leaders are calling on everyone to cooperate.

The free market operates in terms of price signals. There is no price system in bureaucracies. No agency can legally sell services to the highest bidder. There is no system of competition through pricing: buyer versus buyer, seller versus seller. No one in the agency can legally store up profits for himself. He does not have a legal claim to them. Besides, there are no profits to store up. Agencies spend all of the money that the legislature authorized the previous year.

The complexity of the coordination problem grows as the budgets grow. With larger budgets, there is greater responsibility. Agencies exercise greater authority. They have greater influence. This increased responsibility adds to the complexity of the individual bureaucracies. As all of them become more complex, because they all are funded with more money the next year, the system's overall complexity also grows greater. There is no central plan. There is no negative feedback system that encourages senior managers to cut expenses. The opposite is true. They seek to increase expenses in order to fund the hiring of additional staff.

D. Injustice

Point four of the biblical covenant is sanctions. It asks: "What do I get if I obey? Disobey?" How does this apply to bureaucratization?

The system of administrative law transfers the administration of justice away from civil courts to administrative law judges. This rival system of courts transfers power to agencies that are far less responsible to the public than courts governed by the common law: judge-discovered law and legal precedent. The common-law system is far more predictable than any rival system. It restricts the power of both the executive branch of government and the legislative branch. It places a restriction on the expansion of power. Administrative law creates a system of courts that makes the judges agents of the executive branch. These courts are funded by the agencies that administer the law. The agencies hire and fire. This system replaces juries, which are the bedrock institutional foundation of liberty in the West. Administrative law judges interpret the law, administer the sanctions, and answer to the civil courts only when a defendant has enough money to challenge their decision in the civil courts.

With respect to issues of the economy, meaning supply and demand, in a free market, managers are pressured by an organization's owners to pursue profitable lines of activity. Owners issue this two-part instruction to managers: "Buy low. Sell high." This requires managers to identify underpriced resources, buy them, add value to them, and then sell the finished output of these resources to customers. There is nothing comparable to this process in the sphere of government: family, church, or state.

The state is not merely one provider among many. It claims a legal monopoly of violence. It does so in the name of reducing violence and increasing legal predictability. This is the rule of law. But when it extends its jurisdiction into areas where competitive bidding and open entry benefit consumers, it reduces liberty. It grants to bureaucrats greater power to impose unilateral sanctions. This power is easily abused by a legal monopoly.

No rival supplier is allowed to enter the market and offer competing deals to the public. The service is provided legally only by the state or by state-licensed, state-regulated suppliers. This reduces the range of choice available to consumers. This is another way of saying that they are poorer: reduced choice at the same level of income.

In a free market order, consumers have final authority because they possess money: the most marketable commodity. This is not true in civil government. The state has the right to tax, and it has the right to pass laws. These powers shift money to bureaucrats who administer tax-funded programs. They now possess the most marketable commodity, which they extracted from taxpayers. Private citizens no longer do.

The inability of consumers to impose positive sanctions through purchases, and their ability to impose negative sanctions through a refusal to purchase, transfer authority to the state. Point two of the biblical covenant—authority—is closely associated with point four: the legal right to impose sanctions. The state possesses such sanctions in a system of civil government in which the state's authority to tax and regulate is limited by politics only, not by fundamental law.

E. Expansion

Point five of the biblical covenant is succession. It asks: "Does this outfit have a future?" How does this apply to bureaucratization?

Bureaucracies constantly claim the need for greater funding and wider jurisdictions. There are institutional imperatives here, the main one being the need for more subordinates in the careers of those bureaucrats seeking promotions. But there is another aspect of this call for more funding and authority: the vision of the bureaucrats regarding the centrality of whatever they are authorized to regulate. They define justice in terms of their jurisdiction. There is always more justice for them to provide.

With each intervention into the economy, the bureaucracy disrupts market pricing. As prices become less reliable in providing accurate information, the supply system grows unpredictable. Price ceilings produce shortages. Price floors produce gluts. The public demands that the government pass new laws to protect the citizens. The government does this. This creates new areas of jurisdiction for bureaucracies. Then the bureaucracies demand more funding to meet these new requirements. The process of disruption continues. It escalates.

Professor Mises wrote an essay in 1950 on this process: "Middle-of-the-Road Policy Leads to Socialism." But he failed to mention his earlier article: "Economic Calculation in the Socialist Commonwealth." *At some point, the irresistible force of regulatory expansion meets the immovable object of socialism's inability to calculate.* That is when a political crisis occurs. The government-run economy can no longer deliver the goods that consumers want to buy at prices they are willing and able to pay. Either the economy deteriorates, leaving a nation increasingly militarily defenseless, or else the leaders change course. Mainland China reached that point in 1979. The Soviet Union reached it in December 1991. The leaders changed course.

Conclusion

I have identified a universal law of bureaucracy. "There is no law so carefully written by politicians that some bureaucrat will not do something ludicrous by applying the words of that law literally." My law of bureaucracy also applies to rules written by senior bureaucrats for the bureaucracy. It is rare for any bureaucrat to be fired for causing a public embarrassment because of such a blunder. But he may not receive further promotions. Bureaucrats want promotions. So, they attempt to avoid blunders. They do things by the book. The book is long and complicated. This gives them great latitude to interpret it their way.

Bureaucracy is not governed by market prices. It gets funded by politicians. So, most of the time, bureaucrats can safely ignore the public's complaints. Furthermore, it is almost impossible for the public or even politicians to follow the decision-making process inside a bureaucracy, so that specific responsibility can be matched with specific authority for some botched procedure. The system of tax-funding, when coupled with arcane rules governing the bureaucracy and written by the bureaucracy, subsidizes blame-shifting. Autonomous man wants blame-shifting. So does autonomous woman.

> Now they heard the sound of the LORD God walking in the garden in the cool of the day, and the man and his wife hid themselves from the presence of the LORD God among the trees of the garden. Then the LORD God called to the man, and said to him, "Where are you?" He said, "I heard the sound of You in the garden, and I was afraid because I was naked; so I hid myself." And He said, "Who told you that you were naked? Have you eaten from the tree from which I commanded you not to eat?" The man said, "The woman whom You gave to be with me, she gave me some of the fruit of the tree, and I ate." Then the LORD God said to the woman, "What is this that you have done?" And the woman said, "The serpent deceived me, and I ate." (Gen. 3:8–13)

Because there is nothing inside civil government that corresponds to the free market's system of profit-and-loss accounting, bureaucrats are usually able to hide blame for a failure. But the price of their security is this: they cannot profit as owners from any of the bureaucracy's financial successes. Career promotion is based on seniority, not profitability.

It is based on this: not making a mistake, according to written rules. Promotion is not based on having achieved a profitable breakthrough. That is because there are no profits in a government bureaucracy. Therefore, bureaucracy's system of economic sanctions favors inertia, not innovation.

Voters are double-minded about bureaucracy. They laugh at silly things that bureaucrats do, whenever these foibles get reported in the media. They vote for politicians who vote for more government spending. New government programs always expand the authority of bureaucracies, which by law must supervise the distribution of the money. They vote for politicians who favor more government regulations. New regulations require the hiring of more bureaucrats. Then existing bureaucrats get promotions because of all the new bureaucrats to supervise. Voters think that the government should protect them. Bureaucrats do the protecting. The result is always the same: the growth of bureaucracy. Bureaucracy is universal. The leader of a nation cannot administer the laws he is required to enforce. He is not God. He needs specialists to administer the legal system for him.

A society moves from bureaucracy to bureaucratization when the economic resources commanded by the state grow to such an extent that the system of bureaucracy undermines the free market. The economy's productivity then is insufficient to enable the ruler to defend the nation from invasion. The bureaucrats disrupt business to such an extent that the public grows poorer. Their taxes can no longer support the bureaucracy. Great Britain's Prime Minister Margaret Thatcher put it this way: "The trouble with Socialism is that eventually you run out of other people's money." That is how her statement has been summarized. She actually said this in 1976, the year that she took over as leader of the Conservative Party, which was out of office. She said this of the Labor Party:

> I would much prefer to bring them down as soon as possible. I think they've made the biggest financial mess that any government's ever made in this country for a very long time, and Socialist governments traditionally do make a financial mess. They always run out of other people's money. It's quite a characteristic of them. They then start to nationalise everything, and people just do not like more and more

> nationalisation, and they're now trying to control everything by other means. They're progressively reducing the choice available to ordinary people.

This was not quotable, but it was more accurate. Her victory as Prime Minister in 1979 led to her 11-year rule. By 1990, the Labor Party had abandoned its commitment to socialism. It got the memo from the voters. At the end of 1991, the Soviet Union committed suicide. The Communist Party was disbanded. It also got the memo.

Administrative law continues to expand as economies expand. But there are economic limits of this expansion: the solvency of the governments that fund the bureaucracies. There are limits to growth in a bureaucratic society. There are limits to the expansion of the welfare state. At some point, it must default on its promises to the voters. It will either eliminate much of the bureaucracy before this takes place, or else both systems will shrink together. The immovable force of blind central planners will stop the irresistible force of bureaucratic expansion.

Chapter 10

Disinheritance

Now it came about, as soon as Isaac had finished blessing Jacob, and Jacob had hardly gone out from the presence of his father Isaac, that his brother Esau came in from his hunting. Then he also made a delicious meal, and brought it to his father; and he said to his father, "Let my father arise and eat of his son's game, that you may bless me." His father Isaac said to him, "Who are you?" And he said, "I am your son, your firstborn, Esau." Then Isaac trembled violently, and said, "Who then was he who hunted game and brought it to me, so that I ate from all of it before you came, and blessed him? Yes, and he shall be blessed." When Esau heard the words of his father, he cried out with an exceedingly great and bitter cry, and said to his father, "Bless me, me as well, my father!" And he said, "Your brother came deceitfully and has taken away your blessing." Then Esau said, "Is he not rightly named Jacob, for he has betrayed me these two times? He took away my birthright, and behold, now he has taken away my blessing." And he said, "Have you not reserved a blessing for me?" But Isaac replied to Esau, "Behold, I have made him your master, and I have given to him all his relatives as servants; and with grain and new wine I have sustained him. What then can I do for you, my son?"

Genesis 27:30–37

Analysis

Point five of the biblical covenant is succession. It asks: "Does this outfit have a future?"

Esau was a liar and a thief. God hated him. God had hated him even before he was born. Paul wrote:

> For this is the word of promise: "At this time I will come, and Sarah will have a son." And not only that, but there was also Rebekah, when she had conceived twins by one man, our father Isaac; for though the twins were not yet born and had not done anything good or bad, so that God's purpose according to His choice would stand, not because of works but because of Him who calls, it was said to her, "The older will serve the younger." Just as it is written: "Jacob I have loved, but Esau I have hated." (Rom. 9:9–13)

On reading this, most Christians are shocked. They cannot believe it. They ask themselves: "Why did God hate Esau? After all, Esau had done nothing to be hated for." This is a theologically silly question. Esau was a covenantal son of Adam. God hates the covenantal sons of Adam. They are all covenant-breakers, as Adam was. This is the meaning of the doctrine of original sin. God loves only those He has sovereignly elected to regenerate judicial status. A far more astute question is this: "Why did God love Jacob?"

Esau had foolishly sold his birthright to Jacob for a plate of stew and bread (Gen. 25:29–34). That was a valid transaction. It was not made under duress. Esau was intensely present-oriented. He feigned starvation to get a plate of stew from Jacob. Jacob took advantage of his brother's present-orientation. He sold Esau what Esau wanted more than his birthright. Then, after Jacob had gained the blessing from Isaac which his birthright entitled him to, Esau called his brother a thief. Esau had intended to steal the blessing from Jacob, who had bought it from him (Gen. 25). His mother and Jacob had resorted to deception in order to persuade Isaac, who was spiritually blind as well as physically blind, to grant his blessing to the son who deserved it both theologically and financially.

Esau had disinherited himself. He was the elder brother (Gen. 25:25). He was entitled to the double portion of the inheritance, according to Mosaic law (Deut. 21:17). But this was not worth a plate of stew and bread to him. He figured he could steal back the blessing from Jacob, since Isaac liked Esau's meals of meat (Gen. 25:28). He was incorrect. Jacob and their mother outfoxed him.

This is the pattern of inheritance in history. Covenant-breakers believe they can steal the inheritance from the rightful heirs. Who are the rightful heirs? The people to whom God imputes both the perfect moral righteousness and the perfect judicial righteousness of Jesus Christ. Covenant-breakers are not going to be the heirs in history. "A good person leaves an inheritance to his grandchildren, and the wealth of a sinner is stored up for the righteous" (Prov. 13:22). "But the meek shall inherit the earth; and shall delight themselves in the abundance of peace" (Ps. 37:11, KJV). Jesus confirmed this: "Blessed are the meek: for they shall inherit the earth" (Matt. 5:5, KJV).

The struggle between covenant-breakers and covenant-keepers involves a struggle for inheritance in history. The overwhelming majority of Christians have been taught that God has granted covenant-breakers comprehensive cultural and political inheritance in the era of the church. Amillennialists, who have been dominant in the European church tradition, affirm that the political city of man will rule over the political city of God in history. Premillennialists say that this will be true only until Jesus bodily returns to earth to set up a 1,000-year political kingdom. Only postmillennialists interpret literally Jesus' promise of inheritance as applying to covenant-keepers in history prior to Jesus' bodily return in final judgment.

Inheritance necessarily involves disinheritance, just as historical sanctions are both positive and negative. There is a long-term pattern to historical sanctions. They are cumulative. They are also corporate, not just individual. This reflects (represents) God as Trinity, who is both corporate and individual. There are winners and losers in eternity. There are also winners and losers in history. This is because there is a war between two kingdoms. This war has two battlefields: heaven and earth. We do not usually think of heaven as being involved in warfare, but it is. The issues of history are of concern in heaven.

> When the Lamb broke the fifth seal, I saw underneath the altar the souls of those who had been killed because of the word of God, and because of the testimony which they had maintained; and they cried out with a loud voice, saying, "How long, O Lord, holy and true, will You refrain from judging and avenging our blood on those who live on the earth?" (Rev. 6:9–10)

Because covenant-keepers, including leaders, do not perceive the kingdom of God as a civilization, they do not see economic conflicts as being inherently covenantal. They see kingdom issues as applying to souls, families, and churches, but not beyond these tightly constrained personal bonds. In contrast, leaders among covenant-breakers perceive the kingdom of man as a civilization. They see economic conflict as being covenantal. Thus, they are consistent in their pursuit of wealth, influence, and power. They understand that wealth is a tool of social and political change. They seek to change society through comprehensive reform. They seek capital to fund this. Covenant-keepers seek at most to restrain the inroads of the broader culture into their lives: in education, entertainment, and individual moral behavior. But state-funded education is not neutral in any sense. Entertainment reflects the broader culture. Moral behavior is shaped by education, culture, and civil law. Communications technologies have opened the doors of every household to the debaucheries and temptations of the broader culture. Covenant-keepers see all this as a cancer, but they offer no cures, only pain-killers. They lose their children to secular tax-funded education and the secular media. This is the heart, mind, and soul of the battle over inheritance: *the loss of the next generation.*

This is a battle over money, for money is capital. Capital is another word for tools. The super-rich fully understand that their wealth provides them with leverage culturally and politically. They can shape politics with money. They can make it more difficult for economic competitors to replace them. Yet technology waits on no one. The list of the five hundred richest people changes year to year. Also, they face a problem: taxation. If they do not find ways to transfer the money to non-taxable entities, the state will strip away half or more of their wealth when they die. So, they set up charitable foundations to promote their causes. This extends the kingdom of man, but in a less efficient way. Nonprofit organizations rarely innovate. They conserve. They fund conventional projects. They are run by bureaucrats.

There has never been a nonprofit organization with the dynamism of the institutional church. It gains the support of people without much money, but with dedication. It is decentralized. It crosses borders. It is truly international. It persists over time. It innovates. In terms of its millennia of success and systematic expansion, no other institution matches it.

So, the kingdom of man can prosper through voluntary exchange. The market makes covenant-breakers wealthy. But there is no escape from this: "the wealth of a sinner is stored up for the righteous" (Prov. 13:22b).

A. Testator

Point one of the biblical covenant is God's transcendence, yet also His presence. This is the biblical concept of God's sovereignty. It asks: "Who's in charge here?" How does this apply to disinheritance?

The rich man faces the problem of succession. He builds a fortune, but his children will at best conserve it. The modern corporation provides continuity. His heirs will be owners of shares. Others can buy control of his legacy. The non-profit foundation provides continuity, but it will be controlled by upper-middle-class bureaucrats who cannot compete in a competitive market. The testator cannot control what will be done with his legacy. This was understood by Solomon, the richest man in Israel.

> So I hated all the fruit of my labor for which I had labored under the sun, because I must leave it to the man who will come after me. And who knows whether he will be wise or a fool? Yet he will have control over all the fruit of my labor for which I have labored by acting wisely under the sun. This too is futility. Therefore I completely despaired over all the fruit of my labor for which I had labored under the sun. When there is a person who has labored with wisdom, knowledge, and skill, and then gives his legacy to one who has not labored for it; this too is futility and a great evil. (Eccl. 2:18–21)

The testator has a huge problem. He must see the future and control it from beyond the grave. He cannot do this.

In contrast is the Christian doctrine of the testator. "For where a testament is, there must also of necessity be the death of the testator. For a testament is of force after men are dead: otherwise it is of no strength at all while the testator liveth" (Heb. 9:16–17). Who is this testator? The author of the epistle to the Hebrews is clear: Jesus Christ.

Next, consider Paul's doctrine of creation.

> He is the image of the invisible God, the firstborn of all creation: for by Him all things were created, both in the heavens and on earth, visible and invisible, whether thrones, or dominions, or rulers, or authorities—all things have been created through Him and for Him. He is before all things, and in Him all things hold together. He is also the head of the body, the church; and He is the beginning, the firstborn from the dead, so that He Himself will come to have first place in everything. For it was the Father's good pleasure for all the fullness to dwell in Him, and through Him to reconcile all things to Himself, whether things on earth or things in heaven, having made peace through the blood of His cross. (Col. 1:15–20)

The Testator is divine. He is the Creator. He holds title as a Trustee for God the Father. For how long? Until history ends. Paul taught that this trusteeship will expand in influence and dominion in history:

> ...then comes the end, when He hands over the kingdom to our God and Father, when He has abolished all rule and all authority and power. For He must reign until He has put all His enemies under His feet. The last enemy that will be abolished is death. For He has put all things in subjection under His feet. But when He says, "All things are put in subjection," it is clear that this excludes the Father who put all things in subjection to Him. When all things are subjected to Him, then the Son Himself will also be subjected to the One who subjected all things to Him, so that God may be all in all. (I Cor. 15:24–28).

This is his interpretation of Psalm 110.

The New Testament is clear: *the false heirs will be displaced in history*. The Testator remains in charge. He will deliver the inheritance to God the Father. Yet He is the Son, the cosmic heir. Covenant-keepers will inherit as adopted sons.

B. Trusteeship

Point two of the biblical covenant is hierarchical authority. It asks: "To whom do I report?" How does this apply to disinheritance?

History is a struggle over trusteeship. Who acts on behalf of the heir? Who is the heir? Is there more than one?

As we have seen with respect to the testator, the heirs are sons. But whose sons are they? The false heirs claim that they are heirs. Yet they also claim that the state is sovereign, unless they claim this for the free market. Only a handful of economists have claimed this: anarcho-capitalists. The state has the greatest power in society. It is the accepted trustee. It acts on behalf of the masses. But, as we know by now, the super-rich and well-connected gain control. They may act in the name of the masses, but in fact they act on behalf of themselves and their class. This is described in the book by David Rothkopf, *Superclass* (2009). This is the international Old Boy Network. It is humanistic to the core. In terms of wealth, about a thousand people possess wealth equal to that possessed by the bottom 2.5 billion.[1]

This wealth is based on market competition, though the market is not entirely a free market. These people were not made rich by civil governments initially, but they maintain wealth that they gained through competition by means of political competition: domestic tax favoritism, regulation that keeps competitors out of certain markets, and international tax haven nations. They do this through tax strategies devised by skilled lawyers.

Over time, markets change. Demand changes. New technologies replace old ones. Prices change. *Large pools of wealth cannot be maintained permanently in the free market.* Consumers are in charge. The superclass maintains control at the margin, but at the core is market competition: buyers versus buyers, sellers versus sellers. This keeps the existing hierarchy from attaining anything like security from market forces. The members come and go. The system of trusteeship is constantly changing. Men in power would like to maintain it, but history does not permit this. Death does not permit this. Power-seeking men would like to call a halt to all change they do not control. They seek omniscience. They seek omnipotence. They seek omnipresence. But these are noncommunicable attributes of God. To seek them is demonic. It is also futile.

---

1. David Rothkopf, *Superclass: The Global Power Elite and the World They Are Making* (New York: Farrar, Straus and Giroux, [2008] 2009), 66.

C. Protection

Point three of the biblical covenant is law. It asks: "What are the rules?" How does this apply to disinheritance?

The rich and powerful in any generation seek a safe haven from tax collectors. Yet they also seek to use the state to protect them from the relentless competition of consumers, who keep demanding higher quality, lower prices, and better terms of payment. Humanistic elitists want a smaller state with respect to taxation and a stronger state with respect to protection. They cannot achieve both.

They have great control nationally with respect to political influence. Their money helps candidates get elected. Politicians then grant favors to large donors that the voters will not perceive as special-interest legislation that favors the rich and well-connected. Politicians hide arcane tax breaks in tax bills that are 2,000 pages long and written incoherently on purpose. But this strategy ends at a nation's borders. *There is no international civil government that possesses meaningful political sanctions.* The superclass seeks to create such an entity, but this has always failed. Empires rise and fall, but international civil governments are always weak. Voters do not favor surrendering national sovereignty. This greatly hampers the international superclass.

Market competition across borders is increasing. This weakens the ability of national civil governments to establish the terms of trade. As wealth becomes the product of services, and as services become digital, tariffs and import quotas cease to shape the domestic markets around the world. As production becomes computerized, it becomes local. This decentralizes physical production. National governments cannot easily regulate local production. That is the province of local governments. National governments can regulate interstate trade, but as local production becomes more efficient, there will be less trade across state borders. Cross-border trade is the product of huge factories that supply the nation. Factory production is under assault by 3-D printing. This will continue. It will escalate.

The power of nation-states to regulate markets is declining. When the nation-state can no longer meet its obligations to millions of retired voters, which is actuarially inevitable, the ability of the nation-state to extend its power will cease.

D. Decapitalization

Point four of the biblical covenant is sanctions. It asks: "What do I get if I obey? Disobey?" How does this apply to disinheritance?

As the nation-state extends its regulation of business, it reduces productivity. This will eventually reduce the power of the nation-state, which is supported by taxes on successful individuals and businesses. Economic growth will slow.

The Bible is clear that increased wealth is a blessing from God (Deut. 28:1–14). It requires obedience to God's law. *Private property is fundamental to God's law.* To the extent that special-interest groups gain the cooperation of the nation-state to defend their turfs, the economy is hampered. There will be less innovation. State-manipulated prices and markets will distort production. Consumers will have to pay more. They will therefore demand less. They will be paid less. They will then produce less.

Over time, positive economic sanctions accumulate. Profits are reinvested. Output increases. Consumers buy more products. Profits send a clear signal to managers: "Keep doing this." This adds to the capital of a town, region, and nation.

The greater the intervention of the state to protect existing companies from competitors, the less likely that there will be innovation. Regulation is designed to reduce competition in most cases. It protects the procedures of the largest companies, whose lobbyists have the greatest influence because they spend the most money on political action committees. It favors the status quo.

Under these conditions, companies increase profits more from successful legislation than innovation. *Political innovation becomes more profitable than product innovation.* Companies spend less on research and development. They do not need to. The state protects their market share. Reduced investing in research and development then reduces economic growth.

The substitution of political control over markets works against consumers. This is common in regulated economies. The established sellers have an incentive to restrict competition. They have influence politically because they provide campaign money. They also have employees who vote. *The substitution of bureaucracy for market competition trans-*

forms profit-seeking companies into extensions of government bureaucracies. The bureaucrats possess more power to threaten managers than consumers do. Consumers cannot impose fines. They cannot stop the production of specific products. State bureaucrats can and do.

The false heirs want to support the status quo. They possess capital. They have political power. They can pursue their agendas without the degree of competition that a free market offers. The state protects them. The result is decapitalization.

E. Stagnation

Point five of the biblical covenant is succession. It asks: "Does this outfit have a future?" How does this apply to disinheritance?

Without capital accumulation, there can be no economic growth. New ideas require capital to implement them. Someone must save money. He turns it over to entrepreneurs, who use this money to fund development. Without this money, capital wears out. Innovation slows.

The greater the degree of control by bureaucrats, the less economic growth is likely. This is the result of an attitude of resistance to change. The present heirs have no intension of surrendering control. But to insure their safety from outsiders with better ways to serve consumers, the established firms enlist the state to place restrictions on innovation by those not already in the elite: the heirs of the combined economic and political system. This leads to stagnation.

The solution is for the state to limit its interference into the market to protection of life, limb, and property from physical violence and fraud. The state allows people to make voluntary economic transactions. Owners of legal rights to specific pieces of property, including their labor, are allowed to exchange these rights for money. Exchange is an aspect of responsibility.

Consider Esau. He exchanged his birthright for a plate of stew. There should be no question that he possessed this right of exchange. This led to a major benefit for his brother. Esau later regretted that he had made this exchange. He decided that he was entitled to a blessing from his father. This blessing was based on the birthright that Esau had sold to

Jacob. This wealth transfer meant nothing to him. His word meant nothing to him. What mattered was his inheritance. The covenantal problem he faced was this: *he had eaten his birthright.* He wanted this decision overturned by his father. He wanted to seal a revised arrangement.

The legal right to transfer wealth to another person is basic to the free market social order. Such an exchange possesses authority. If it did not, property would be insecure. The right to own it could be revoked. That was what Esau wanted. Isaac knew better. He had wanted to bless his oldest son, but he stood by his word. He had spoken a blessing to Jacob by mistake. But this word was judicially binding. It was part of the family covenant: inheritance.

Conclusion

The biblical covenant extends to inheritance. It also involves disinheritance. The sanctions are both positive and negative.

The Bible is clear with respect to inheritance in history. It goes to covenant-keepers. This was not the teaching of the church until the seventeenth century. Some Puritans and some Scottish Presbyterians adopted this view. It transformed historical thinking from linear to linear and progressive. This introduced the concept of inter-generational economic inheritance. It laid the theological foundation for the concept of compound economic growth. This was a new idea. It rested on a new eschatology: postmillennialism.

There had always been postmillennialism: the postmillennialism of covenant-breakers. They believed that the kingdom of God would not manifest itself as a systematic, self-consciously biblical worldview with power. That benefit was supposedly reserved for covenant-breakers.

To defend their cultural and political turf, covenant-breakers have made it difficult for covenant-keepers to accumulate capital. With capital, covenant-keepers might redeem—buy back—the world. Covenant-keepers accept such suppression as normal. These circumstances are normal chronologically, but they are not normative. They are not permanent. They will be overturned. Psalm 110 says so.

Conclusion to Part II

Part II deals with the economic world we have lost due to sin. This affected men's view of economics.

The covenantal structure of biblical economics reflects the five-point covenant: God, man, law, sanctions, and time. The pre-fall structure of economics was this: ownership, stewardship, property, imputation, and inheritance. After the fall of man, mankind adopted this structure, but substituted new content: chance, autonomy, theft, bureaucratization, and disinheritance. Covenant-breakers want to establish their own kingdoms in history. Their view of economics reflects this goal.

Part III will explore the issue of redemption. Jesus Christ's incarnation, ministry, death, resurrection, and ascension have definitively transformed the world. Jesus announced His authority after His resurrection, but before His ascension:

> And Jesus came up and spoke to them, saying, "All authority in heaven and on earth has been given to Me. Go, therefore, and make disciples of all the nations, baptizing them in the name of the Father and the Son and the Holy Spirit, teaching them to follow all that I commanded you; and behold, I am with you always, to the end of the age." (Matt. 28:18–20)

That which has been definitively accomplished in history by Christ must now be progressively implemented in history by Christians. We are heirs of the promise. This means that economic theory must be redeemed, i.e., bought back. The original five points are foundational, but they are now burdened by the curses that God imposed on Adam and the ground. It is the task of redemption to reduce the effects of those curses.

This leads us to Part III: redemption.

PART III

Redemption

Introduction to Part III

"The bricks have fallen down, but we will rebuild with smooth stones; the sycamores have been cut down, but we will replace them with cedars."

ISAIAH 9:10

The fall of man brought mankind under a series of curses: biological and environmental. But there was also hope: "And I will make enemies of you and the woman, and of your offspring and her Descendant; He shall bruise you on the head, and you shall bruise Him on the heel" (Gen. 3:15).

The dominion covenant of Genesis 1:26–28 was not repealed. Mankind is still required to subdue the creation for the glory of God. Mankind is still a collective steward under God. There has been no reduction of personal or corporate responsibility. But mankind is now divided into two branches within one family: the adopted heirs and the disinherited, the covenant-keepers and the covenant-breakers.

The earth is under a curse.

> Then to Adam He said, "Because you have listened to the voice of your wife, and have eaten from the tree about which I commanded you, saying, 'You shall not eat from it'; cursed is the ground because of you; with hard labor you shall eat from it all the days of your life. Both thorns and thistles it shall grow for you; yet you shall eat the plants of the field (Gen. 3:17–18).

But this curse will be progressively removed in history.

> For the eagerly awaiting creation waits for the revealing of the sons and daughters of God. For the creation was subjected to futility, not will-

> ingly, but because of Him who subjected it, in hope that the creation itself also will be set free from its slavery to corruption into the freedom of the glory of the children of God. For we know that the whole creation groans and suffers the pains of childbirth together until now. And not only that, but also we ourselves, having the first fruits of the Spirit, even we ourselves groan within ourselves, waiting eagerly for our adoption as sons and daughters, the redemption of our body. For in hope we have been saved, but hope that is seen is not hope; for who hopes for what he already sees? But if we hope for what we do not see, through perseverance we wait eagerly for it. (Rom. 8:19–25)

What is God's program of progressive redemption in history? What is His program of restoration? It is a program of redemption: to buy back. It is covenantal. It is therefore judicial. But it is necessarily also ethical, for all covenants are tied to ethics. Law is inescapably tied to sanctions: positive and negative. Sanctions in turn point to inheritance and disinheritance: in history and then eternity.

We have seen what mankind possessed pre-fall. This is the world we have lost. We have seen what covenant-breaking men have substituted for God's economy. It is under a curse. Now we must see what God offers as a way to regain part of what we have lost before the final judgment. In Part III, I discuss a reconstruction of economics. There has to be a reconstruction of economic theory and practice because the fall of man has corrupted economics. The economy before the fall was different from the economy after the fall. Covenant-breaking man adopted a new worldview, one which proclaims man as God. This is the essence of humanism.

Humanism was implied by the fall. Adam decided that he would decide whether God's word was true or the serpent's word. Man was the decision maker. Man would choose. In affirming his position as the judge of the rival words, Adam elevated himself into the sovereign over history. He would decide. He would choose.

The reconstruction of every area of life is based on a replacement of humanism with Christianity. There is no neutrality in the world. Neutrality is a myth. It is used by humanists to persuade Christians to surrender intellectual leadership to the spiritual and philosophical sons of Adam. Adam also pretended to be a neutral investigator. But he was not neutral. He had rejected God's word.

In reconstructing economic theory, I begin with God's dominion covenant: God, man, law, sanctions, and time. Humanistic man has a parallel covenant. Instead of God, there is an impersonal universe which is said to operate in terms of an eternal struggle between pure physical law versus pure chance: determinism versus randomness. All theories of both nature and history reveal this dualism. They go back and forth between the two. If we are determined, we lose our freedom. If we are not determined, then how do we change the deterministic world around us? By mathematics? Then those people who have the best formulas and the fastest computers will become our masters. What about tools? What about robots? Will they become our new masters? Back and forth, back and forth: there is never any resolution.

Humanism makes man the king of creation. But is this individual man? If so, how can society operate? If this is collective man, how will freedom survive? Back and forth, back and forth: there is never any resolution.

Christianity calls men to honor God's covenants: the dominion covenant, plus individual, family, church, and state covenants. It calls us to see the world God's way. I cover this in Part IV.

How does this reconstruction affect economic theory? By offering a theory of redemption: to buy back the ethically lost world. How? By restoring what mankind lost in the fall and reducing the curses that God imposed. There are two aspects of this reconstruction, both covenantal. One aspect is judicial. The other is economic. One has to do with delegated legal sovereignty. The other has to do with delegated economic authority. Both are hierarchical. Both are ethical. Both have to do with sanctions in history. Both have to do with inheritance, both individual and corporate.

If Adam and Eve had not rebelled, they and their children would not have died. Second, the earth would not have been cursed by God. So, the birth rate would have been high, the death rate would have been zero, and mankind would have filled the earth within a few hundred years. Second, they would have increased their per capita wealth through the entire period. Instead, we still labor long and hard to earn our daily bread, and only in the last few decades has there been legitimate hope that the billions of people who live in subsistence poverty will be delivered from this curse within a few decades.

Beginning sometime around 1800 in Great Britain and the United States, the world began to experience compound economic growth and compound population growth. The world today bears almost no resemblance to the world of 1800. Yet all that it his taken to achieve this worldwide transformation has been compound growth of about 2% to 3% per year per capita. Economic historians are not agreed on how this unprecedented achievement has taken place. Therefore, they are not agreed on how this growth can be sustained.

In the next five chapters, I will describe how God requires covenant-keepers to implement the dominion covenant in a world that God has cursed because of the sin of Adam. The same five points remain in force. Mankind is still responsible for extending dominion by means of God's covenant laws. I am going to cover the ways that these covenantal laws are supposed to be obeyed in the New Covenant era.

If we want to understand how, beginning around 1800, compound economic growth and compound population growth for the first time were sustained for over two centuries, we should begin studying the historical records in terms of five economic issues: the providence of God, the service-based economy, God's leasehold, entrepreneurship, and compounding.

Chapter 11

Providence

He is the image of the invisible God, the firstborn of all creation: for by Him all things were created, both in the heavens and on earth, visible and invisible, whether thrones, or dominions, or rulers, or authorities—all things have been created through Him and for Him. He is before all things, and in Him all things hold together.

Colossians 1:15–17

Analysis

Are there economic laws? Yes. How can Christians be sure? Because these laws are manifestations of the providence of God. The regularities that we see in nature, including human nature, exist only because God is in complete control of everything. He is not capricious. The universe reflects His orderliness. The strongest biblical testimony to this fact is God's self-revelation in Job, chapters 38 to 42. *If you have any doubts with respect to God's sovereignty, read those chapters now.* Then return to this chapter. I mean this. It is far more important that you understand Job 38 to 42 than that you understand this chapter or this little book. First things first.

What if human beings could not perceive this orderliness? What if they had no capacity to understand the regularities of nature and therefore the predictability of these regularities? Would there still be economic laws? Yes. Would people be able to put these laws to productive use? No. If they could not understand them, what good would it do them in making sense of the world around them? None. Could human beings exercise dominion if they did not perceive nature's regularities? No.

There are economic laws. We know this because of the dominion covenant (Gen. 1:26–28). We know this because of God's revelation of Himself and His sovereignty in history. We know this because we can and do make sense of the orderliness of the world around us. The world is orderly. Our minds are orderly. *The orderliness of our minds corresponds to the orderliness of the world around us.* Apart from faith in God, this correspondence between our minds and the world around us would make no sense. It would not be logical. Eugene Wigner won the Nobel Prize in physics in 1963. Three years earlier, he wrote an article for a mathematics scholarly journal: "The Unreasonable Effectiveness of Mathematics in the Natural Sciences." It is online. I suggest that you read it. It is readable, unlike most articles in mathematics journals. He ended it with these words: "The miracle of the appropriateness of the language of mathematics for the formulation of the laws of physics is a wonderful gift which we neither understand nor deserve. We should be grateful for it and hope that it will remain valid in future research and that it will extend, for better or for worse, to our pleasure, even though perhaps also to our bafflement, to wide branches of learning." There is a theological word for a wonderful gift which we neither understand nor deserve. That word is "grace."

What Wigner wrote about the amazing yet scientifically unexplained relationship between mathematics and physics applies to every other field of study. *The coherence between the logic of our minds and the regularities of the world outside our minds is a gift.* Specifically, it is a gift from God. This gift rests on the providence of God. He created the universe, and He also sustains it. He is sovereign over it. The English word "providence" is related to the word "provide." God has provided gifts: laws of nature. There are laws of economics only because there are providentially sustained regularities in nature, including human nature. *Every science should begin with the doctrines of God's creation and providence.* So should every academic discipline. So should every human enterprise. This is why I am beginning Part III with the doctrine of God's providence.

A. Omnipotence

Point one of the biblical covenant is God's transcendence, yet also His presence. This is the biblical concept of God's original sovereignty. It asks: "Who's in charge here?" How does this apply to providence?

God's omnipotence is a non-transferable attribute of God. Two others are omniscience and omnipresence. God has control over all the cosmos: hundreds of billions of galaxies with an estimated hundred billion stars in each galaxy. Also, don't ignore all the electrons, protons, and neutrons. Throw in the quarks. The universe looks immense to us, but not to God. He runs the whole show. This is the biblical doctrine of omnipotence.

Humanists deny that such a God exists. They are joined by innumerable Christians who say that while God could control everything, He chooses not to. Yes, they admit, God may well control two trillion galaxies and their stars, along with their electrons, neutrons, and protons, but He does not control you and me—not completely, anyway. He has exempted us from such all-embracing controls.

The Bible teaches otherwise.

> "As for you, you meant evil against me, but God meant it for good in order to bring about this present result, to keep many people alive." (Gen. 50:20)

> The king's heart is like channels of water in the hand of the LORD; He turns it wherever He pleases. (Prov. 21:1)

> "It is I who made the earth, and created mankind upon it. I stretched out the heavens with My hands, and I ordained all their lights. I have stirred him in righteousness, and I will make all his ways smooth. He will build My city and let My exiles go free, without any payment or reward," says the LORD of armies. (Isa. 45:12–13)

> Then Job answered the LORD and said, "I know that You can do all things, and that no plan is impossible for You." (Job 42:1–2)

> But our God is in the heavens; He does whatever He pleases. (Ps. 115:3)

> What shall we say then? There is no injustice with God, is there? Far from it! For He says to Moses, "I will have mercy on whomever I have mercy, and I will show compassion to whomever I show compassion."

> So then, it does not depend on the person who wants it nor the one who runs, but on God who has mercy. For the Scripture says to Pharaoh, "For this very reason I raised you up, in order to demonstrate My power in you, and that My name might be proclaimed throughout the earth." So then He has mercy on whom He desires, and He hardens whom He desires. You will say to me then, "Why does He still find fault? For who has resisted His will?" On the contrary, who are you, you foolish person, who answers back to God? The thing molded will not say to the molder, "Why did you make me like this," will it? Or does the potter not have a right over the clay, to make from the same lump one object for honorable use, and another for common use? (Rom. 9:14–21)

For the purpose of establishing the foundations of Christian economic theory, I begin with Genesis 50:20. Joseph spoke to all but one of his brothers, some of whom had sought to kill him, and all of whom sold him into slavery. "As for you, you meant evil against me, but God meant it for good in order to bring about this present result, to keep many people alive." There were the plans of the many: the brothers. There was the plan of the One: God. God's plan was sovereign; the brothers' plans were not. God possessed omnipotence; the brothers did not. Yet the brothers were responsible before God for their evil deed. They knew this. They feared Joseph. This is why he comforted them. He showed mercy to them. He showed grace. So had God.

What has this to do with economic theory? This. People make decisions to buy or sell, to save or consume, to invest or donate. They are completely responsible for these decisions. They may even be legally liable for the outcomes of some of these decisions. But not one decision is made outside of the providence of God. Not one of them comes as a surprise to God. God never says: "Well, what do you know about that? Who would have guessed?"

Here is God's promise to covenant-keepers. "And we know that God causes all things to work together for good to those who love God, to those who are called according to His purpose" (Rom. 8:28). This should give covenant-keepers confidence in making decisions. The outcomes of their decisions are unclear to them. They seem uncertain. But they are not random. The world is orderly. That is because it is sustained by an omnipotent God who has a decree for all of history.

B. Covenantal Order

Point two of the biblical covenant is hierarchical authority. It asks: "To whom do I report?" How does this apply to providence?

God's order is at bottom covenantal. This means that it is moral. It reflects God's moral character. Covenant-breakers deny this.

> For the wrath of God is revealed from heaven against all ungodliness and unrighteousness of people who suppress the truth in unrighteousness, because that which is known about God is evident within them; for God made it evident to them. For since the creation of the world His invisible attributes, that is, His eternal power and divine nature, have been clearly perceived, being understood by what has been made, so that they are without excuse. For even though they knew God, they did not honor Him as God or give thanks, but they became futile in their reasonings, and their senseless hearts were darkened. (Rom. 1:18–21)

The Bible teaches the doctrine of *cosmic personalism*. The universe is not impersonal. It is inherently personal because God created it out of nothing and continues to support its operations providentially. It is not the product of impersonal forces.

The affairs of men are governed by ethical laws. Moses warned the generation of the inheritance of Canaan not to forget the God who had delivered their enemies into their hands.

> "Otherwise, you may say in your heart, 'My power and the strength of my hand made me this wealth.' But you are to remember the LORD your God, for it is He who is giving you power to make wealth, in order to confirm His covenant which He swore to your fathers, as it is this day." (Deut. 8:17–18)

This passage is the heart, mind, and soul of Christian social theory. If this passage is not true, then the affairs of men are governed by non-covenantal forces. These forces are therefore autonomous: self-law, not God's providential law. These supposedly autonomous forces are then discovered, one by one, by covenant-breaking intellectuals and scientists. *If this passage is not true, then there is no such thing as biblical social theory, including economics.* There are at best competing humanistic social theories, which are then "baptized" by academically employed Christians, who know their place in life: subordinates to covenant-breakers.

C. Economic Laws

Point three of the biblical covenant is law. It asks: "What are the rules?" How does this apply to providence?

The laws of economics include these: (1) supply and demand, (2) high bid wins, (3) when the price falls, there is an increase in the quantity demanded, (4) producers compete against producers, while customers compete against customers, (5) sooner is better than later at the same price, (6) there is a hierarchy of economic values, (7) this hierarchy is subjective, (8) it is ordinal (first, second, third), not cardinal (exactly so much more), (9) more is better than less at the same price, (10) there are no free lunches, (11) at zero price, there is greater demand than supply, and my favorite: (12) it is better to be rich and healthy than it is to be poor and sick. This last one involves an ethical judgment: better.

Are these laws in the same way that the law of gravity is a law? No. What are the most important differences? First, no one can explain the law of gravity, but almost anyone who reads this book and understands it can explain economic laws. Economic laws make sense. The law of gravity doesn't. Am I exaggerating? How can you answer this? "Why is there attraction at a distance in an interstellar vacuum between objects with mass?" Newton discovered the mathematical laws of gravity. To explain them, he appealed to the providence of God. This appears in the section of the *Principia* titled "General Scholium." He wrote: "This most beautiful system of the sun, planets, and comets, could only proceed from the counsel and dominion of an intelligent being. And if the fixed Stars are the centers of other like systems, these, being formed by the like wise counsel, must all be subject to the dominion of One. ...This Being Governs all things, not as the soul of the world, but as Lord over all: And on account of his dominion he is wont to be called Lord God παντοκρατωρ, or Universal Ruler." He also wrote: "I have not as yet been able to discover the reason for these properties of gravity from phenomena, and I do not frame hypotheses." He was wiser than his successors, who think they can leave God out of their explanations.

Second, economic laws are not governed by mathematical formulas. The laws of gravity are. So, astrophysicists make far better predictions regarding the trajectories of planets in the solar system than economists make regarding the timing of recessions. Economists offer explanations for recessions. These explanations do not agree; there are rival explanations. Most of them possess at least a surface plausibility. In contrast, astrophysicists do not offer coherent explanations for why planets are attracted to the sun in unbreakable recurring patterns across a vacuum. There are invisible cosmic strings that link the planets, stars, and galaxies. But if you don't believe in a sovereign creator God, your explanation for this will not make sense to anyone except you. Also, your theory will be replaced soon by another even more complex, incoherent, and implausible theory.

Why any economist would want to imitate physics as a science is beyond me, but a lot of them do. They write articles and books that are as unreadable for non-economists as physicists write. Physicists are not trying to persuade non-physicists. Economists whose articles resemble physicists' articles are also not trying to persuade non-economists. This puts them at a disadvantage with those of us who do write for non-economists. You are reading this book. You are not reading a scholarly journal in economics. This is good for me. Let me assure you, this is also good for you.

Economic laws are imposed by a providential God. The laws governing scarcity in the post-fall world are the result of God's curse of Adam's body and the ground (Gen. 3:17–19). Similarly, the laws governing individual self-interest are also the result of God's curse on Adam and the ground. These effects are consistent with the effects of sin in people's lives. They are the result of individuals' assertion of their autonomy from the God of the Bible. Adam Smith, a theological deist, did invoke God in his book, *The Theory of Moral Sentiments* (1759; revised in 1790), but not in *The Wealth of Nations* (1776). *The Wealth of Nations* is implicitly atheistic. There is no trace of theistic causation in *The Wealth of Nations.* Mankind is described as if people were autonomous. Economists ever since have imitated *The Wealth of Nations*, just as physicists have imitated those parts of *Principia* other than "General Scholium." Newton did not believe in either human or cosmic autonomy. Neither did Smith. But their self-professed heirs do.

There are patterns of behavior in people's lives that allow economists and economic forecasters to predict events with greater accuracy than the vast majority of people who have never studied economics. *These patterns are the result of human nature in a providential world.* They are also the result of differences in geographical environments: location, rainfall, soil fertility, and similar attributes. If these patterns of behavior were not pervasive, we could not make long-run economic decisions with accuracy. We would all be flying blind. This includes economists.

D. Predictable Sanctions

Point four of the biblical covenant is sanctions. It asks: "What happens if I obey? Disobey?" How does this apply to providence?

Every covenant has positive commands and negative commands. Every covenant also has corresponding sanctions: positive and negative. This is the model for all social life. Economists have been far more productive than other social scientists in specifying economic sanctions and their consequences, both individual and corporate.

Consider this positive sanction: profit. The entrepreneur who forecasts future conditions of supply and demand more accurately than his competitors do will be able to buy or sell production goods in terms of his forecasts. Because his competitors are not actively bidding for production goods today, he can buy low now and sell high later when demand unexpectedly increases, meaning unexpected by his competitors. Also, if he thinks demand will fall, he can sell his production goods for cash today, and wait for prices to fall. Then he can buy back similar capital goods more inexpensively. This is sell high and buy low. Both approaches produce a profit. The opposite decisions produce losses: buy high, sell low.

If economic sanctions were random, we could not plan successfully. We would be making investment mistakes at least half the time. This would keep us from fulfilling the dominion covenant. God wants mankind to fulfill this covenant; hence, He has created a world in which there are predictable economic sanctions. *These sanctions are providential.* This is true of sanctions in every area of life, but they are more consistently true in economic affairs. The science of predictable sanctions is far more developed in economics than in any other social science.

E. Inheritance/Disinheritance

Point five of the biblical covenant is succession. It asks: "Does this outfit have a future?" How does this apply to providence?

Covenants have positive and negative commands. They have positive and negative sanctions. These sanctions have social effects over time: the expansion of some people's wealth, and a reduced expansion or even reduction of other people's wealth. This also applies to groups. These effects are consistent with what the Bible teaches.

> As for the saints who are on the earth, they are the majestic ones; all my delight is in them. The pains of those who have acquired another god will be multiplied; I will not pour out their drink offerings of blood, nor will I take their names upon my lips. (Ps. 16:3–4)

> But the humble will inherit the land and will delight themselves in abundant prosperity. The wicked plots against the righteous, and gnashes at him with his teeth. The Lord laughs at him, for He sees that his day is coming. (Ps. 37:11–13)

> The righteous will inherit the land and dwell in it forever. (Ps. 37:29)

> You indeed put them on slippery ground; You dropped them into ruin. How they are destroyed in a moment! They are utterly swept away by sudden terrors! Like a dream when one awakes, Lord, when stirred, You will despise their image. (Ps. 73:18–20)

The ethical battlefield of covenantal history is not level. It has been tipped by God against covenant-breakers who violate His laws, which are at bottom ethical laws. Those who conform to His laws benefit. Those who do not are led into paths of destruction: slippery places.

The process of compound growth, generation after generation, has transformed the world. It has made the world a far better place to live for vastly more people. There were about a billion people in 1800. Today, it is more than seven times that many. The extension of private property and the rule of law produced this compounding. So has a new respectability of business profits, which itself was the product of a change in outlook, beginning in the Netherlands in the seventeenth century.

This has to do with inheritance and disinheritance. "A good person leaves an inheritance to his grandchildren, and the wealth of a sinner is stored up for the righteous" (Prov. 13:22). This is the twofold effect of the covenantal structure of history.

Conclusion

The doctrine of God's providence is an extension of the doctrine of God's creation. The doctrine of creation is an affirmation of God's omnipotence.

The doctrine of God's providence stands in stark contrast to the doctrine of nature's dualism between absolute law and absolute chance. Humanists ground their analysis on cosmic impersonalism. They claim that economic theory must be value-free. Then they bring ethical criticisms against the free market. This is inconsistent.

Critics of the free market argue that the system of profit-and-loss accounting does not take into consideration the macro effects of individual profits. They say that there are negative macroeconomic effects that arise from microeconomic profits. An example is pollution. Businesses that emit pollutants profit from this. They transfer costs to society: victims of pollution. Corporate profits rise. So, the fact that a transaction is regarded as profitable by the participants is not recognized by collectivists as a valid argument that society is better off. It may be worse off. Similarly, defenders of individualism speak of the loss of wealth that comes from government regulation. What seems good to state officials is not good for the broad masses of humanity.

The inability of secular economists to resolve this fundamental disagreement over the relationship between free market pricing and its social effects has led to a permanent division within the camp of the economists. This representative example of the one/many dualism in secular philosophy has never been solved to the satisfaction of the competing schools of economic opinion. The hypothetical cosmically impersonal system of free market pricing, which is based on the auction's principle of "high bid wins," works well for individuals, according to most economists, but apart from the concept of God's providence, defenders of the free market cannot show logically that the auction's competition benefits society, which is a collective concept. It is illogical to begin with the assumption of methodological individualism, and then expect it to lead to truths regarding what are good or bad outcomes for collectives.

The doctrine of God's providence teaches that the results of the private property system are beneficial to individuals and also to society. This system did not evolve from a hypothetical social contract. It is the product of God's intervention into the lives of the Israelites under Moses. It is the product of a Trinitarian (One/Many) God. It is therefore consistent with a covenant-based collective social order and also the individual participants who constitute this social order. The allocation system based on "high bid wins" brings greater wealth and a wider range of choices to productive people who own something of value to bid with. It also provides poverty-stricken people opportunities to work and accumulate capital by participating in the market.

Chapter 12

Service

"For it is just like a man about to go on a journey, who called his own slaves and entrusted his possessions to them. To one he gave five talents, to another, two, and to another, one, each according to his own ability; and he went on his journey. The one who had received the five talents immediately went and did business with them, and earned five more talents. In the same way the one who had received the two talents earned two more. But he who received the one talent went away and dug a hole in the ground, and hid his master's money. Now after a long time the master of those slaves came and settled accounts with them."

Matthew 25:14–19

Analysis

The owner transferred assets to his stewards. This was a test. He did not tell them that it was a test. He simply transferred the assets and departed. But they knew that there would be a day of reckoning. This was the day when the open accounts would be settled. This parable appears as the introduction to Jesus' description of the final judgment.

The transfer of assets was an act of delegation. The owner transferred *legal sovereignty to his stewards.* They had full control over the assets. They acted *in his name.* But this was also an act of delegating wealth. They had capital to work with. They were his economic agents. They acted *on his behalf.* Their competition would be economic. Economic competition here is an analogy for comprehensive competition. In Luke's version of this parable, the owner transferred political control over cities to the winners in the economic competition (Luke 19:11–27).

There are two branches of the human family: adopted heirs and disinherited members. They compete for wealth in history, but they also compete in all other areas of life. Economic competition is readily understandable. This is why Jesus preached what I call pocketbook parables. He knew that his listeners would get the point faster and clearer this way.

The two families compete with each other in history. It is the competition between two kingdoms. The two kingdoms represent God and mammon. Jesus said: "No man can serve two masters: for either he will hate the one, and love the other; or else he will hold to the one, and despise the other. Ye cannot serve God and mammon" (Matt. 6:24, KJV). Mammon was a Syrian god of wealth. The New American Standard Bible translation reads: "No one can serve two masters; for either he will hate the one and love the other, or he will be devoted to one and despise the other. You cannot serve God and wealth." The word mammon implies more than money. It means riches in general. I interpret it as follows: "More for me in history."

The issue here is competition between the kingdom of God versus the kingdom of man. It manifests itself in every area of life. But this competition is seen above all in the realm of economics. The dividing line is covenantal representation: point two of the biblical covenant. The dividing line is not riches versus poverty. It is riches on behalf of God versus riches on behalf of man. This also applies to institutions. It is covenantal conflict. It is a war to the death. But this war is seen in economic affairs as competition.

Socialists always said this: "There should be cooperation, not competition." This meant that they wanted politically appointed central planners to decide who gets what and on what terms. Then the masses without power or independent sources of money were supposed to cooperate with the central planners by accepting whatever resources the planners allocated without complaint. This system of allocation invariably led to tyranny: *monopoly control by political elite*. It also led to falling production and widespread poverty. This was why socialism was abandoned in practice and then in theory in the final quarter of the twentieth century.

Men put up with tyranny, but they would not put up with socialist poverty in the midst of capitalist plenty. China abandoned socialist ownership in the late 1970s. The Soviet Union shut down on December 25, 1991.

Competition in economics is always based on an offer: "Buy this from me, not from someone else." It is analogous to marriage: "Marry me, not someone else." It is analogous to church membership: "Join our church, not another one." It is analogous to politics: "Vote for me, not someone else." Competition is basic to life. It is inescapable.

Rival economic systems are in competition. So are rival businesses. So are rival economic theories. Ultimately, *rival confessions of faith* are in competition. This is not well understood in the modern era of humanism, which preaches the religious neutrality of economics, politics, education, and all other areas of public life outside the four walls of the church. Neutrality is a myth.

The essence of competition is *competition for authority*, meaning decision-making for ourselves and for others under our authority. This is at bottom *competition for responsibility* to act on behalf of the sovereign. There is no agreement on who this sovereign is: God or mammon. This competition over authority and responsibility will go on until the end of time.

> Jesus presented another parable to them, saying, "The kingdom of heaven is like a man who sowed good seed in his field. But while his men were sleeping, his enemy came and sowed weeds among the wheat, and left. And when the wheat sprouted and produced grain, then the weeds also became evident. And the slaves of the landowner came and said to him, 'Sir, did you not sow good seed in your field? How then does it have weeds?' And he said to them, 'An enemy has done this!' The slaves said to him, 'Do you want us, then, to go and gather them up?' But he said, 'No; while you are gathering up the weeds, you may uproot the wheat with them. 'Allow both to grow together until the harvest; and at the time of the harvest I will say to the reapers, "First gather up the weeds and bind them in bundles to burn them; but gather the wheat into my barn."' " (Matt. 13:24–30)

Note: nothing intervenes to separate the wheat and tares (weeds) in history. The weeds and the wheat compete without any period of separation: not seven years or three-and-a-half years. There is no temporary period of rest and recreation in heaven for the wheat before they return to history. The only way out of history is death.

Point two of the biblical covenant is authority. This can also be described as hierarchy. In every organization there is a hierarchy. The person at the top of this hierarchy has the authority to give lawful commands. Those beneath him have a responsibility to obey.

Point two of the biblical covenant is associated with the covenant itself. It is the arrangement by which God rules His kingdom. All men are responsible to God as His creations, but covenant-keepers acknowledge this obligation.

The dominion covenant found in Genesis 1 sets forth the chain of command: God over mankind over creation.

> God blessed them; and God said to them, "Be fruitful and multiply, and fill the earth, and subdue it; and rule over the fish of the sea and over the birds of the sky and over every living thing that moves on the earth." (Gen. 1:28)

Mankind represents God to the creation, and also represents the creation to God. Put differently, mankind must serve the creation. "Then the LORD God took the man and put him in the Garden of Eden to cultivate it and tend it" (Gen. 2:15). Mankind is in the middle.

This original, pre-fall hierarchy serves as the model for a Christian society. Jesus made it clear that the means of success in His kingdom is service to others. *The path to leadership is a servant's path.* He contrasted this with rulers among the gentiles. They sought authority as a way to command others. This is not the correct approach, Jesus said—not in the church, not in the family, and not in the state.

What about in the economy? The economy is not covenantal. It is not established by a formal public oath before God, unlike church, family, and state. Market exchanges are contractual. They are promises. A contract is analogous to a covenant, but it does not have the same degree of authority. If Jesus' words apply to binding covenants, then they surely apply to contracts. *The means of success is service.*

In the hierarchy of the free market social order, consumers possess final economic authority. This is because they possess money. *Money is the most marketable commodity.* When you walk into a store, you do not have to plead with a salesman to take your money. You do not have to offer him a discount to take your money. Far more likely is this scenario: the salesman pleads with you to part with your money. He may even offer a discount for cash. Why? Because what he is selling is not the most marketable commodity.

The seller is not in authority. The buyer is. Let me clarify this. The seller of goods and services is not in authority. The seller of money is. We call the seller of goods a seller. We call the person who spends money a buyer. But both of them are sellers, and both of them are buyers. Both parties surrender ownership. Both parties take ownership. This is what every sale is: *a transfer of ownership.*

The seller must serve the buyer because the buyer owns the most marketable commodity: money. Nevertheless, the buyer must serve the seller by handing over his money. If there is not mutual service, there will be no sale. This is why Jesus' words apply to the free market economy. *The free market economy is a gigantic system of mutual service.* The study of economics is the study of how this system operates.

A. Incarnation

Point one of the biblical covenant is God's transcendence, yet also His presence. This is the biblical concept of God's original sovereignty. It asks: "Who's in charge here?" How does this apply to service?

The Christian doctrine of authority by means of service begins with the doctrine of the incarnation of the Second Person of the Trinity in the Person of Jesus Christ.

> Do nothing from selfishness or empty conceit, but with humility consider one another as more important than yourselves; do not merely look out for your own personal interests, but also for the interests of others. Have this attitude in yourselves which was also in Christ Jesus, who, as He already existed in the form of God, did not consider equality with God something to be grasped, but emptied Himself by taking the form of a bond-servant and being born in the likeness of men. And being found in appearance as a man, He humbled Himself by becoming obedient to the point of death: death on a cross. For this reason

> also God highly exalted Him, and bestowed on Him the name which is above every name, so that at the name of Jesus every knee will bow, of those who are in heaven and on earth and under the earth, and that every tongue will confess that Jesus Christ is Lord, to the glory of God the Father. (Phil. 2:3–11)

The incarnation involved the ultimate service by the ultimate being. This service was unto death: the supreme sacrifice for others. Yet this was not designed to humiliate Jesus permanently. On the contrary, it was designed to elevate Him. The path of incarnation was this: God became a man, who surrendered power to the state and the church of His day, thereby establishing the judicial foundation of total authority. As the resurrected Jesus announced to the disciples,

> "All authority in heaven and on earth has been given to Me. Go, therefore, and make disciples of all the nations, baptizing them in the name of the Father and the Son and the Holy Spirit, teaching them to follow all that I commanded you; and behold, I am with you always, to the end of the age." (Matt. 28:18–20)

When Jesus contrasted the way to authority in the church versus the way to authority among the gentiles, He was presenting a model of dominion. It was the same model that God had established for the redemption of mankind. This is God's way to overcome the kingdom of Satan, which is the kingdom of self-proclaimed autonomous man. The competition between the kingdom of God and the kingdom of man is not based on power. It is based on ethics. Might does not make right. *Right eventually makes might.* But it takes time for covenant-keepers to figure this out. They read it. Jesus taught it. But they find it difficult to believe. It is not the familiar way of autonomous man.

B. Four-Way Authority

Point two of the biblical covenant is hierarchical authority. It asks: "To whom do I report?" How does this apply to service?

Covenantal authority is both hierarchical and horizontal. This fact is not intuitive.

Authority brings responsibility. To whom is someone in authority responsible? First and foremost, he is responsible to God. God is sovereign. He is the Creator. He providentially maintains the creation. He brings preliminary judgments in history. He answers prayers. He brings final judgment. He is in charge. This is standard Christian doctrine. It is not controversial.

God demands service to others as the means of demonstrating allegiance to Him. In the passage on the final judgment, Jesus said:

> "But when the Son of Man comes in His glory, and all the angels with Him, then He will sit on His glorious throne. And all the nations will be gathered before Him; and He will separate them from one another, just as the shepherd separates the sheep from the goats; and He will put the sheep on His right, but the goats on the left. Then the King will say to those on His right, 'Come, you who are blessed of My Father, inherit the kingdom prepared for you from the foundation of the world. For I was hungry, and you gave Me something to eat; I was thirsty, and you gave Me something to drink; I was a stranger, and you invited Me in; naked, and you clothed Me; I was sick, and you visited Me; I was in prison, and you came to Me.' Then the righteous will answer Him, 'Lord, when did we see You hungry, and feed You, or thirsty, and give You something to drink? And when did we see You as a stranger, and invite You in, or naked, and clothe You? And when did we see You sick, or in prison, and come to You?' And the King will answer and say to them, 'Truly I say to you, to the extent that you did it for one of the least of these brothers or sisters of Mine, you did it for Me.'" (Matt. 25:31–40)

The covenantal doctrine of *authority* is inherently a doctrine of *representation*. Jesus made it clear: the poor are representatives of God. How people treat the weak and poor reflects their view of God's treatment of them. Covenant-keepers perceive that they are weak and poor in the sight of God. So, there must be *submission upward*. But this is demonstrated by *service downward*: service to those who cannot repay.

There is more. There is also service outward. We serve those who can repay. In voluntary exchanges, this service is immediately repaid. Adam Smith put it famously in *Wealth of Nations*:

> But man has almost constant occasion for the help of his brethren, and it is in vain for him to expect it from their benevolence only. He will

> be more likely to prevail if he can interest their self-love in his favour, and show them that it is for their own advantage to do for him what he requires of them. Whoever offers to another a bargain of any kind, proposes to do this. Give me that which I want, and you shall have this which you want, is the meaning of every such offer; and it is in this manner that we obtain from one another the far greater part of those good offices which we stand in need of. It is not from the benevolence of the butcher, the brewer, or the baker that we expect our dinner, but from their regard to their own interest. We address ourselves, not to their humanity but to their self-love, and never talk to them of our own necessities but of their advantages. Nobody but a beggar chooses to depend chiefly upon the benevolence of his fellow-citizens.[1]

So, we must serve others. Why? Because we want their cooperation. Why? Because we need help. This leads us to a consideration of the fourth authority: ourselves. We are self-interested. This means there is *service inward.* Smith grounded his book on this crucial insight. *We serve in order that we may be served.* We are all buyers. We are all sellers. We need help. To obtain it, we offer help.

In covenantal economics, covenant-keepers are told to serve others. But this service need not be a one-way street in every case, or even in most cases. *There is mutually advantageous service.* It is negotiated for the sake of our own goals and comforts, and also for those under our jurisdiction.

C. The Extra Mile

Point three of the biblical covenant is law. It asks: "What are the rules?" ow does this apply to service?

Jesus preached to Israelites. These people were under the domination of Rome. They were not citizens of an independent nation.

Jesus did not teach revolution as a legitimate way to throw off bondage. He taught service.

> "You have heard that it was said, 'Eye for eye, and tooth for tooth.' But I say to you, do not show opposition against an evil person; but whoever

1. Adam Smith, *The Wealth of Nations* (1776), book 1, ch. 2.

> slaps you on your right cheek, turn the other toward him also. And if anyone wants to sue you and take your tunic, let him have your cloak also. Whoever forces you to go one mile, go with him two. Give to him who asks of you, and do not turn away from him who wants to borrow from you." (Matt. 5:38–42)

This was prudent advice to people in political bondage. If someone in power decides to single you out for poor treatment, respond with above-average service. The archetype of this was Jesus on the cross. "Father, forgive them; for they do not know what they are doing" (Luke 23:34b). Go the extra mile with those above you. Go the extra mile with those below you.

What about our relationship with judicial equals? Do the same. In a free market, two bargainers both own assets. They wish to gain an exchange. The best approach is to offer a better deal. Go the extra mile. If you are selling something, ask for less in return. The transaction is more likely to take place. In the free market, this is the strategy of *price competition*. This is the insight of a fundamental law of economics: "When the price is reduced, more is demanded."

The principle of going the extra mile governs employee relations. The employee should do more than what is expected. Why? Because this is a competitive way to avoid being fired when the economy sags. If you are on the "short list" of employees to be kept on the payroll, this is an advantage.

Jesus gave this advice to oppressed people. The correct way to deal with people who do not appreciate you is to identify yourself as a cooperative person. Such people are hard to find. The same holds true for any group. If the Jews had not rebelled militarily against the Roman emperor Vespasian in AD 69, Vespasian would not have sent his son Titus to besiege the city of Jerusalem in AD 70. The Romans burned the city and the temple. This ended the Mosaic sacrificial system. This was what Jesus had predicted would happen a generation earlier.

> "But when you see Jerusalem surrounded by armies, then recognize that her desolation is near. Then those who are in Judea must flee to the mountains, and those who are inside the city must leave, and those who are in the country must not enter the city; because these are days of punishment, so that all things which have been written will be fulfilled. Woe to those women who are pregnant, and to those who are nursing babies

> in those days; for there will be great distress upon the land, and wrath to this people; and they will fall by the edge of the sword, and will be led captive into all the nations; and Jerusalem will be trampled underfoot by the Gentiles until the times of the Gentiles are fulfilled." (Luke 21:20–24)

Better to have gone the extra mile.

D. Trust

Point four of the biblical covenant is sanctions. It asks: "What happens if I obey? Disobey?" How does this apply to service?

There are positive economic sanctions and negative economic sanctions. These are the key economic sanctions: *profit and loss.*

When someone performs well on a long-term basis, those who do business with him want to maintain the relationship. It takes time and effort to locate someone who is reliable, whose word can be trusted.

I have written for many years that there are three keys to business success.

1. Do what you said you would do.
2. Do it at the price agreed on, or lower.
3. Do it on or before the deadline agreed on.

It boils down to these: *quality, price, and time.* Anyone who consistently performs as promised, or a little better, will find that he is seldom out of work. There will be demand for his services.

If someone gains the reputation that he will not cheat a buyer, he will have clients. Wherever this internal commitment to not cheating is widespread in a group or a society, a cost of doing business will fall. There will be an increase in the number of voluntary exchanges. The market will be extended. Why? Because of this rule: "When the price falls, more is demanded." The division of labor will increase. Specialization will increase. Efficiency will increase. Per capita wealth will increase.

Trust takes time to develop. It can be lost in one transaction. It is a valuable resource, but it is a fragile resource. It is a capital asset. It makes a trusted person, company, or group more valuable to others. This increase in value can be converted into money. There will be repeat business.

E. Repeat Business

Point five of the biblical covenant is succession. It asks: "Does this outfit have a future?" How does this apply to service?

In business, most of the net income usually comes from repeat business. It costs a lot of advertising money to generate a new customer. The profit from this new customer comes from repeat sales. *It is much less expensive to generate a repeat sale than the first sale.* There is a marketing concept called the lifetime value of the customer. How many sales will there be? What is the expected average profit per sale? These estimates are crucial for estimating how much money must be devoted to advertising.

Businesses that get repeat business from the same customers for years are profitable. Their marketing costs are low in relation to the profits generated over years. But to achieve this desirable situation, a company must deliver high-quality goods on a predictable basis. The customers must trust the company not to cheat them. But even this is not enough. The company should also go the extra mile.

The company that continues to improve quality and service will grow. If a company continues to satisfy its customers and attract new ones, it will expand its sales, profits, and market share. This is the basis of long-term expansion. This is how a few firms become dominant in the market place. The continual reinvestment of profits, the continual improvement of product quality, and constant attention to what customers want and are willing to pay for are marks of dominant companies in any market niche.

Conclusion

Jesus called the disciples to a life of service to the members of the church. They were not to lord it over others. They were to serve faithfully. *This strategy leads to success whenever it is implemented systematically.* If this becomes the outlook of the church's leaders, the church will grow.

What is true of the church is true of business. When a business's owners and senior managers set the pattern of above-average customer service, they will be imitated by their institutional subordinates. The business will grow. The business will be able to serve a larger number of customers. This will generate repeat business. The business will prosper. Everyone connected with the business will benefit financially. Their ability to save money for the future will help generate future profits. Their dominion will increase.

The dominion covenant is all about responsibility. Mankind rejected this covenant at the fall. Redemption is the program by which God is restoring the original dominion covenant. This involves the restoration of responsibility. This means individual responsibility. It also means institutional responsibility.

One means of increasing responsibility is capital. It is a tool of production. The Christian is to view wealth as a means of dominion. It provides capital. Capital enables covenant-keepers to subdue the earth to God's glory at a lower cost. As wealth increases, so does responsibility.

Christians should not pursue wealth unless they are also pursuing responsibility. Wealth is usually regarded as an end in itself. It should not be pursued for the sake of increased consumption. To do so is a covenantal error. Wealth should be regarded as a means to an end. To regard wealth as an end is to misunderstand the dominion covenant. Wealth is primarily a tool of production. Some of it may be lawfully consumed as a reward, but not all of it. If all of it is consumed, there can be no inheritance of capital.

Most people do not want any more responsibility. They much prefer leisure. But almost everybody wants more money. This is illogical. *You cannot get more money without getting more responsibility.* But people prefer not to admit that there is an unbreakable connection between money and responsibility.

If Christians understood this, and if they would structure their household budgets accordingly, they would begin to increase their influence in society. Thrift requires the adoption of a future-oriented worldview, one stretching down through the generations until the final judgment.

Dominion requires increased responsibility. Here is a law of political power: "Power flows to the person who takes responsibility." In economics, wealth flows to the person who takes responsibility. The Christian way to power is different from the power seeker's way: service. So is the Christian way to wealth: service.

But Jesus called them to Himself and said, "You know that the rulers of the Gentiles domineer over them, and those in high position exercise authority over them. It is not this way among you, but whoever wants to become prominent among you shall be your servant, and whoever desires to be first among you shall be your slave; just as the Son of Man did not come to be served, but to serve, and to give His life as a ransom for many." (Matt. 20:25–28)

Chapter 13

Leasehold

"The Lord will command the blessing for you in your barns and in everything that you put your hand to, and He will bless you in the land that the Lord your God is giving you. The Lord will establish you as a holy people to Himself, as He swore to you, if you keep the commandments of the Lord your God and walk in His ways."

Deuteronomy 28:8–9

"But it shall come about, if you do not obey the Lord your God, to be careful to follow all His commandments and His statutes which I am commanding you today, that all these curses will come upon you and overtake you: Cursed will you be in the city, and cursed will you be in the country. Cursed will be your basket and your kneading bowl. Cursed will be the children of your womb, the produce of your ground, the newborn of your herd, and the offspring of your flock. Cursed will you be when you come in, and cursed will you be when you go out."

Deuteronomy 28:15–19

Analysis

God's dominion covenant had to be modified after the fall of man. Mankind became subject to death. This meant that God would have to renew the dominion covenant with each new generation. This transformed private property into what we call a leasehold. Delegated ownership was no longer permanent. Each generation died off.

Before the fall of man, there would not have had to have been detailed leasehold agreements. People would not have stolen from each other. Any disputes over ownership would have been settled amicably. There was no need for the civil government to intervene. There would have been no civil government had man not sinned. But man did sin, and this meant that God's arrangements with mankind had to be modified. This was because of the effect of sin in the lives of men. Leasehold agreements had to become far more specific than before the fall. Disputes were constant. Disagreements were not ordinarily amicable. The terms of each agreement would have to be spelled out in detail. This was true of the covenantal agreement between God and mankind. It was also true of the agreements among mankind. Boundaries had to be specified. Rules governing the use of property also had to be specified.

Leviticus 26 and Deuteronomy 28 are leasehold agreements. They are parallel passages. They are long chapters. They contain promises of blessings and curses. The sections that deal with the curses are three times as long as the sections that deal with the blessings.

Written contracts have terms. The parties agree to the terms of a contract. There are specified penalties for any violation of the contract. There are usually benefits listed for performance according to the terms of the contract. But the penalties are the crucial section. Both parties to the contract understand that the terms must be fulfilled, and fear of the penalties serves as a motivation for both parties to the contract to perform as promised.

One of the insights of the field known as behavioral economics is this: *people fear a loss with greater intensity than they desire a comparable amount of gain.* This has been demonstrated in numerous psychological experiments. This is reflected in the story of the forbidden tree. Adam was told that he had access to all of the trees of the garden, including the tree of life. But God did not go into details about these benefits. The negative sanction of death was the focus of the agreement. God did not even mention the fact that the tree of life would guarantee eternal life to Adam. He never did tell Adam that this was the case. But, after the fall, He placed a barrier around the garden so that Adam could not re-enter the garden, eat from the tree, and gain eternal life. It was sufficient that the contract specified that a violation of the terms of the lease would result in death. That threat did not impress Adam, so he came under the curse. He came under a whole series of curses. So do we.

A leasehold agreement has this crucial goal: *to keep the tenant from exploiting the property that has been transferred to him.* The owner knows that the tenant will be tempted to misuse the property, thereby reducing its market value. For example, if he does not rotate crops or otherwise fertilize land, the productivity of the land will decline over time. He benefits from the productivity during the terms of the lease, and then he turns the property back to the owner in a depleted condition. He de-capitalizes the owner. Therefore, the owner is careful to specify what the tenant is allowed to do with the property. The owner wants the property returned to him in its original condition or even in a more productive condition.

A lease is not the same as a permanent transfer of property. A lease is not full ownership; it merely establishes the right of someone to use a specific piece of property for a limited period of time. Because of Adam's sin, all humans occupy for temporary time. We die. *The lease ends when the tenant dies.* It may be a transferable lease, but the terms of occupancy do not change. This is how the owner of the property preserves the value of the property.

There is no question that the terms of the leasehold for the dominion covenant are rigorous. They are overwhelmingly ethical. They do not change except when the owner authorizes such a change. The tenants do not have the authority to modify the terms of the lease.

Modern theologians assume that the terms of the lease which God granted in a series of revisions from Adam to Christ do not extend into the New Covenant. They assume that Christians can safely ignore the terms of the original lease. They assume that God has quietly and without any public announcement modified the lease agreement in such a way that almost none of the Mosaic economic and civil laws persevere in the New Covenant.

Why would God abandon virtually all of the economic terms of the lease without explaining why? Why does God expect Christian tenants to return His property in good condition, despite the fact that the terms of the lease have been abandoned, and therefore there are no negative sanctions associated with failure to comply with those terms? At the same time, why do modern theologians assume that the blessings of the original agreement have also been annulled by God? Why do they think that the specified benefits are no longer awarded to reward honest production? Why do they think that the whole program of dominion, which requires an increase of capital over multiple generations, no longer applies to covenant-keepers?

There were positive and negative sanctions in the garden of Eden. There were positive and negative sanctions associated with the Abrahamic covenant. These were covenantal laws. For example, Abraham tithed to Melchizedek (Gen. 14:20). Israelite land owners under the Mosaic law were required to tithe to the Levites (Num. 18). There was covenantal continuity. Yet there are few theologians today who argue that God still requires the tithe payment to the institutional church. We are told that God has abandoned the requirement of the tithe, despite the fact that Jesus is a high priest in the order of Melchizedek and therefore deserving of a tithe (Heb. 7). Isn't that strange? I don't believe it. I have written a book refuting the idea: *The Covenantal Tithe* (2011). I hold the position that the terms of the Melchizedekan tithe remain in force.

A. Owner

Point one of the biblical covenant is God's transcendence, yet also His presence. This is the biblical concept of God's original sovereignty. It asks: "Who's in charge here?" How does this apply to the leasehold?

God is the absolute owner of the creation. He is the owner because He created everything. He is not the God of pantheism. He is not part of the creation. He is transcendent over the creation. Second, He maintains His ownership as the providential administrator of the entire creation. He is not the God of deism. He is present with the creation.

God created mankind to exercise dominion over the earth. As the owner of the earth, God established a contract between Himself and Adam. We correctly call this a covenant, but it had the characteristic features of any leasehold agreement. There was a statement of what Adam and Eve were required to do: exercise dominion and multiply biologically. There was also a representative test of Adam's capacity as God's caretaker. He had to avoid eating from a specific tree. There was a negative sanction associated with a violation of the leasehold agreement: death. That would certainly have ended the lease. But God in His grace did not execute Adam on that day. He extended the lease to Adam's heirs down through the ages. You and I come under the terms of the lease.

B. Stewardship Under Law

Point two of the biblical covenant is hierarchical authority. It asks: "To whom do I report?" How does this apply to the leasehold?

When Adam demonstrated that he was a thief, he made it clear to himself, his wife, and his heirs that he was no longer a reliable caretaker. He was willing to steal from the owner. He was therefore willing to extract part of the capital value of the leasehold in order to benefit personally. He would count as personal income the depleted value of the original capital.

This was exactly the opposite of what God had told Adam to do before the fall. They were required to administer God's property to God's advantage. Their heirs were also to serve as stewards of God's property. They were given a lease, but God did not transfer full ownership of the property to them. Therefore, they were not to deplete the value of the original capital assets; on the contrary, they were required to increase its value. But Adam could no longer be trusted to do this.

Biblical law sets forth the terms of the lease. The reason why there has to be this law-order is that mankind, now corrupted by sin, simply cannot be trusted to administer God's property apart from specified rules and the appropriate sanctions. There have to be rewards, and there have to be punishments. Without these, mankind would rob God blind. God is not blind, so He has specified terms of the lease. *This limits man's authority.*

The terms of the lease are part of the hierarchical structure of authority. There could be no safe transfer of this authority apart from the terms of the lease. The terms of the lease should be seen as benefits. *The terms of the lease establish what man is required to do. This is the judicial foundation of man's authority in the hierarchy of dominion.* God did not kill Adam. Instead, he extended the lease. This was an act of grace on God's part. If you are a covenant-keeper, and therefore redeemed by the life, death, resurrection, and ascension of Jesus Christ, then you are a beneficiary. You should rejoice in the fact that you have been given this honor. But without the leasehold agreement, God could not trust you. For that matter, you could not trust you. "The heart is more deceitful than all else and is desperately sick; who can understand it?" (Jer. 17:9). The sin of self-deception has been around ever since the Garden of Eden. Basically, Adam and Eve committed suicide. They were involved in a suicide mission. They were successful.

The existence of the leasehold and its terms testifies to the legitimacy of our office as stewards. The leasehold testifies to God's grace. Never forget: *grace precedes law.* Adam was given life before he was told not to eat of the forbidden tree. The grace of God is vastly more powerful than the wrath of God. The grace of God extends to all eternity. It is progressive in eternity. It compounds. The wrath of God just sits there, burning covenant-breakers. There is no progress in the wrath of God.

C. Theft

Point three of the biblical covenant is law. It asks: "What are the rules?" How does this apply to the leasehold?

The fundamental principle of Christian economics is the creation. Secondarily, it is the providence of God in sustaining the creation. *This is where economic theory should begin: original ownership and providence.* But this is not where other economists begin. Far more often, they begin with the concept of scarcity and the division of labor. Scarcity is not the central principle of economic science. Neither is the division of labor. Adam Smith began with the division of labor, and this set back the cause of liberty for at least 180 years. He should have started with ownership. A socialist can claim to be in favor of the division of labor. A socialist is never in favor of widespread private ownership.

There is no question that the story of the fall of man focuses on an act of theft. So, theft should be the focus of all discussions of economic law. The overwhelming bulk of economic laws in the Old Testament and the New Testament focus on restrictions against theft. The laws specify what constitutes theft. In other words, the heart of Christian economics, after the doctrines of creation and providence, and after the doctrine of the dominion covenant, is the integrity of private property. If this were not true, this would not have been the only prohibition in the garden of Eden. That prohibition should make it clear to all of us: *theft is the archetype sin of mankind.* It is the alpha and omega of sin. Joseph's brothers stole his liberty by selling him to slave traders (Gen. 37). A subsequent Pharaoh enslaved the Israelites, stealing their liberty (Ex. 1). Jezebel stole Naboth's vineyard to benefit her husband (I Kings 21). Judas was a thief (John 12:6).

The details of Christian economics can best be found in the details of the laws against theft. If we study the laws against theft, we prepare ourselves for understanding the operations of the market order. Understanding ownership and property rights is fundamental to a correct understanding of all economics, and Christian economists have a moral obligation to make this clear. If they don't get this clear, who will?

D. Policing

Point four of the biblical covenant is sanctions. It asks: "What happens if I obey? Disobey?" How does this apply to the leasehold?

In a sharecropping arrangement, the owner is entitled to a share of the output of his property. This is also true of business income.

It is always difficult for an owner to police this aspect of the lease. A sharecropper can hide some of the output. The owner cannot monitor everything. This, of course, is not true of God, but the old adage still applies: "The best fertilizer is the owner's shadow." After God left the garden, Adam and Eve acted as though He was not present in their midst.

Every lease has to have success indicators. Every employment contract has to have success indicators. In businesses, accounting concepts of monetary profit and loss are the most common success and failure indicators. These are monetary concepts. They are objective. But the problem with them is this: *those who are closest to the system's local operations can cheat.* The specialized knowledge which they possess is not possessed by the owner, who is more distant. This is especially true in a division-of-labor economy with extensive international trade. If the low-level employee or the business trading partner is in a position to take advantage of the owner, the owner is hard-pressed to monitor all of these opportunities for cheating. This is why the self-discipline involved in a refusal to cheat or to take advantage of an owner is beneficial for society. *This is a matter of self-government.* The owner cannot expend sufficient resources to police every transaction. Furthermore, people who are closer to the transactions have the ability to structure the transaction so as to benefit them. This is called "gaming the system." This is always the problem with objective success indicators. They can all be gamed. They are supposed to motivate decision-makers to do what is profitable for end users: the service function. Instead, they are used to benefit the employees at the expense of users and also owners.

Here is a familiar example of this problem. Parents tell their child to earn good grades at school. Grades are supposed to tell everyone how well the student understands the material. But what if the student cheats? Teachers tell the student not to cheat. But what if the student finds a way to cheat without getting caught? This undermines the purpose of grading. If it becomes widespread, this will undermine the reputation of the school. The cheating students who graduate will not be able to perform as expected in college... unless they find ways to cheat without getting caught in college. Over time, widespread cheating erodes trust in the performance of educational institutions. This is not a hypothetical problem. Cheating is widespread in higher education in the United States. It is far worse than it was in my college days in the early 1960s. There are online companies that sell term papers for students to submit as their own work. There is a large market for this service.

Ethical people who refuse to take advantage of the ignorance of trading partners will find over time that they have more opportunities to become involved in profitable ventures. But even here, it is difficult to gain the reputation, because the cheating is not observed. So, refusing to cheat is not observed. But God observes it. *The battlefield of ethics is tilted against covenant-breakers.* An omniscient God is not fooled.

The system of double-entry bookkeeping does reduce the amount of cheating. The capitalist world has depended on this accounting procedure for half a millennium. It has given Western economies a tremendous advantage over the rest of the world. It has reduced the cost of monitoring cheating. It enables owners to know the condition of their businesses.

If Christians obeyed God's laws regarding theft, then they would possess a major competitive advantage in every society. If they were self-disciplined in not taking advantage of others, they would gain reputations of honesty that would increase the number of offers for joint ventures. *This begins with self-government under God.* Christians should be sufficiently afraid of the negative sanctions of God to persuade them to avoid cheating.

E. Economic Growth

Point five of the biblical covenant is succession. It asks: "Does this outfit have a future?" How does this apply to the leasehold?

God promised to bless his covenant people if they obey his laws (Deut. 28:1–14). This involved the economic blessings. This was an intergenerational promise. It was not just to the first generation of Israelites who would conquer the Canaanites. It was a promise to Israel through the generations. This promise ended in AD 70 when Rome destroyed Israel. The church then replaced Israel. It became the Israel of God (Gal. 6:16).

This is the issue of compound economic growth. Even a relatively low rate of growth transforms any economy within a century. The rate of economic growth in Great Britain and the United States began to compound around 1800. With only one decade of stagnation, the 1930s, the economy of the United States and Great Britain continued to grow at somewhere between 2% and 3% per annum per capita. This has led to the complete transformation of the world. There were about a billion people in 1800. There are over seven times this today. Never before in the recorded history of man has there been comparable economic growth and population growth. All of this has taken place because of the compound economic growth and compound population growth at or below 3% per capita per year. This steady increase, year after year, has led to a completely new world, a world of wealth so great that it would have been inconceivable in 1800. Yet, incredibly, this took place within three generations of one family: President John Tyler (1790–1861) to his two grandsons, who were still alive in 2019. (I interviewed Lyon Tyler in 2010.)

The most important historical question that historians can conceivably answer by an appeal to historical records is this one: "What took place around 1800 that launched a period of compound economic growth that lasted for over two centuries?" So far, economic historians have not come to any agreed-on answers.

The texts of Leviticus 26 and Deuteronomy 28 testify to the fact that God promised something like this in the middle of the fifteenth century BC. Compound growth could have begun then. It did not. Historians want to know why a trend began in a particular location at a particular period of time. Why didn't this enormous transformation of the world economy begin in Israel sometime around 1450 BC? The biblical answer is simple: the Israelites did not remain obedient to the stipulations of the leasehold agreement that gave them control over the geography of the tiny nation of Israel. The nations around them also did not abide by these stipulations.

Conclusion

God was quite specific in His revelation to Moses regarding His law. It was a systematic law-order. It was supposed to be enforced by sanctions: self-government, family government, church government, and state government. This did not take place on a systematic basis in the history of Israel.

If the Mosaic system of economic and civil laws and sanctions is no longer in force, then there is no such thing as Christian economic theory or Christian social theory. Christians from the first century onward have denied that this system of law and sanctions is still mandatory in the New Covenant era. This has stripped Christians of their ability to come up with alternatives to the prevailing secular legal systems and social systems of the world around them. Whenever they have sought power, they have sought control over the existing social and political order. They have contented themselves to occupy the existing seats of power. Their social theories have always been some form of baptized paganism. There have been a few exceptions. The New England Puritans were exceptions. But their experiment lasted less than three generations (1630–1700). Subsequent generations adopted the prevailing social theories of the time.

If it is true that all of the Mosaic laws governing economics and civil government were automatically annulled by the ministry of Jesus, even though Jesus never said that this was the case, then Christianity is impotent except for individuals, families, and congregations. This means that the kingdom of God should not extend outside the four walls of Christian families and Christian churches. This therefore means that *the kingdom of man has been granted a free pass by Christ.* Such an outlook relies on a theory of covenantal neutrality between the kingdom of God and the kingdom of man. This view of neutrality is not taught in the Bible, but it is assumed by virtually all modern Christian social and political thinkers. Jesus said this: "The one who is not with Me is against Me; and the one who does not gather with Me scatters" (Matt. 12:30). This is not the view of modern Christian social theorists. Therefore, Christians don't take biblical law seriously, and non-Christians don't take Christians seriously. *Christians pose no threat to the prevailing social order.* They are part of the "loyal opposition." This means loyal to the kingdom of man, not to the kingdom of God. As a result, modern Christians have voted for the modern welfare state. They have adopted this view of the eighth commandment: "You shall not steal except by majority vote."

Chapter 14

Entrepreneurship

For now we see in a mirror dimly, but then face to face; now I know in part, but then I will know fully, just as I also have been fully known.

I Corinthians 13:12

Analysis

Only God is omniscient. Only He knows the future perfectly. No creature should ever aspire to possess knowledge equal to God's. Such a goal is inherently demonic. Nevertheless, it is wise to seek to understand better what is likely to affect you in your areas of responsibility. You do not want to be blind-sided by some event that sets your plans back a year or a decade. You cannot foresee such an event, but you may be able to buy insurance to compensate you if a similar kind of event upends you. Insurance is one of the great discoveries in history. Take advantage of it. Just don't pay more than you have to.

Insurance is possible only because there are statistical patterns in life. Certain kinds of events take place on a mathematically predictable basis. These mathematical laws are referred to collectively as *the law of large numbers*. Some events that are unpredictable individually are part of a class of events whose frequency is predictable collectively. Statisticians who are called actuaries understand these patterns. This knowledge enables them to advise insurance companies on how to design policies that can be sold profitably to people seeking a way to minimize the economic impact of such an event.

The insurance industry rests on a knowledge of risk. The industry insures against the economic effects of certain classes of events. It does not insure against events that are not part of a class of events that are subject to the law of large numbers. Most events are not part of such a class. Therefore, most events cannot be insured against. But most of the individually devastating ones can. These are events that are common to mankind and nature.

What about events that cannot be insured against? They are part of life's innumerable uncertainties. Economists distinguish between risk and uncertainty. Risk is subject to the law of large numbers. Uncertainty is not. This analytical distinction goes back to a 1921 book by a young economist named Frank H. Knight: *Risk, Uncertainty, and Profit.* This insight on the difference between risk and uncertainty is considered conventional among economists.

This brings us to the topic at hand: entrepreneurship. There is an analytical distinction between an entrepreneur and a manager. Both of them must deal with an unknown future in a business enterprise. An entrepreneur deals mainly with uncertainty. A manager deals mainly with risk. An entrepreneur forecasts events that are not part of a class. A manager forecasts events that are part of a class. An entrepreneur cannot buy insurance policies to hedge against the economic effects of events. A manager can. They may be the same person in a small business, but if this is the case, then the person must take care to distinguish between the two types of forecasting. They are not the same. *The tasks of entrepreneurship are far greater than the tasks of management.* Not many people are good business entrepreneurs. The skill is limited in society.

Nevertheless, everyone who makes responsible decisions must be an entrepreneur. No one sees the future clearly. Uncertainty is universal. We must all deal with uncertainty. We cannot buy an insurance policy to deal with every bad event that might happen to us. Even if such policies were available, we could not afford to buy all of them.

The free market rests on the decisions of entrepreneurs who specialize in forecasting future supply and demand. Without entrepreneurs, most of us would die, and most of the survivors would live in what today would be regarded as extreme poverty.

A. Omniscience

Point one of the biblical covenant is God's transcendence, yet also His presence. This is the biblical concept of God's original sovereignty. It asks: "Who's in charge here?" How does this apply to entrepreneurship?

God is omniscient. No other being is. Omniscience is a non-communicable attribute of God. God is also omnipotent. No other being is. Omnipotence is a non-communicable attribute of God. The fact that God knows everything and exercises power over everything offers this comfort to covenant-keepers: *life is not a threat to them.* It is an opportunity. Paul wrote this:

> And we know that God causes all things to work together for good to those who love God, to those who are called according to His purpose. For those whom He foreknew, He also predestined to become conformed to the image of His Son, so that He would be the firstborn among many brothers and sisters; and these whom He predestined, He also called; and these whom He called, He also justified; and these whom He justified, He also glorified. (Rom. 8:28–30)

The entrepreneur must be an optimist regarding the outcome of his ventures. No one commits time, money, and emotion to a project that he thinks will probably fail. He thinks he can beat the odds. Besides, there are no odds in a truly uncertain endeavor. If there were odds, then there would be statistics on similar outcomes. There would be evidence of the law of large numbers. The project would then be mostly managerial, not entrepreneurial.

A covenant-keeper presumably thinks that God is calling him to pursue some venture. He ought to believe that God is both omniscient and omnipotent. He should not think that God is a cosmic deceiver, let alone a cosmic trickster. He thinks that God has a wonderful plan for his life. So, he is willing to take what are commonly called risks, but which are not risks. They are uncertainties.

Sustaining a covenant-keeping entrepreneur internally is faith: *optimism.* He does not think that he may get lucky in the latest venture. He thinks that he is operating in a providential world in which the cosmic battlefield tipped in his favor.

B. Forecasting

Point two of the biblical covenant is hierarchical authority. It asks: "To whom do I report?" How does this apply to entrepreneurship?

God knows the future perfectly. Man is made in God's image. Man can also make judgments about the future, but imperfectly. Man is supposed to think God's thoughts after Him. This ability is the basis of accurate forecasting.

The heart of entrepreneurship is forecasting. An entrepreneur seeks a profit from buying low and selling high. But how can he buy low? If the free market is competitive, why can anyone buy low? Why isn't there a single price for every asset in a class? Doesn't competition lead to equalized prices? No, it doesn't. That is because people are not omniscient.

An entrepreneur thinks that he knows better than his competitors regarding future customer demand. Maybe he thinks that customers will pay more for what he wants to sell, or maybe he thinks that they will buy far more units if he lowers the price. His competitors do not share his estimate. They have not entered the markets for labor, raw materials, and warehouse space. They have not bid up prices. So, he thinks there is an opportunity for buying low and selling high. He enters specific markets for production goods and starts buying, hiring, and leasing. If he is correct in his forecast, he will reap a profit. If he is wrong, he will reap a loss.

Because men are not omniscient, there is great uncertainty regarding the future. The entrepreneur comes with a unique forecast. He puts his money or his investors' money or his lenders' money where his forecast is. He re-organizes existing producers' goods to create new opportunities for future customers.

Economists have the same task that all scholars have. They must make sense out of the constantly changing world around them. They must impute order to what seems to be chaos. We do not live in chaos. There are continuities in life. There are familiar patterns. Theorists attribute these regularities to laws. They offer different theories about how such laws operate. They offer rival theories of how such laws even exist. They attempt to link together stable economic laws and the flux of historical events. They face what physicist Eugene Wigner pointed to in his 1960 article, "The Unreasonable Effectiveness of Mathematics in the Natural Sciences." Any correlation between the laws of human logic and the regularities of the external world is unreasonable. But scholars keep trying to discover even more reasonable unreasonable correlations.

Economists compare their theories' accuracy with a fixed standard. There are two main standards for economic causation. One standard is omniscience. The other is randomness. The standard of omniscience is called equilibrium. There are neither profits nor losses under the assumptions that are said to govern the utterly hypothetical world of equilibrium. *The concept of equilibrium is nonsense.* If there were omniscience, no one would hold money. People hold money because they are uncertain about the future. But if no one held money, all money prices would be infinite. Money would not function. *There could be no price system under equilibrium.* But there is no scientific economic theory without money pricing. So, any economist who uses equilibrium conditions as a standard is faking it. It cannot exist. How useful for understanding the real world is a theoretical model that cannot exist even in theory?

The rival procedure is to identify deviations from pure randomness as evidence of causation. This also has major problems. First, pure randomness does not exist. There is always some orderly deviation from randomness. Second, the model presupposes a world without any structured causation. This is not God's world. So, statistical deviations from pure randomness do not prove anything definitive. Economists rely on statistical correlations to explain causation. But, as critics always insist, statistical correlation is not causation. This criticism is correct.

Then why is there cause and effect? Because of God's providence. How can anyone make sufficiently accurate predictions to produce a profit? Because man is made in God's image. Man is responsible to God: point two of the biblical covenant.

C. Pricing

Point three of the biblical covenant is law. It asks: "What are the rules?" How does this apply to entrepreneurship?

The Bible mandates the private ownership of property. There is a prohibition of theft (Ex. 20:15). There are rights of property. These are legal rights to exclude. This leads to a conclusion: the right to own property is necessarily the right to disown property, i.e., sell it.

How does someone sell an asset in a free market economy? He places a price on it. This is the first step in making an offer to sell it. Then he finds a way to communicate to potential buyers his offer to sell at a specific price.

He faces competition from other sellers. They also are making offers to sell. Sellers compete against sellers. On the other side of these offers are offers to pay. This usually means payment in money. We call people "buyers" if they are willing to pay money. Buyers compete against buyers. Out of this system of competition—sellers versus sellers, buyers versus buyers—comes an array of prices for goods and services.

This system of competition is best described in terms of an auction. Most people can understand an auction. People with money come to an auction. They want to bid for one or more items. The auctioneer shows an item. Then he calls for bids. The bids begin. He is paid on a commission basis: a fixed percentage of the sale price of each item. The higher the bids, the more money he makes. So, it is in his interest to get potential buyers bidding against each other. He uses familiar techniques to keep people bidding. "Do I hear a thousand?" He wants to hear this. Then he wants to hear a higher bid.

There is only one item offered for sale in each bidding session. *Bidders compete against bidders.* Who will take it home? The person who bids the highest price. Here is the rule of all auctions: *high bid wins.* All over the world, auction participants understand this rule. It is easy to understand. When the person making the highest and therefore the final bid hears the word, "sold," he is happy. When others who made bids hear this, they may be happy or sad. Maybe they think, "That person paid way too much. I'm glad I stopped bidding." Or they may think: "Maybe I should have stayed in the bidding." But no one thinks this: "It's just not fair." Everyone knows the rule: high bid wins. Everyone also knows that only one person will leave the auction as the new owner.

If there were only one auction, there would be only one seller. But there are many auctions going on at one time. *Auctioneers compete against auctioneers.* They advertise. "Come to my auction on Saturday." Each auctioneer wants a large crowd: more bidders. More bidders mean higher prices.

Who sets prices in any bidding session? The bidders. The auctioneer can beg. He may try to humiliate bidders. He has time-proven techniques to keep bidders bidding. But he is not in control. Why not? Because bidders own the most marketable commodity: money. Money talks. Money screams. *High bid wins.*

This is how the free market works. Critics of this process of production and distribution complain, "It's just not fair." Why isn't it fair? Is an auction inherently unfair? In what way?

D. Accounting

Point four of the biblical covenant is sanctions. It asks: "What happens if I obey? Disobey?" How does this apply to entrepreneurship?

The entrepreneur has an idea of what customers will buy, at what price, and in what quantities. I have already covered the economics of entrepreneurship under "Forecasting" (Section B). The issue here is the system of accounting. We call it double-entry bookkeeping.

The entrepreneur makes a judgment regarding the future. This is a forecast involving economic value. What will customers value in the future? At what price? There is a relationship between economic value and price. What is it?

Economic value is imputed subjectively by buyers and sellers. Each person has a scale of values at any time: first, second, third, etc. He first satisfies the want that is highest on his list, if he can afford it. Price will determine this.

Prices are the result of the auction process. They are objective: exactly this much money for this item. These prices may be public. Today, prices are more public on the Web than at any time in history. The ignorance factor of buyers and sellers is shrinking constantly.

The businessman uses accounting techniques to assess either profit or loss. These techniques have been widely known since around 1550. Businessmen have great familiarity with double-entry bookkeeping. If they do not have this familiarity, they had better get it.

The businessman is held to a numerical standard. He must reap a monetary profit. The success or failure of the business is made in terms of a monetary standard: black ink (profit) versus red ink (loss). There may also be a minus sign to mark losses, or parentheses. The point is, others besides business owners can accurately assess profit or loss. There has been a huge expansion of the number of people who can read a profit-and-loss statement and a balance sheet. This means that others can exercise judgment.

The entrepreneur wants to make profits. These are monetary profits. A business may have intangibles of value, but these rarely count for much in the price of the shares of a company. Investors look at profit and loss in the immediate past. They look at the trend. Then they make judgments about the share price in the future. Then they buy, sell, or hold. Out of today's orders to buy or sell emerges a price for the shares.

E. Innovation

Point five of the biblical covenant is succession. It asks: "Does this outfit have a future?" How does this apply to entrepreneurship?

If an entrepreneur makes a discovery that leads to above-average profits, he will get imitators. *Through imitation, productive techniques spread around the world.* The once-unperceived advantages of a particular production technique become a common practice. The initially high rate of profit gets lower and may even disappear. Customers benefit.

A successful entrepreneur dares not rest on his laurels. He must find new ways to repeat his success. New techniques become old, fast. They cease to generate profits, fast. Imitation removes the initial advantage.

The free market order is inherently innovative. People seek to better themselves through voluntary exchange. Competition is continual. Producers must find new ways to meet future customer demand. *This process of innovation is intensely future-oriented.*

The result of the quest for profits is economic growth. Compound economic growth is the result of innovation. It is not sufficient to reinvest profits. This is necessary, but not sufficient. Profits will decline as the result of imitation and competition. For a business to have profits to reinvest, it must discover new, previously unrecognized ways to please customers in the future. The carrot of profits and the stick of losses promote innovation.

There is nothing automatic about profits. Profits result when an entrepreneur sees what others do not perceive. He works to reduce uncertainty. He is not a manager. He is not dealing with risk. He is dealing with uncertainty. He cannot reduce uncertainty by applying known risk-reduction techniques in familiar ways. The law of large numbers does not apply to uncertainty.

Conclusion

At the heart of the biblical economy is the entrepreneur. He attempts to reduce the costs of uncertainty by means of innovative techniques of production and distribution. He imagines the future, and he estimates demand. Then he attempts to meet this demand at a profit. He buys low in order to sell higher. He can buy low because he imagines what competing entrepreneurs do not imagine or else reject. So, they do not bid up the prices of production assets in this limited market niche.

There are opportunities for profit because God is omniscient. He can see the future perfectly. Men cannot. God has granted to some people a remarkable ability to see the economic future. If men could all see the future as God does, there would be neither profits or losses. There would be no unexploited opportunities for profit. There would be no errors that would produce losses. This is the general equilibrium model. It assumes that human omniscience is the best way to explain economics in a world of ignorance. This model is not merely useless. It leads to major conceptual errors. The main one is this: *an incommunicable attribute of God is supposedly a legitimate standard of performance for man.* It would make as much sense to establish the standard of God's omnipresence as the ideal for computerized digital monitoring.

Chapter 15

Compounding

"The Lord will command the blessing for you in your barns and in everything that you put your hand to, and He will bless you in the land that the Lord your God is giving you. The Lord will establish you as a holy people to Himself, as He swore to you, if you keep the commandments of the Lord your God and walk in His ways. So all the peoples of the earth will see that you are called by the name of the Lord, and they will be afraid of you. And the Lord will give you more than enough prosperity, in the children of your womb, in the offspring of your livestock, and in the produce of your ground, in the land which the Lord swore to your fathers to give you."

Deuteronomy 28:8–11

Analysis

Compound growth is the most socially transforming process in world history. Beginning around 1800, economic development in Great Britain and English-speaking North America began to exhibit compound economic growth. So did population. This has been maintained for over two centuries. Nothing like this had ever happened before. Always before, famines, plagues, and wars had reversed growth. In 1800, almost no one saw what was about to come. Ben Franklin was the main exception. In 1751, he had foreseen extensive population growth in the United States.

Steady economic growth at 2% or 3% per capita per year has completely transformed the world. The historian asks: "Why did this happen where it did and when it did?" Economic historians have no agreed-on explanation. There are dozens of explanations, but none of them seems to be supported by the evidence.

The possibility of long-term economic growth and population growth first appears in ancient literature in Leviticus 26 and Deuteronomy 28. The Christian worldview teaches linear time: creation, fall, redemption, and final judgment. No other worldview taught this in the ancient world. The biblical worldview also teaches progress.

Moses spoke of positive corporate sanctions. These promises were ethically conditional: "if you keep the commandments of the LORD your God and walk in His ways" (Deut. 28:9). *These were covenantal corporate sanctions.* God promised these blessings to a nation of covenant-keepers. Clearly, the following promise was corporate, not individual: "So all the peoples of the earth will see that you are called by the name of the LORD, and they will be afraid of you" (Deut. 28:10).

This passage and the parallel passage in Leviticus 26 are crucial in developing an explicitly Christian economics. Why? Because of the unbreakable connection between covenant law and covenant sanctions. The bulk of both passages is devoted to negative sanctions. These are also covenantal and corporate. The correlation between covenant-keeping and prosperity, like the correlation between covenant-breaking and poverty, makes it clear that *God intervenes in history to confirm His national covenant.* This is covenantal confirmation. This is a detailed development of God's announcement to them regarding covenantal thankfulness.

> "Otherwise, you may say in your heart, 'My power and the strength of my hand made me this wealth.' But you are to remember the LORD your God, for it is He who is giving you power to make wealth, in order to confirm His covenant which He swore to your fathers, as it is this day." (Deut. 8:17–18)

The blessings and the cursings were guaranteed by God *as visible signs of His covenantal authority.* They were to persuade the other nations of the benefits of obeying God's Bible-revealed law.

> "See, I have taught you statutes and judgments just as the LORD my God commanded me, that you are to do these things in the land where you are entering to take possession of it. So keep and do them, for that is your wisdom and your understanding in the sight of the peoples who will hear all these statutes and say, 'Surely this great nation is a wise and understanding people.' For what great nation is there that has a god so near to it as is the LORD our God whenever we call on Him? Or what great nation is there that has statutes and judgments as righteous as this whole Law which I am setting before you today?" (Deut. 4:5–8)

Prosperity was a matter of obedience to God's law. The crucial but practical question is this: Is this still true under the New Covenant? If it isn't, then there is no possibility of developing a uniquely Christian economics. The passages in Leviticus 26 and Deuteronomy 28 also speak of political success. Are these also part of the New Covenant? If there are no covenantal connections between national covenant-keeping and visible national civil sanctions, then there is no possibility of developing a uniquely Christian theory of civil government. It all hinges on visible corporate sanctions as testimonies to the continuing reliability and legitimacy of Christian economics and Christian political theory. In short, it all hinges on *covenantal judicial continuity*.

In modern times, the vast majority of Christian theologians deny this continuity. This is equally true of the relatively small number of people who call themselves Christian social theorists. They do not declare with the psalmist, "Teach me, the way of Your statutes, LORD, and I shall comply with it to the end. Give me understanding, so that I may comply with Your Law and keep it with all my heart. Make me walk in the path of Your commandments, for I delight in it" (Ps. 119:33–35). They dismiss biblical civil law as Christ-annulled civil guidelines of a now long-defunct nation, Israel. This legal system supposedly never had any covenantal continuity with the New Testament social order. They do not offer judicial details about what exactly constitutes the New Testament legal system, but they are adamant that it has no covenantal continuity with Mosaic Israel. They are incorrect. The Ten Commandments provide this continuity (Ex. 20). So do the Mosaic laws implementing the Ten Commandments (Ex. 21–23). The land laws and seed laws have been annulled. So have the priestly laws. But all of the Mosaic laws and their sanctions that Paul refers to in I Timothy 1:9–10 are still in force: "law is not made for a righteous person but for those who are lawless and rebellious, for the ungodly and sinners, for the unholy and worldly, for those who kill their fathers or mothers, for murderers, for the sexually immoral, homosexuals, slave traders, liars, perjurers, and whatever else is contrary to sound teaching".

Christian economics is authoritative because God still imposes corporate sanctions in terms of His law. When Christians deny that God still does this, they must then accept humanistic economics in the name of Jesus. Dominion will then take place, if at all, only in terms of the kingdom of man. Is the economic kingdom of man what you want to proclaim in the name of Jesus?

A. Redemption

Point one of the biblical covenant is God's transcendence, yet also His presence. This is the biblical concept of God's original sovereignty. It asks: "Who's in charge here?" How does this apply to compounding?

Christian theologians speak of three ages in history: creation, fall, and redemption. To redeem something means to buy it back. What has been bought back? From whom? The Christian doctrine of redemption teaches that the redeemed sons of God have been bought back from God's wrath by Jesus Christ's perfect life, crucifixion, resurrection, and ascension to heaven (Rom. 5:6–11). This is the legal basis of God's grace. God brings *soul-saving special grace* to the redeemed, who become covenant-keepers, and He brings life-preserving common grace to covenant-breakers for the sake of covenant-keepers. "[F]or He causes His sun to rise on the evil and the good, and sends rain on the righteous and the unrighteous" (Matt. 5:45b). The two kingdoms grow in the same field until the end of time. This is the meaning of the parable of the wheat and the tares (Matt. 13:24–30, 36–43).

What is the legal nature of redemption? It is the payment of a ransom to God on behalf of previous covenant-breakers. "For even the Son of Man did not come to be served, but to serve, and to give His life as a ransom for many" (Mark 10:45). This is special grace. Yet He also died for all mankind, to delay the wrath of God. "For there is one God, and one mediator also between God and mankind, the man Christ Jesus, who gave Himself as a ransom for all, the testimony given at the proper time" (I Tim. 2:5–6). This is common grace.

Of covenant-keepers, Paul wrote: "In Him we have redemption through His blood, the forgiveness of our wrongdoings, according to the riches of His grace" (Eph. 1:7). He wrote of Christ, "who gave Himself for us to redeem us from every lawless deed, and to purify for Himself a people for His own possession, eager for good deeds" (Titus 2:14). He also wrote, "for all have sinned and fall short of the glory of God, being justified as a gift by His grace through the redemption which is in Christ Jesus" (Rom. 3:23–24), This brings liberation from sin. It therefore brings liberty. "It was for freedom that Christ set us free; therefore keep standing firm and do not be subject again to a yoke of slavery" (Gal. 5:1).

Christ's model of redemption governs the New Covenant era. It governs Christian economics.

B. Adoption

Point two of the biblical covenant is hierarchical authority. It asks: "To whom do I report?" How does this apply to compounding?

All of humanity is the family of God. Paul spoke about God in Athens: "He made from one man every nation of mankind to live on all the face of the earth, having determined their appointed times and the boundaries of their habitation, that they would seek God, if perhaps they might feel around for Him and find Him" (Acts 17:26–27). But the family of man is not unified. Because of Adam's rebellion, God disinherited the covenantal sons of Adam. Were it not for special grace, all mankind would perish. But God has redeemed some of these disinherited children. He has adopted them into the inherited family. "He predestined us to adoption as sons and daughters through Jesus Christ to Himself, according to the good pleasure of His will" (Eph. 1:5).

> But when the fullness of the time came, God sent His Son, born of a woman, born under the Law, so that He might redeem those who were under the Law, that we might receive the adoption as sons and daugh-

> ters. Because you are sons, God has sent the Spirit of His Son into our hearts, crying out, "Abba! Father!" Therefore you are no longer a slave, but a son; and if a son, then an heir through God. (Gal. 4:4–7)

The covenantal sons of Adam are under God's curse of disinheritance. Not so with the covenantal sons of Christ, whom Paul called the last Adam.

> So also it is written: "The first man, Adam, became a living person." The last Adam was a life-giving spirit. However, the spiritual is not first, but the natural; then the spiritual. The first man is from the earth, earthy; the second man is from heaven. As is the earthy one, so also are those who are earthy; and as is the heavenly one, so also are those who are heavenly. Just as we have borne the image of the earthy, we will also bear the image of the heavenly. (I Cor. 15:45–49)

As God's adopted sons, covenant-keepers are the heirs of the whole world *definitively*. This is a matter of God's judicial declaration. Adopted sons are required by God to extend their dominion *progressively*. After the final judgment, they will inherit *finally*. Christian theologians debate over how much of this progressive inheritance by Christians will have been secured by the end of time. They do not disagree over whether or not it will be secured after the final judgment: the new heavens and new earth (Rev. 21–22).

Paul spoke of a guaranteed inheritance.

> In Him we have redemption through His blood, the forgiveness of our wrongdoings, according to the riches of His grace which He lavished on us. In all wisdom and insight He made known to us the mystery of His will, according to His good pleasure which He set forth in Him, regarding His plan of the fullness of the times, to bring all things together in Christ, things in the heavens and things on the earth. In Him we also have obtained an inheritance, having been predestined according to the purpose of Him who works all things in accordance with the plan of His will, to the end that we who were the first to hope in the Christ would be to the praise of His glory. In Him, you also, after listening to the message of truth, the gospel of your salvation—having also believed, you were sealed in Him with the Holy Spirit of the promise, who is a first installment of our inheritance, in regard to the redemption of God's own possession, to the praise of His glory. (Eph. 1:7–14)

There is another way of inheritance by covenant-keepers. A covenant-breaker hears the gospel of deliverance through faith in the saving work of Christ. He accepts this offer of salvation. He becomes a covenant-keeper. Now all that he owns and controls belongs to a covenant-keeper. The wealth that had belonged to the kingdom of man now belongs to the kingdom of God.

C. Acquisition

Point three of the biblical covenant is law. It asks: "What are the rules?" How does this apply to compounding?

Redemption means to buy back. It applies to all mankind: special grace and common grace. Christ has paid a ransom. This has liberated covenant-keepers. To do what? To exercise dominion under God, according to the dominion covenant (Gen. 1:26–28).

The world is not yet under the authority of covenant-keepers. It is under covenant-breakers. They own real estate, capital goods, and banks. They own most of the educational institutions. This is contrary to the dominion covenant. It is the result of sin. But it is far more the result of covenant-keepers' defection from the tasks associated with increasing their productivity. It is a rejection of covenantal responsibility by covenant-keepers. All of this must be purchased from them by covenant-keepers.

If covenant-keepers buy the capital goods of covenant-breakers, they must surrender ownership of an asset: money. *This is the most marketable commodity.* Why does this transfer economic authority to covenant-keepers? The exchange is legally mutual. But it is not mutual in terms of the economics of dominion. Covenant-keepers are supposed to be future-oriented—far more future-oriented than covenant-breakers. So, covenant-beakers sell long-term capital assets in exchange for short-term consumer goods. God expects covenant-breakers to be decapitalized by covenant-keepers. This is the biblical process of disinheriting covenant-breakers in history. The post-fall theology of covenantal inheritance necessarily includes covenantal dis-inheritance.

The archetypal biblical story of such a transaction is Jacob's purchase of his brother Esau's birthright. Esau was a covenant-breaker. God had told Rebekah when she was pregnant that Jacob would be the lawful heir (Gen. 25:23). Yet Esau was the firstborn (Gen. 25:25). Jacob bought the birthright from Esau for some stew (Gen. 25:33). Esau either did not value his birthright or else he thought he could defend it easily. He was wrong.

Before this, Abraham had purchased a cave for Sarah's tomb. He would not accept it as a gift from a Canaanite (Gen. 24:10–16). He was a stranger in a strange land. His heirs would inherit this land, God had assured him. But he paid for the cave anyway. He paid a lot of money. Moses' subsequent conquest of Canaan by military force was a one-time covenantal event. It was not to become a model for Israel. The purchase of the cave was.

Dominion by covenant-keepers requires the legal transfer of property from covenant-breakers to covenant-keepers. "A good person leaves an inheritance to his grandchildren, and the wealth of a sinner is stored up for the righteous" (Prov. 13:22). Covenant-keepers are supposed to buy property from covenant-breakers. This is the proper way to transfer the inheritances of covenant-breakers to covenant-keepers. "Again, the kingdom of heaven is like a merchant seeking fine pearls, and upon finding one pearl of great value, he went and sold everything that he had and bought it" (Matt. 13:45–46). He obtained the money, and he then paid the price.

D. Profit and Loss

Point four of the biblical covenant is sanctions. It asks: "What happens if I obey? Disobey?" How does this apply to compounding?

Judgment has to do with applying God's laws to specific circumstances. It requires an understanding of the sanctions, positive and negative, that are associated with each of God's laws. In economics, the two main sanctions are profit and loss.

The parable of the talents is the archetype. The property owner plans to go on a long journey. He leaves his stewards with coins. One steward is given five coins. One is given two coins. One is given one coin. At his return, the owner demands an accounting. The man who had been given five coins now has ten coins. The man who had been given two coins now has four. The man with one coin has produced no profit at all. He returns the coin. The owner condemns him, and then gives this coin to the most productive steward, who had doubled the owner's money, but with more initial capital than the second steward had received (Matt. 25:14–31). In Matthew's version, Jesus follows with the story of the final judgment. In Luke's version, we learn something different. A steward with one coin made ten more. He received ten cities to command. Another steward with one coin earned five more. He received five cities (Luke 19:17, 19). They had prospered in terms of business. They were then rewarded by civil rulership. This meant dominion in the broadest sense.

Profit is a business residual after all expenses have been paid. The entrepreneur seeks to buy low and sell high. The only reason why this is possible in a competitive market is because other entrepreneurs are ignorant of the future conditions of supply and demand. They fail to bid up the price of relevant capital goods and labor. This leaves an opportunity for the entrepreneur who trusts his prediction of future market demand.

E. Reinvestment

Point five of the biblical covenant is succession. It asks: "Does this outfit have a future?" How does this apply to compounding?

The story of Isaac's dual blessings of his two sons is the story of the inheritance that each son received. Because of God's prophecy that the younger son would inherit, and because Jacob had purchased Esau's birthright, and because of the joint deception by Rebecca and Jacob, Isaac gave the main blessing to Jacob (Gen. 27:28–29). This left little for Esau (Gen. 27:39–40). Esau was not completely disinherited, but he received only the remainder.

How extensive will the inheritance be? Kingdom-wide. This means worldwide. "For the earth will be filled with the knowledge of the glory of the LORD, as the waters cover the sea" (Hab. 2:14). Jesus said: "All authority in heaven and on earth has been given to Me. Go, therefore, and make disciples of all the nations, baptizing them in the name of the Father and the Son and the Holy Spirit, teaching them to follow all that I commanded you; and behold, I am with you always, to the end of the age" (Matt. 28:18b–20).

To fulfill the dominion covenant, there must be multiplication of capital. This means that there must be a steady reinvestment of profits. God requires His adopted sons to steadily replace the disinherited sons in history. So, covenant-keepers must spend less than they receive as post-tithe, post-tax income. There must be a surplus. This reinvested capital extends the businesses owned and run by covenant-keepers. It multiplies. Some of the profits are also reinvested, and they multiply. This program requires two things to be successful: thrift and entrepreneurial wisdom. It is not good enough to reinvest profits. There must later be more profits. The investor must accurately predict future supply and demand for his product or service. Then he must buy low. He must do this over and over. So must all of his heirs in order to speed up the dominion process.

So, there must be compounding. This process changes the world. The world has experienced this, 1800 to the twenty-first century. A fairly constant annual positive rate of return after price inflation of at least 2% to 3% per capita transformed the world in two centuries.

God wants covenant-keepers to replace covenant-breakers in high positions of authority and great wealth. This process of long-run inheritance necessarily involves the disinheritance of covenant-breakers. God wants the great reversal, as described by Mary in her testimony to Elizabeth. "He has done mighty deeds with His arm; He has scattered those who were proud in the thoughts of their hearts. He has brought down rulers from their thrones, and has exalted those who were humble. He has filled the hungry with good things, and sent the rich away empty-handed" (Luke 1:51–53). Everyone gets richer (common grace), but covenant-keepers become dominant (special grace). They inherit most of the earth. They are on top. Covenant-breakers are subordinate. This is not achieved through coercion. It is achieved through the redemption of covenant-breakers by God and purchase of covenant-breakers' capital assets by covenant-keepers.

Conclusion

The dominion covenant defines mankind. It remains in force today. God has commanded mankind to subdue the earth as His stewards. He had delegated ownership to all mankind. The command to exercise dominion includes covenant-breakers.

With the fall of man, God divided mankind into disinherited children and children of the inheritance. The judicial distinction is between biological children and adopted children. God sent Jesus Christ into history to serve as the redeemer of His people. His program of redemption was to buy back sinners through a redemption payment to God the Father. This is the model for Christians. It provides God's post-fall strategy of dominion: the conversion of souls by God, the purchase of capital assets by covenant-keepers, and both successful entrepreneurship and the reinvestment of profits.

Conclusion to Part III

Part I introduced you to the five points of the biblical covenant as it applied to economics prior to the fall of man. These points were applications of what I have called the dominion covenant. The dominion covenant encompasses all of life and all of creation, while economics relates to the issues of resource allocation.

Part II introduced you to the five points of the biblical covenant as it applies to economics after the fall of man. The fundamental economic categories did not change, but their applications did. This was the result of Adam's sin and God's negative sanctions on Adam's body and the ground. The earth is now under a curse.

One of the requirements associated with the dominion covenant is to reduce the impact of God's curses on the ground and his curses on Adam's body. This has to do with medical science. It has to do with agronomy. It has to do with chemistry. But it obviously has to do with economics. As we work out the implications of the economic aspects of the dominion covenant, we should expect relief from the curses.

Let me give an obvious example. One of the curses on Adam was sweat. Residents in the economically developed world now live in temperature-controlled comfort because of air conditioning. Air conditioning was an invention of the early twentieth century. It was first used commercially to cool large movie theaters. It is now in most homes in the United States. This has made our leisure time more comfortable in summer, but it has also made us more productive in the heat of the day. In other words, air conditioning should be regarded as a consumer good, but it should also be regarded as a producer good. It is a blessing of God, but it is also a tool of production. I think it is representative of all of God's economic blessings. It is also easy to understand.

You have now read those sections of this book that deal with Christian economic theory. In Part III, I deal with applications of the theory. But this is only the beginning. I intend to follow this book with three supplemental books, much longer and much more detailed. This book is designed to get you started.

I have not covered the bulk of the topics that you find in any college-level economics textbook. I have not dealt with monetary theory and monetary policy. I have not dealt with the issue of cartels. What about pollution? What about labor policy? What about the stock market? All of these topics are institutional applications of market pricing and government policy. They all can be explained in terms of a handful—actually, two handfuls—of fundamental principles of economic analysis. They began with the dominion covenant (one hand), as revised by God after the fall of man (another hand).

I do not expect you to remember the five-point breakdown that I supplied in each chapter. I do expect you to remember the governing concept in each chapter. Before the fall, the five-point covenantal structure of economics was this: God's absolute ownership, man's subordinate responsibility as a trustee, the ethical requirement of private property, the judicial requirement to impute economic value accurately, and the economically mandatory requirement to leave an inheritance. I derived these from a relatively simple exegesis of the first two chapters of Genesis. I have developed these in detail in my economic commentary on the book of Genesis, *Sovereignty & Dominion.*[1]

After the fall, the dominion covenant remained in force, but it was restructured by the imposition of the curses on Adam's body and the ground. The world now labors under God-cursed scarcity. The five points of the dominion covenant today are these: God's providence, the principle of service, the terms of the leasehold agreement, entrepreneurship, and compound growth. Whenever a society honors these principles in morals and also in civil law, the curses that God imposed on the ground are steadily removed. This is God's program of redemp-

1. *Sovereignty & Dominion: An Economic Commentary on Genesis* (Moulton, Alabama: Axehead Press, [1982, 2012] 2022). An earlier version was published as a hardback in 1982: *The Dominion Covenant: Genesis.*

tion. Redemption is not limited to the saving of souls. It extends to the healing of societies.

You can count the five points of the Christian economics, pre-fall and post-fall, on the fingers of two hands, plus both thumbs. The two thumbs are these: God's absolute ownership, which is based on his original creation, and His providential sustaining of the universe. This includes His sustaining of economic coherence in a world governed by private property, the profit-and-loss system, double-entry accounting techniques, and money. We therefore have legitimate confidence that economic decisions that are beneficial for individuals and families, in a society governed by biblical law, produce benefits for the entire social order. The pursuit of private profit in a social order based on the principle of the rule of law and the principle of private property will not produce negative consequences for society.

I have attempted to keep my analysis simple. I have also done my best to show why my analysis is an extension of biblical revelation. My analysis is not grounded on a theory of autonomous man in a universe whose origin came from the unexplainable explosion known as the Big Bang. *Man did not evolve out of the impersonal cosmos. The laws of economics did not evolve out of the unplanned actions of autonomous men and women.*

The Scottish moral philosopher Adam Ferguson wrote in 1767 that society is the product of human action but not of human design. He was arguing in favor of social evolution. He ignored the crucial point. Society is the product of God's design, which in His total sovereignty allows for responsible individual action. So is the economy. This is why Christian economics is fundamentally different from humanistic economics. The differences have to do with rival assumptions about the locus of sovereignty. They have to do with the differences between the doctrine of God's creation of the universe out of nothing and the rival doctrine of impersonal cosmic evolution. There is no way to reconcile these differences. These differences are at the core of the conflict between the city of God in the city of man.

Every social science must be re-structured in terms of the five points of the biblical covenant. My work in developing a self-consciously Christian economics is the first attempt to do this. I hope it will be a model for other scholars.

PART IV

Covenantal Reform

Introduction to Part IV

Christianity teaches that history has three phases: creation, fall, and redemption. In Part I, I covered creation. In Part II, I covered the fall. In Part III, I covered redemption. You now have some idea of how God calls Christians to reformulate their thinking, their lives, and their societies in terms of the dominion covenant. You are waiting for specific guidance from God and from me: "What now?" I hope that God and I agree. You should, too.

A. Covenants

The dominion covenant applies to mankind in general. It defines mankind. It defines covenant-breaking man, and it also defines covenant-keeping man. Because it is a covenant, it applies to the four covenants that Christianity acknowledges as valid: individual covenant, family covenant, church covenant, and civil covenant. Each of these is established by an oath before God. Men are not allowed to invoke God's name in a judicial sense outside one of these four covenants. To do so is a violation of God's name, which is prohibited by the third commandment (Ex. 20:7).

An individual establishes the individual covenant by making a confession of faith. Paul wrote: "if you confess with your mouth Jesus as Lord, and believe in your heart that God raised Him from the dead, you will be saved" (Rom. 10:9). The individual must also subordinate himself to the institutional church. He does this by the oath-sign of baptism, and he renews this covenant regularly by means of the oath-sign of the Lord's

Supper, also called communion or holy communion. The fact that the individual must swear an oath to the institutional church is evidence that there is no pure individualism according to Christian theology.

Second, there is the family covenant. This covenant is established by mutual vows between a man and a woman. These are legally binding oaths. Both the church and the state are judicially involved, and both can bring negative sanctions against a violation of the marriage vow. There is no biblically mandated oath-sign for the family covenant, but it is common in the West to exchange rings. Rings are symbolic of being under restraint.

Third, there is the church covenant. The church administers the sacraments, meaning oath-signs. These sacraments bring church members under the judicial sanctions associated with the church: blessings and cursings. The primary negative sanction is excommunication. This cuts people off from the Lord's supper. This is judicially symbolic of the negative sanction of hell.

> "Now if your brother sins, go and show him his fault in private; if he listens to you, you have gained your brother. "But if he does not listen to you, take one or two more with you, so that on the testimony of two or three witnesses every matter may be confirmed. And if he refuses to listen to them, tell it to the church; and if he refuses to listen even to the church, he is to be to you as a Gentile and a tax collector. Truly I say to you, whatever you bind on earth shall have been bound in heaven; and whatever you loose on earth shall have been loosed in heaven." (Matt. 18:15–18)

Fourth, there is the civil covenant. It is also established by oath, but usually this oath is implicit rather than explicit. Individuals are assumed to have sworn loyalty to a particular civil government by reaching the legal age of adulthood. There are negative sanctions associated with violations of civil law. The recurring oath-sign is voting in elections.

B. Economics

What are the obligations of each of the covenant law-orders with respect to economics? I provide selective answers to this question in each of the chapters that follow. We live in the era of the welfare state. This state is inherently messianic. It promises to heal. It is a false god. I have explained why this is the case in Part II. *It is therefore the responsibility of members of each of the four covenants to reject the claims of the modern welfare state.* Each individual is required by God to do what he can to overturn this modern god.

Part IV offers suggestions that are tied to money. The best way to reform or overturn any institution is to cut off its funding. This does not involve revolution. It does not involve violence. If an institution cannot collect the funds to keep the doors open, it goes out of existence. This is true of the free market, and it is true with respect to both church and state.

In the case of the church, a member can switch his membership to another congregation or denomination. With respect to the state, it is much more difficult to switch membership. Membership is geographical. The individual must move to a new jurisdiction. But in free societies, this is legal. It was not legal under Communist regimes that put up walls and fences to keep citizens from leaving the Communist paradises. The early warning of the dissolution of the Soviet Union began when the Berlin wall was torn down in 1989, and the Soviet Union did not invade to put the wall back up. On December 25, 1991, the Soviet Union dissolved itself.

If churches had not defected with respect to the preaching of the gospel and the preaching of the covenant, the once-Christian West would not be in the present disastrous situation in which it finds itself. The modern welfare state would not have come into existence. The bankruptcy-producing unfunded liabilities of the West's national governments to fund old-age retirement plans and health care for the aged were voted into existence by politicians elected by Christians. If pastors had preached the laws of Christian economics, and if church members had believed them, this would not have happened. But the pastors did not preach this, so the welfare state gained support from the broad masses of Christians. From 1885 on, the idea of the welfare state began to gain support of pastors in the large northern Protestant denominations in the United States. This new theology was known as the social gospel. It was dominant in large Northern Protestant denominations by 1925.

In 1901, Vladimir Lenin wrote a pamphlet that was published in 1902, *What Is to Be Done?* He stole the title from another Russian revolutionary, Nicholas Cherneshevsky, who wrote a novel with that title in 1863. The question is always legitimate in every generation. I regard Part IV as my preliminary contribution to the answer to the question, "What is to be done?"

Chapter 16

Individual Covenant

"Why do you look at the speck that is in your brother's eye, but do not notice the log that is in your own eye? Or how can you say to your brother, 'Let me take the speck out of your eye,' and look, the log is in your own eye? You hypocrite, first take the log out of your own eye, and then you will see clearly to take the speck out of your brother's eye!"

Matthew 7:3–5

Analysis

There is an innate desire in covenant-breaking people to avoid additional responsibility. Adam blamed Eve. Eve blamed the serpent. "It's not my fault. It's someone else's fault." Yet at the same time, people want the blessings that always accompany responsibility. They want these blessings at zero cost or at least a steep discount.

I am a great believer in taking on additional responsibility. *Taking on additional responsibility is an inescapable aspect of exercising dominion.* I also take this attitude: as long as you are willing to take on additional responsibility, you might as well welcome the accompanying blessings. Use a share of these blessings as consumption items. But be sure to tithe, be sure to exercise charity, and be sure to save. I agree with John Wesley in Sermon 50 (1760): "The Use of Money." He said this: gain all you can, save all you can, and give all you can. But notice carefully: *it takes additional responsibility to accomplish each of these goals.*

We are not judicially responsible to God or man in those areas of life in which we have neither influence nor power. This is why everyone needs to take a careful inventory of those areas of life in which he has influence and power.

You are under the terms of four covenants, in addition to the dominion covenant: individual, family, church, and state. Only in rare cases are individuals outside of a family covenant: unmarried orphans. I assume that this is not you. I begin this section of this book with a discussion of the individual covenant. This is where you have the greatest responsibility. You know more about you than any other human being does. Where there is greater knowledge, there is greater responsibility (Luke 12:47–48).

You see yourself as a Christian. If you are a Christian, you should have been baptized: an oath-sign. You have confirmed your judicial position covenantally, or else your parents did this on your behalf. You are therefore under the laws of the individual covenant. You are also under these laws' sanctions. Furthermore, you take the Lord's Supper: an oath-sign. Each Lord's supper renews your covenant. There is no escape. You are trapped. But you were also trapped under Adam's covenant. We cannot escape from a personal covenant: either Adam's or Christ's. Christ's is better.

A. Acknowledge God's Sovereignty

Point one of the biblical covenant is God's transcendence, yet also His presence. This is the biblical concept of God's original sovereignty. It asks: "Who's in charge here?" How does this apply to your economic affairs?

Every covenant has a sovereign. God is sovereign. There is no other. "Then God spoke all these words, saying, 'I am the LORD your God, who brought you out of the land of Egypt, out of the house of slavery. You shall have no other gods before Me'" (Ex. 20:1–3). God requires everyone to make this confession in history. Most people refuse. You have already confessed this publicly and judicially: baptism and communion. You must now think through every aspect of your life in terms of this confession. This includes economics.

God is sovereign over all economics. He is in control. This means that everyone must search the Bible to find out what God requires. Few people ever do this. I have. It took from 1960 until 2017. I wrote 31 volumes of economic commentaries as a preliminary exercise: "homework."

Because God is sovereign, we can safely trust His revealed word for information. We must never trust our interpretations unconditionally, but we can safely trust the Bible. The Bible represents God: point two of the biblical covenant. The Bible therefore possesses supreme authority in history: point two.

B. Assume More Responsibility

Point two of the biblical covenant is hierarchical authority. It asks: "To whom do I report?" How does this apply to your economic affairs?

You represent God in everything you do. Therefore, God's public reputation is at stake. Covenant-breakers are ready to show contempt for God by way of showing contempt for you. Do not give them any opportunity by providing good cause for their scorn. Jesus provided the model in his representation of God the Father (John 14:8–9).

The strategy of dominion is service. This makes it more difficult for critics to criticize God by criticizing you. If you care for the weak and give to the poor, you will gain support, sometimes grudging. Grudging support is still support.

Power and influence flow to those who exercise responsibility. Most people prefer to limit their exposure to uncertainty. They prefer avoiding the limelight whenever public failure is a possibility. They want to avoid failure, but especially public failure. They fear the public's imputation: "Loser!" They ignore God's imputation: "Courageous!" God's imputation is not yet public. So, they do not take responsibility when it is available. Yet there can be no organization or society that is not exposed to the uncertainties of life. So, there will always be opportunities to bear responsibility. Who will take charge? Covenant-keepers or covenant-breakers?

It is best to begin taking low-level responsibility is one organization you belong to. Start small. Be there at every meeting. Get there early to set up chairs. Stay late to help clean up. Do not show signs of wanting power. Just be a dutiful servant. There are not many of them. Word will get out. Then, if a new level of responsibility appears, and it is offered to you, accept it. Do a good job. Be predictable. This is a long-term strategy. Be content to do without praise. Most people will never adopt this strategy in any area of life outside of their families.

As you exercise greater responsibility, you will find that you are placed in charge of more capital. This is basic to covenantal cause and effect. The tools that you need to fulfill your tasks will be provided, possibly in unusual ways. When you see this pattern, make further use of it. Keep a diary of these occurrences. One of the best examples in history was the Christian orphanage run by George Müller in Great Britain in the second half of the nineteenth century. The money always came. A similar ministry was run by Hudson Taylor: China Inland Mission. He was a contemporary of Müller's.

Continue your upward path to positions of influence, and perhaps even power. Do not grab the robes of authority prematurely. That was Adam's sin. Here is the model.

> Now He began telling a parable to the invited guests when He noticed how they had been picking out the places of honor at the table, saying to them, "Whenever you are invited by someone to a wedding feast, do not take the place of honor, for someone more distinguished than you may have been invited by him, and the one who invited you both will come and say to you, 'Give your place to this person,' and then in disgrace you will proceed to occupy the last place. But whenever you are invited, go and take the last place, so that when the one who has invited you comes, he will say to you, 'Friend, move up higher'; then you will have honor in the sight of all who are dining at the table with you. For everyone who exalts himself will be humbled, and the one who humbles himself will be exalted." (Luke 14:7–11)

C. Do Not Steal

Point three of the biblical covenant is law. It asks: "What are the rules?" How does this apply to your economic affairs?

The Bible teaches this: "You shall not steal" (Ex. 20:15). It does not say this: "You shall not steal except by majority vote."

The modern welfare state rests on the second version of the commandment. There are always special-interest groups that seek subsidies from the state. They often justify these subsidies in the name of social justice. These payments are political pay-offs: money for having enough votes to grab it. These handouts are funded by taxation, by government debt, and by central bank monetary inflation. There is no third source.

You must stop asking the government for handouts. Do not vote for them. Do not support political candidates who promise them. Most important, you must stop deceiving yourself. You must stop trying to justify these handouts. You must stop saying to yourself: "These are not political handouts. They are owed to me. They are moral obligations on the part of the government. Handouts are what all those other special-interest groups want. I am not like them. I am morally superior. My cause is morally superior to theirs. I deserve the money. So does my cause." No, you aren't morally superior. No, you don't deserve the money. No, your cause doesn't, either.

Stop voting for government handouts of any kind.

If the government plans to pay for a project, evaluate who will pay, and how much. Find out who is behind the group that is promoting the project. Find out how much money specific organizations will receive. Most of all, determine whether the project will help the general public without discrimination. Then determine why the private sector has not already built the project. There has to be a reason. What is it?

Never vote for a bond issue that is not solving a true emergency. If some predictable project is worth doing, the government should have the money saved up to pay for it. *Bond issues subsidize governments that refuse to set money aside.* Governments ask for loans when they need extra money. They do not plan ahead. This is also what alcoholics do. It is what bums do.

There are private forms of theft. People borrow, but they do not repay. Here is what the psalmist said: "The wicked borrows and does not pay back" (Ps. 37:21a). This is a widespread sin in Christian circles. If you agree to do something, do it. If you sign a contract, fulfill it.

D. Pay the Tithe

Point four of the biblical covenant is sanctions. It asks: "What happens if I obey? Disobey?" How does this apply to your economic affairs?

Abraham paid a tithe to the high priest Melchizedek (Gen. 14:18–20). The Epistle to the Hebrews identifies Jesus Christ as the New Covenant's high priest after the order of Melchizedek (Heb. 7). If you have any doubts about the obligation of the tithe, read Hebrews 7. "Now observe how great this man was to whom Abraham, the patriarch, gave a tenth of the choicest spoils" (Heb. 7:4). God therefore requires you to turn over 10% of your net income to your local church. If you are allowed by the civil government to deduct this donation from your taxable gross income, do this. If the government does not allow this, the government is a thief. It steals from God. In this case, you owe the tithe on your after-tax income. Think of this income as the grain left over after the locusts have eaten their fill. You don't owe a tithe on the grain that came up before the locusts arrived.

By paying your tithe to your local congregation, you do the following. First, you acknowledge that God is the source of your money. Second, you acknowledge that God has a legal claim on 10% as a covenantal obligation. Third, you acknowledge that the local congregation represents God covenantally. You are not lawfully in control over where this money goes. God is. He has designated the church: the common storehouse. "Bring the whole tithe into the storehouse, so that there may be food in My house, and put Me to the test now in this," says the LORD of armies, "if I do not open for you the windows of heaven and pour out for you a blessing until it overflows" (Mal. 3:10). There is only one designated storehouse. You choose which church to join. That is the limit of your authority to choose where your tithe money goes.

God lets you keep 90% of your earnings. The state will collect a percentage, but the rest is up to you. You are like a salesman who gets a 90% commission. But no salesman ever gets this high a commission.

God is generous. He supplied your capital, including your life. Never forget this: *grace precedes law.*

There are covenant sanctions associated with the tithe. They are positive and negative. This is why we know they are covenantal.

> "For I, the LORD, do not change; therefore you, the sons of Jacob, have not come to an end. From the days of your fathers you have turned away from My statutes and have not kept them. Return to Me, and I will return to you," says the LORD of armies. "But you say, 'How shall we return?' Would anyone rob God? Yet you are robbing Me! But you say, 'How have we robbed You?' In tithes and offerings. You are cursed with a curse, for you are robbing Me, the entire nation of you! Bring the whole tithe into the storehouse, so that there may be food in My house, and put Me to the test now in this," says the LORD of armies, "if I do not open for you the windows of heaven and pour out for you a blessing until it overflows. Then I will rebuke the devourer for you, so that it will not destroy the fruit of your ground; nor will the vine in the field prove fruitless to you," says the LORD of armies. (Mal. 3:6–11)

Pay a tithe. Start today if you have not done so before. Don't pray to God for blessings unless you are ready for added responsibility. You acknowledge this added responsibility when you pay the tithe.

E. Leave an Inheritance

Point five of the biblical covenant is succession. It asks: "Does this outfit have a future?" How does this apply to your economic affairs?

You have a moral obligation to leave an inheritance to your covenant-keeping children. There should be no debate over this. "A good person leaves an inheritance to his grandchildren, and the wealth of a sinner is stored up for the righteous" (Prov. 13:22).

To leave an inheritance means that you must save more money than you spend. You must also invest wisely, so as not to lose this money. Every generation owes this to at least two generations down the covenant line: children's children. The best example of obeying this grandfather's law of inheritance in American history is the Tyler family. John Tyler was born in 1790, the first full year of George Washington's presidency. He was elected Vice President in 1840. President Harrison died a month later, so Tyler became the first Vice President to become President. He brought the Republic of Texas into the Union in March 1845. He joined the Confederacy in 1861, the year of his death. His two grandsons were still alive in 2019. I know the older brother, Lyon, who is a member of my daughter's church. Harrison Tyler, the younger brother, lives on the Tyler estate in Virginia. In 2004, he donated $5 million to William and Mary College, where his father had been president from 1888 to 1919. He did so in the memory of his father. These three generations lived in the era in which the entire world was completely changed by economic growth. John Tyler was 13 years old when the first locomotive was invented. He was 17 when the first steamboat was launched.

Even more important than money as a legacy is a Christian education. Parents should be sure that their children know the difference between secular humanism and Christianity. This is especially true in the debate over creationism versus Darwinian evolution. Children should understand that the two worldviews are not compatible. The tax-funded public schools teach evolutionism. In the United States, teaching any view other than evolutionism is prohibited by law.

Conclusion

Each individual is responsible before God to bring his thoughts and deeds into conformity to biblical law. This includes economics.

Each individual is also required to think through the presuppositions and implications of whatever he has been taught about how the world works. If he has been taught by evolutionists, he has a lot of rethinking to do.

This book is my attempt to think through economics from a creationist, providentialist, anti-evolution mindset. Evolutionists have discovered accurate facts about how the world works. They have offered theories of how the world works that are compatible with what Christianity teaches. "You shall not steal" means much the same for a free market humanist as it does—or should—to a Christian. But when it comes to explaining why we should not steal, and what we risk if we do steal, the humanist economist and the Christian economist do not agree. When Adam Smith wrote about the invisible hand, he did not have in mind this invisible hand: "Reach out with Your hand from on high; rescue me and save me from great waters, from the hand of foreigners whose mouths speak deceit, and whose right hand is a right hand of falsehood" (Ps. 144:7–8).

Chapter 17

Family Covenant

"Honor your father and your mother, so that your days may be prolonged on the land which the Lord *your God gives you."*

Exodus 20:12

Analysis

Unlike the individual and the church, the family does not persevere into eternity. It is bounded by history. There is no marriage in the world beyond the grave (Matt. 22:30).

The family is the primary welfare institution in every society. It is bound by law, and is bound by love. Any attempt by the state or the church to replace the family's welfare functions should be regarded as an assault on the family until proved otherwise by Scripture. Because people are sinners, they are always looking for ways to compel other people to pay for the expenses of their families. This is true in the church, and it is also true in the state. But in modern times, the state is by far a greater threat to the family than the church. This is because membership in a church is voluntary. People can transfer this membership if they do not like what a church is doing. The members have a veto. In contrast, membership under the jurisdiction of one or another state is inescapable. Also, the state has the power to force a redistribution of wealth. It therefore has the economic capacity to replace the family in many areas of life. This is why there is a fundamental conflict going on in the modern world between the state and the family.

1. Sanctions

Economic theory applies only to marketable property. It rests on the existence of a system of economic sanctions that is governed by this accounting principle: *monetary profit and loss.* The pricing of goods in the market place is based on this principle: *high bid wins.* Ultimately, economic theory rests on this fundamental legal foundation: *the right to use whatever you own or sell whatever you own without interference from others.* This principle of ownership/disownership does not apply in three covenantal institutions: family, church, and state.

You do not have the right to sell your wife. She does not belong to you. You also do not have the right to sell your children. Therefore, the complex, logical, and highly sophisticated intellectual discipline known as economics does not work either predictably or plausibly when it is applied to the family. This failure has to do with the absence of a self-policed system of sanctions that lies outside a specific family's jurisdiction. A business faces independent sanctions: customers' decisions either to buy or not buy the output of the business. It faces competition from other businesses. Every law needs a system of sanctions to enforce it. In a free market, the sanctions are monetary profit and loss. These are imposed by the market itself. Economists say that market sanctions are endogenous: generated from within the institutional arrangement. They are accounting-based sanctions, which in turn are based on a money economy.

So, with respect to the family, the economist must look beyond the family in search of sanctions. What sanctions are absent from a family that must be supplied by either church or state? The answer is usually this: state sanctions. These involve the state's right to inflict physical punishment or even death.

This raises the crucial moral and practical question: who decides which agency is in authority in any given case: family (endogenous) or state (exogenous)?

2. *Welfare*

We come now to a practical matter: welfare. Biblically speaking, the family is responsible for the welfare of its members. Parents are responsible for the welfare of minor children. Adult children are responsible for the care of their parents.

The modern welfare state, beginning in the late nineteenth century in authoritarian Prussia, began with the first tax-funded national pension plan. This idea has spread across the West. To this has been added universal medical care for the aged. In the United States, half of the federal government's budget expenditures goes to support the aged: Social Security's old age pension program (25%) and Medicare (25%). These percentages are expected to increase as tens of millions of people reach the ages of eligibility: 62 for Social Security, 65 for Medicare.

These programs' future expenses have not been funded by purchasing investment assets, as every private pension must. Instead, they are "pay as you go." Professor Laurence Kotlikoff of Boston University has estimated that, using the government's figures, in 2015 the *present value* of the future unfunded liabilities of Social Security, Medicare, and Medicaid totaled $210 trillion. Other nations have comparable unfunded liabilities. To meet these obligations, governments must raise taxes significantly (impossible politically), reduce benefits significantly (impossible politically), or both. Politicians in the West refuse to face this publicly. This phrase used to describe what they do: "kick the can down the road." So, Western governments will eventually default. They will have no other option. The controversial political questions as to which voting blocs will get hurt most, and by how much, and in what sequence, have not been decided. At some point, politicians will have to decide.

Also beginning in Prussia in the late eighteenth century was compulsory, tax-funded education for children. This also has spread across the West. The state controls the content of the curriculum materials. This means that public school materials are in conformity with the theories of tax-funded welfare. The welfare state uses the public schools as propaganda tools. The state has numerous agendas. These agendas are taught in the schools as if they were morally legitimate. Opposition views are not.

The state is attempting to replace the family. Politicians have used the voters' desire for subsidies to strengthen the state's control over the family.

The state's bureaucrats serve as substitute parents. These bureaucrats must be supported financially. The state imposes taxation to fund them. The state needs continual funding. Families do not. Parents need support in their old age, which usually does not last for long. Parents expect their children to be independent as adults. They train their children for two decades to gain enough maturity to leave home. Parents do not expect their children to begin funding them as soon as they leave home. In contrast, the state wants children to leave home, get jobs, and pay taxes... immediately.

The West finds itself in a statistically inescapable crisis because voters decided generations ago that they preferred taxpayers to pay for welfare expenses that historically have been funded by individual families. They voted to impose their expected financial obligations on others. They adopted this poem as their family's financial plan: "Don't tax you. Don't tax me. Tax the guy behind the tree."

A. Define the Family as Male/Female

Point one of the biblical covenant is God's transcendence, yet also His presence. This is the biblical concept of God's original sovereignty. It asks: "Who's in charge here?" How does this apply to the family?

God is a Trinity. Two persons of the Trinity are described in the same language as the persons of the family: Father and Son. Mankind is made in God's image. In terms of defining the family biologically, this is clear: "So God created man in His own image, in the image of God He created him; male and female He created them" (Gen. 1:27). This judicial definition can be altered by covenant-breaking men, but not without negative sanctions.

The male-female family was the origin of the division of labor. God gave Eve to Adam as a helper (Gen. 2:18). There was gender hierarchy from the beginning. It was a hierarchy of legal responsibility before God. This is definitional. It is judicial. It is covenantal. Any attempt to undermine this judicial hierarchy is covenant-breaking. This is grounded in God as the Creator and God as the providential Sustainer. It has to do with the absolute sovereignty of God. The authority of the family (point two) rests on the sovereignty of God (point one).

Any attempt by the state to define a family as anything except a union physically between a male and a female is a judicial assault on the family. The church must support the family's legitimate claim to renounce the legitimacy of all definitions of a family that are not male/female. Churches must excommunicate all members who establish such a union in the name of marriage.

B. Set Up a Budget

Point two of the biblical covenant is hierarchical authority. It asks: "To whom do I report?" How does this apply to the family?

Parents must provide for minor children. This was built into the creation. Infants and young children are not able to care for themselves. So, the family before the fall was a welfare agency. It required a budget that placed the needs of children before the wants of parents. Parents had to abide by this budget. This means that budgeting is a major responsibility. It is one that most families are forced to honor.

Who does the budgeting in your family? Is this a joint venture? How successful are you in adhering to this budget?

A budget lets you establish greater control. Budgeting helps people to increase their authority over many areas of their lives. They do not have the feeling that events are overwhelming them. They feel that they have greater control over their lives when they budget months in advance. They become future-oriented. They pay attention to expected costs and unexpected costs. This form of discipline helps families stay out of trouble.

Do you go into debt in order to avoid staying within a monthly budget? You cannot do this indefinitely. You will exhaust your lines of credit. The longer that you defer the task of budgeting, the more difficult it will be for you to escape this habit. Remember this: "The rich rules over the poor, and the borrower becomes the lender's slave" (Prov. 22:7). The dominion covenant mandates a hierarchy. So does God's law. Debt is a threat. "The stranger who is among you will rise above you higher and higher, and you will go down lower and lower. He will lend to you, but you will not lend to him; he will be the head, and you will be the tail" (Deut. 28:43–44). You must not allow creditors to gain control over you. You must stay out of consumer debt. Even business debt is risky. Be very careful about taking on debt.

Budgeting involves forecasting. You must make guesses about which unexpected expenses might come up in the near future. Are you systematically setting aside money, so that you will not be caught short of money when the unexpected bills arrive?

C. Pay for Educating Your Children

Point three of the biblical covenant is law. It asks: "What are the rules?" How does this apply to the family?

Education is ultimately covenantal. Therefore, it is ethical. It is related to law. It raises the issues of truth and falsehood, good and bad, right and wrong. It can never be neutral on matters of ethics. But politicians want the public to accept the state's role as the source of funding for education, and therefore also for the source of basic presuppositions regarding ethics. So, politicians and educational bureaucrats go before the voters and tell them that state education is neutral. It doesn't matter what you believe about God, man, law, sanctions, and time. You will get a subsidized education, but it renounces the biblical doctrines of God, man, law, sanctions, and time.

Most people in the United States believe that it is wrong for the government to tax people in order to fund specific religious denominations. That idea went out of fashion in the early nineteenth century. The last state to abolish tax-supported churches was Massachusetts. That was in 1833. Yet within four years, the state of Massachusetts set up a tax-funded educational system. This was a replacement church, but without an official theology. Voters around the world have accepted an idea that they would not accept if the politicians used the word "church," but they do accept when the politicians use the word "school."

Education should reflect the worldview of the parents. The parents are responsible for their children's education. Parents should be careful to make certain that whatever is being taught to their children by any school and by any teacher is consistent with what they believe is true about God, man, law, sanctions, and time. When I say time, I also mean eternity.

Every Christian should vote no on every bond issue devoted to funding education.

Every Christian should pull his child out of the public schools and provide an educational alternative, either a Christian classroom program or a Christian homeschool program. If the parent uses any other kind of materials to teach the students, such as in physics or chemistry, the parent should intervene in order to explain to the children why they need to consider the doctrine of creation and the doctrine of the providence of God in order to understand whatever it is that the child is studying. This means that the parent has to have specific insights into the ways in which the ideas of Darwinian evolution influences the content of academic disciplines. Most parents do not know how to explain this. You had better understand how to explain it.

Obviously, with respect to church, you should take your children to church every week. They need to understand the basic doctrines of the faith. They need to learn how to sit still. They need to learn how to pay attention. This should begin in church, not in school.

D. Teach Your Children Biblical Causality

Point four of the biblical covenant is sanctions. It asks: "What happens if I obey? Disobey?" How does this apply to the family?

Every philosophy of life has a theory of causation. This is certainly true of Christianity. Your children should understand the enormous differences between a Christian worldview and rival worldviews. There are radically different concepts of God, man, law, sanctions, and time.

You must tell your children from an early age that the world is governed by ethical cause and effect. They must understand that what they think and do will have consequences in their lives. You must teach them not to believe in a system of causality that is consistent with Darwinian evolution. You must teach them why causality is covenantal. You must teach them why there is predictability in the world. That is because of the original creation and God's providence in history.

I keep saying: "You must." That is because you must. Nobody else is going to do it. Nobody else is equally responsible for doing it.

It is important that you discipline your children in a consistent fashion. You should let them know early that if they do not learn how to budget their time and money, they will suffer negative consequences for the rest of their lives. You must help teach them how to do basic budgeting. You must also teach them about dealing with other children in an honest way. You must teach them the importance of gaining a reputation for fairness and wisdom. They should see both of these character attributes as tremendous benefits.

You must teach them systematically that the welfare state is built on anti-biblical, anti-Christian presuppositions. They must understand that the welfare state rests on theft. They must understand also that the crises that are inevitably going to come onto welfare states around the world are well-deserved. They must understand these terrible events as the judgment of God in history against a philosophy that says theft is all right if voters vote for it.

E. Leave an Inheritance

Point five of the biblical covenant is succession. It asks: "Does this outfit have a future?" How does this apply to the family?

You must teach your children that they are the heirs of a family tradition. They are also the heirs of a cultural tradition. They must understand something about the history of these traditions. They must understand about causation, which is based on covenants. They must understand that they are intermediaries in a long chain of inheritance stretching back to Adam and Eve. They must see themselves as responsible agents in the transmission of a Christian inheritance to their children.

Inheritance is mainly covenantal. Parents are responsible for training their children in the five points of the covenant. The children must learn to exercise judgment in applying the Christian worldview to their lives. If they do this correctly, they will leave an inheritance. They will build up a capital base. You must teach them to understand the importance of building up a capital base. This involves money, education, and everything associated with exercising dominion in history.

The family does not stretch into eternity. Like the civil government, it will end at the final judgment. Since there will be no sin in heaven or after the resurrection, there will be no need for civil government. Since there will be no marriage in heaven or after the resurrection, there will be no need for a family. "For in the resurrection they neither marry nor are given in marriage, but are like angels in heaven" (Matt. 22:30). But until the end of time, the family will remain the primary agency of inheritance.

We know that people will sacrifice for their families when they will not sacrifice for anyone else or any other institution. We should therefore harness that widely shared emotional commitment to the family in order to extend the kingdom of God in history. We should tell our children how important it is for them to be disciplined about family budgets, so that they can leave an inheritance to their children. But, to persuade them that we are serious, we will have to leave inheritances to them.

It is a mistake to leave an inheritance to a covenant-breaker. In doing this, you subsidize the kingdom of man. Do not subsidize the kingdom of man. The inheritance is covenantal. It is based on ethics. If one of your children is clearly unethical, you should cut him off. You should disinherit him. This is what God did with Adam, and it is what we must do with covenant-breaking children. We must not place the family above the kingdom of God.

The child who is willing to bear the responsibility of caring for parents in their old age is the child who should be the primary beneficiary of the inheritance. This goes back to the rule of the Mosaic law governing the firstborn child of the first wife.

> "If a man has two wives, the one loved and the other unloved, and both the loved and the unloved have borne him sons, and the firstborn son belongs to the unloved, then it shall be on the day that he wills what he owns as an inheritance to his sons, he is not allowed to treat the son of

> the loved wife as the firstborn, at the expense of the son of the unloved, who actually is the firstborn son. On the contrary, he shall acknowledge the firstborn, the son of the unloved wife, by giving him a double portion of everything that he owns, for he was the beginning of his strength; to him belongs the right of the firstborn." (Deut. 21:15–17)

With all blessings comes responsibility. With the blessing of a large inheritance comes the responsibility of caring for aged parents. The child who is committed to the primary care of the parents should receive the double portion. If any of the other children think this is unfair, ask those children what they are going to do to provide their share of support for the parents.

Inheritance is mostly covenantal, mostly about worldview, and mostly about ethics. Do not neglect these in preparing your children to be recipients of whatever they will receive from you.

Conclusion

The family is under assault by the state in the modern world. It is a moral obligation of the head of the family to resist this invasion of his authority in his household. Christians should be alert to any attempt by church or state to substitute its funding for the funding that the head of the household is responsible for in the eyes of God. With the transfer of responsibility for funding comes an inevitable and inescapable transfer of authority to the agency that is providing the funding. There is no escape from the strings attached to what is popularly regarded as free money. There is no such thing as free money.

The rise of the welfare state in the twentieth century represented the greatest single threat to the integrity of the family in the history of man. No other societies in the history of man have been more systematic in transferring family responsibility to the state, and the lure in almost all cases has been the promise of free money. It is obvious in the area of education. It is also obvious in the area of old age security, meaning pensions from the state and medical care from the state. Christians have submitted to this transfer. They have not understood the fundamental rule of all taxation: *the power to tax is the power to destroy.* They have assented to a vast expansion of taxation by various levels of civil government, always in the name of providing benefits for the people. But the benefits have come mainly at the expense of the family, because the family is the primary institution of social welfare in every society.

The refusal of Christians to challenge the expansion of the state in the area of education and old age security is evidence of the fact that Christians no longer believe the Bible offers the theological, moral, and judicial foundations of social theory. They have surrendered to the state in almost every area of life, because they do not believe that they are responsible, as Christians, to preach and then implement a system of institutional governments: family, church, and state. These are oath-bound institutions, and the stipulations of the respective oaths are presented in the Bible. Because Christians do not believe this, they have continually surrendered to rival systems of government with rival oaths and rival stipulations.

The legalization of abortion represents the most important assault against the Christian concept of the family in the modern world. God-hating pagans who refuse to accept responsibility for the children that their sexual activity produces are ready to kill their children. They want the benefits of sexual activity, but they do not want any of the liabilities. They have gone to the state and demanded that the state legalize their murder of their own children. Christians have generally accepted this development. There has been some resistance, but it has not been systematic. Christians have verbally identified abortion as murder, but they do not really believe this. On the one hand, they insist that the death penalty is mandated by the Bible for murder. On the other hand, they have refused to call for the execution of abortionists as murderers. They are schizophrenic: judicially, covenantally and intellectually. This surrender to the mass murderers of the modern world is representative of the widespread defection of political responsibility by Christians. They have accepted the doctrine of neutral civil government, despite the fact that neutral civil government authorizes the murder of the innocents. Until Christians steadfastly oppose the murder of the innocents, there is little hope that the city of man will face a serious threat from Christianity.

Chapter 18

Church Covenant

"I know your deeds, that you are neither cold nor hot; I wish that you were cold or hot. So because you are lukewarm, and neither hot nor cold, I will vomit you out of My mouth. Because you say, 'I am rich, and have become wealthy, and have no need of anything,' and you do not know that you are wretched, miserable, poor, blind, and naked..."

Revelation 3:15–17

Analysis

Churches today, as with every other institution, are rich beyond the wildest dreams of men in 1800. The vast outpouring of productivity which the free market has produced since 1800 has transformed all of us. By historical standards, we are fantastically wealthy. Yet the church is miserable, poor, and blind today, just as the church of Laodicea was in John's day. It is neither hot nor cold. It has lost its impact in society.

How did this come about? How is it that the church of Jesus Christ, which has been granted a covenant by God himself, should have proven to be so impotent culturally, economically, educationally, and politically ever since the mid-nineteenth century?

It has to do with theology. It has to do with an unwillingness to challenge the central orthodoxies of the city of man. It has to do with the surrender of authority to the city of man. The question is: "Why did the church surrender this authority?"

A. Defend the Bride of Christ

Point one of the biblical covenant is God's transcendence, yet also His presence. This is the biblical concept of God's original sovereignty. It asks: "Who's in charge here?" How does this apply to the institutional church?

The church is called the Bride of Christ.

> Husbands, love your wives, just as Christ also loved the church and gave Himself up for her, so that He might sanctify her, having cleansed her by the washing of water with the word, that He might present to Himself the church in all her glory, having no spot or wrinkle or any such thing; but that she would be holy and blameless. (Eph. 5:25–27)

Therefore, the church has a unique covenantal connection to God. The doctrine of the Trinity teaches that Jesus Christ is the incarnation of the Second Person of the Trinity. This means that the church is favored above all other institutions. God is transcendent to the church, yet He is also present with the church.

Church members and church leaders must defend the integrity of the church against all challengers. They must do this with the same degree of commitment that they defend the doctrine of the Trinity. They must believe that they separate themselves from the bride of Christ when they refused to join a church. They must see their connection with Christ in terms of their membership in a local church. Churches must defend the doctrine of the church. Membership in the church is not optional. It is a covenantal responsibility. Churches must preach this, teach this in Sunday school, and remind people of this whenever there is an excommunication.

B. Accept No State Subsidies

Point two of the biblical covenant is hierarchical authority. It asks: "To whom do I report?" How does this apply to the institutional church?

Churches should not accept money from any unit of civil government for any program operated by the church. This includes charitable ministries, free public school textbooks for church-operated schools, or any kind of direct subsidy. Whenever a church receives money from any institution, it becomes dependent on that institution. The church's budget is threatened if such subsidies are removed. *The church must never become dependent on external sources of income from any other institution.* Churches should be supported by the donations of their members. The only major exception would be in those rare instances where churches have television ministries, and they ask for financial support from nonmembers who watch the broadcasts. This would be a payment for spiritual services rendered. This donated money is not extracted from the taxpayers. Such is not the case with subsidies from the civil government.

Pastors should preach against the idea that tax exemption is an indirect subsidy from the state. This idea is pernicious. It rests on a philosophy of civil government that says that the state owns everything in principle, but it graciously exempts certain individuals or institutions from having to pay taxes. This is why pastors should preach against the idea of tax exemption for churches. They should preach the doctrine of *tax immunity* for churches. This is completely different from tax exemption. The idea of tax immunity is based on the superior jurisdiction of the church above the state. The church is the bride of Christ. The church extends into eternity. The state has no legitimate authority whatsoever over what the church does with its income.

Tax immunity is not based on the idea that the state graciously grants to the church an exemption from taxation. Such an idea places the state above the church in terms of its authority and lawful jurisdiction. Churches should never accept such an idea. Churches should not apply for tax exemption. They should simply say that they are churches, and that they are not subject to taxation. This is possible in the United States. Churches do not need to apply to the Internal Revenue Service in order to be granted tax exempt status under what is known as the 501(c)(3) section of the Internal Revenue Code. They should not apply for this status. They should simply declare that they are churches, and therefore they do not have to file any papers or money with the Internal Revenue Service, other than for salaries paid to individuals who work for the church. From the point of view of economic analysis, the church does not pay these taxes; the employees do.

In a famous American Supreme Court decision, the Chief Justice of the court declared this: "The power to tax is the power to destroy" (*McCulloch v. Maryland*, 1819). This is an accurate assessment of the threat of taxation. This is why churches should not be subject to any taxation. To tax the church is the power to destroy it. It is not that the state has graciously granted tax exemption to churches. Rather, they are tax-immune in the eyes of God. *God does not grant to the state the right to tax churches.* Christians should defend this principle politically. They should not surrender to the idea that a supposedly religiously neutral state has the right to tax churches, but has graciously granted exemptions to them. This idea of tax exemption acknowledges far too much authority on the part of politicians to determine whether or not to tax churches.

C. Operate Charities

Point three of the biblical covenant is ethics. It asks: "What are the rules?" How does this apply to the institutional church?

The welfare state has used taxpayers' money in order to set up charitable services. These are not charities. Charities are supported by voluntary contributions. These so-called charities are in fact vote-getting devices. *The politicians extract money from one group of taxpayers in order to support another group of taxpayers.* The supported taxpayers, who always outnumber the taxpayers, are then expected to vote for the politicians. These votes are payments for services rendered.

One of the justifications that defenders of the welfare state use is this: churches have defected on their responsibilities for caring for the poor. This criticism is correct. But this is no legal or moral justification for the state to use coercion in order to extract money in a gigantic vote-getting system of wealth redistribution.

Churches should set up ministries under the control of their diaconates. The deacons should determine which requests for support are legitimate, and which are not. The church has biblical responsibilities for doing this. This is why the diaconate was created in the first place (Acts 6). Deacons should gain experience in giving away money when times are relatively good. This will prepare them for a wave of requests from members and nonmembers to receive money when times get bad.

The church has a legitimate healing function. *Healing is related to salvation.* The English word "salve" reflects this. A salve is a healing ointment. When the state uses taxpayers' money to imitate the church in providing this form of healing, it becomes messianic. *The modern welfare state is messianic.* This is one reason why every modern welfare state is involved in supplying money for medical care. The state is invading the sanctuary of the church. The state is attempting to persuade voters that the state's power of coercion, not the churches' authority to ask members for financial support, should be the basis of healing in modern society. The voters have accepted this implicit claim by the state. Welfare states are notorious for their secularism. They are attempting to replace the church, and the means of doing so is money that has been extracted from the taxpayers, and which is then spent on pseudo-charities, especially healthcare services. Welfare states are attempting to undermine the authority, legitimacy, and influence of churches by means of money extracted from the voters. This arrangement extends the bureaucracy of the state into every area of life in which the state funds operations.

Because the vast majority of Christian theologians and pastors believe that civil law is neutral, they rarely preach against specific violations of biblical law by the state. They remain generally silent about the activities of the state. The idea that the state should enforce biblical law has been unpopular since the days of the Roman Empire. When they got into control of the Roman Empire in the early fourth century, Christian leaders used Roman law, not biblical law, to administer the Empire. This set a precedent for the church that is still honored by the church. The resulting problem is this: the church is tempted to drift with the social, moral, and legal orders of the non-Christian world outside of the institutional churches. The church refuses to serve as salt and light within civil affairs. But in the kingdom of man, civil affairs are regarded as sovereign in almost every area of life. About the only area of life that is considered off-limits to the government has to do with sexual activity. The modern state tolerates and even encourages sexual debauchery. Except for marital affairs, the state is regarded as sovereign in the affairs of men.

It is important that Christians resist the idea that the modern welfare state operates in terms of legitimate ethical law, which is biblical law. The modern welfare state is in rebellion against biblical law. Modern Christians are also in rebellion against biblical law, which is why there is a political alliance between the secular humanists and the pietists. The pietists have surrendered any degree of authority in civil affairs, and this is strongly supported by the humanists who are in control of civil affairs.

Christians have adopted the ethics of the rewritten eighth commandment: "You shall not steal except by majority vote." They are as supportive as pagans are of tax-funded education, government-funded pensions for all citizens, and universal health care for the aged. Christians go along with the city of man in order to get along with the city of man. They do not think it is imperative that the city of man be replaced by the city of God in history.

D. Preach the Tithe

Point four of the biblical covenant is sanctions. It asks: "What happens if I obey? Disobey?" How does this apply to the institutional church?

Point four has to do with church sacraments, for they are oath-signs that place members under the sanctions of God's church covenant. This is the covenantal basis of the tithe.

Abraham paid a tithe to the high priest Melchizedek (Gen. 14:17–20). Jesus Christ is a high priest in the order of Melchizedek (Heb. 7). Therefore, church members owe a tithe to the local church.

The local church is entitled to the tithe, or 10% of family income. Because most churches no longer preach the covenantal requirement of the tithe, they have not been able to redirect the flow of authority in their direction. Authority flows in the direction of those institutions that bear social risks and take responsibility. The churches have not called upon their members to make available the funds that God says His church is entitled to. Churches, like families, have thereby transferred power to the state.

The tithe is built into man's affairs. Either we pay it to the church or else we will pay it to the state. The church limits its lawful demands to

10%; the state extracts all it can get. The modern welfare state demands far more than the tithe. The combined level of taxation of all branches of government in the United States exceeds 40% of all national income. This is sinful. It is also the judgment of God on rebels. It happens every time men rebel against the tithe. The taxes of Egypt in Joseph's day were only half of this, or 20% (Gen. 47:24). The prophet Samuel came before the Israelites and warned them that the king they wanted would eventually take 10% of their wealth: "And he will take a tenth of your seed and your vineyards and give it to his high officials and his servants" (I Sam. 8:15). Christians live in a country that extracts four times the tithe from them, and they vote for politicians who promise even more government spending. They are in bondage, but they fail to recognize it. They are in Egypt, but they fail to recognize it.

E. Preach Victory in History

Point five of the biblical covenant is succession. It asks: "Does this outfit have a future?" How does this apply to the institutional church?

Modern churches have completely rejected the idea that members of the city of God are to spend their lives working against the city of man in economic and civil affairs. They believe that there is moral, covenantal, and judicial neutrality in the realm of economics and civil affairs. Therefore, pietistic Christians insist, Christians should not challenge the prevailing social and economic order. They do not believe that there is so intense a competition in history between the city of man in the city of God that members of the city of God should work to replace members of the city of man in civil affairs. They insist that Christians must remain in what is functionally the loyal opposition. They do not ask this question: "Why should Christians be loyal to the city of man?"

Christians do not believe that they are morally required to spend less money than they earned after taxes and tithe, so that they leave an inheritance to their children. This is supposed to help them to become wealthier, more influential, and more powerful than members of the city of man. Christians normally expect their children to become less wealthy, less influential, and less powerful than members of the city of man. *They have accepted social defeat as a way of life.* They have invented theologies of inevitable defeat which predict that the church will be a failure historically in implementing the Great Commission of Matthew 28:18–20. "All authority in heaven and on earth has been given to Me. Go, therefore, and make disciples of all the nations, baptizing them in the name of the Father and the Son and the Holy Spirit, teaching them to follow all that I commanded you; and behold, I am with you always, to the end of the age."

Because they have given up hope in the future, they are unwilling to commit to a program of comprehensive redemption. They have a theology which says that the city of man in the realm of civil affairs is legitimately exempt from the gospel, and therefore it is legitimately exempt from biblical law. They believe that Christianity has nothing unique and covenantally authoritative to say in the realm of civil government. They believe the same with respect to economic theory.

Conclusion

First and foremost, pastors should preach the obligation of members to tithe. Churches should not be in the position of begging members for money. When members don't tithe, they are stealing from God. Pastors should preach this theology on a regular basis. If some members leave because of such preaching, this is to the benefit of the local congregation. A tithing church is a faithful church. It is a church made up of self-disciplined members. It is in a position to confront the modern welfare state. These are the kinds of churches the world needs.[1]

Second, churches should take at least 10% of their income from people's tithes and offerings and set this money aside for welfare activities. They should care for the poor, or work with other local churches that have ministries to the poor. In the worldwide division of labor, certain churches should specialize in certain kinds of charitable activities. They should make available training materials, free of charge, to other

1. Gary North, *The Covenantal Tithe: The Providential Plan for Fruitful Stewardship* (Moulton, Alabama: Axehead Press, [2011] 2026).

churches that want to start such programs. These materials can be distributed free of charge on the World Wide Web.

Third, churches should revamp their diaconates. They should make it clear to all members that access to free money in times of crisis is only available to members who have taken care to purchase insurance against the worst effects of these unexpected crises. There are no free lunches in life, and churches should not encourage members to believe that the church is just another government welfare agency. Insurance is one of the great inventions of the modern world. It enables families to reduce the impact of life's unpredictable setbacks. Every adult church member should be warned in advance that the deacons will not provide money for families that have not purchased insurance that would have covered expenses that the heads of households later ask the deacons to pay for.

Here is the rule: do not use church funds to support improvident families that need money because they failed to purchase insurance. To do so is unfair to those members of the church who have protected their families by purchasing insurance, and who are now being asked to support improvident families. This is what the welfare state does. It should not be what churches do.

Churches should see to it that the wife of every head of household has sufficient low-cost term life insurance written on her husband's life to protect her and the children. She should own the policy, paying for it from her own personal, exclusive checkbook. This establishes her as the owner of the policy. Why should she own it? What if he quits the church, divorces her, and remarries? If he owns the policy, he will name the new wife as the beneficiary, leaving the first wife without alimony income if he dies. If he dies, the covenantally faithful wife is protected, and the church is not responsible for supporting her.

What if a family is really poverty-stricken? What if it really can't afford money for basic health insurance protection? In that case, deacons need to step in and give the family enough money to meet the annual premium payment to the insurance company. Why? Because the church has this obligation biblically. The deacons are acting in the name of God, in the name of the family, and in the name of the congregation, which also needs protection from these costs. The deacons should then ask the family for proof that it used the money to buy such insurance.

The church becomes responsible if there is an accident or illness, and the family is impoverished because of medical costs. Deacons should intervene by going to the hospital to inform the hospital that the family is impoverished. Deacons should negotiate with the hospital to get the hospital to reduce the bill.

The church therefore has a legitimate police function to make sure that each member has adequate health insurance coverage. This should be high-deductible health insurance, which is cheaper to buy. A wise church makes it clear to all members that they are responsible for buying insurance in order to become eligible for aid from the deacons. Insurance reduces or eliminates this risk to churches. If members don't do this, the church can legitimately tell these members in a crisis that there will be no free money.

Churches should assist non-church ministries that specialize in aiding the poor: hospitals, charitable ministries, rescue missions, and so forth. Let those who better understand the needs (and "hustles") of the poor administer the funds. *Pastors should preach regularly on the topic of church responsibility to the poor.* They should also make it clear that such teaching is in open opposition to the modern doctrine of the state's responsibility to the poor. They must call for a replacement operation, not a church-financed supplement to the modern welfare state. Anyone who preaches for more private charity without also calling for a reduction in tax-financed charity is a guilt-manipulator and an accomplice to the welfare state.

Poverty programs must be accompanied by preaching and instruction concerning the moral responsibility of the able-bodied to work. Paul wrote, "if anyone is not willing to work, then he is not to eat, either" (II Thess. 3:10b). The world doesn't owe any able-bodied person a living. Neither does God. To aid laziness is to aid evil. *The long-term goal of most charity programs should be to make the recipients financially independent.* State-run poverty programs are programs for extending poverty. Rome had similar programs in the era of the early church. These programs bankrupted the Empire financially, but Rome had been bankrupt morally long before. The proof of this moral bankruptcy was the existence of the politics of bread and circuses. It is no different today.

Pastors should teach the biblical principles of financial success: self-discipline, thrift, hard work, customer service, thrift, future-orientation, saving for retirement, thrift, profitability, low or zero debt, thrift, long hours, family sacrifice, reduced lifestyle, and thrift. They should prepare their people for the worst, so that people will be capable of handling the best, when it comes.

Churches need to train their members in the theology and specifics of Christian dominion in every area of life. Christians are supposed to inherit the earth. In fact, we have inherited the earth by God's declaration (definitive inheritance), but we have not yet occupied it (progressive inheritance). We have not yet established authority by service. Adam inherited the earth before he sinned and gave it away, but even in his sin-free state, he had to take possession of his inheritance. He received title, but he didn't receive it completed. He first had to take communion at the tree of life. Through Christ, we have inherited the earth. We, too, must now take possession of our inheritance. We have title, but we have not been given occupancy. That takes a program of dominion.

The church's self-imposed impotence, meaning its refusal to accept social responsibility, has made possible the rise of the welfare state. Liberal theologians have applauded this turn of events, while conservative Christians have grumbled a lot, but they have done little institutionally to fight it. Let us assume that the welfare state system continues. Taxes will remain high. Government budget deficits will continue. Governments will eventually default on welfare payments. There is no long-run statistical alternative to default. We will have a series of devastating financial crises, just as Rome had after the year 200, and just as France had just before and during the French Revolution (1785–1795). When these crises hit, local churches will be subject to economic pressures that they have not seen since the Great Depression of the 1930s. Giving will drop unless members are highly self-disciplined. Members will lose jobs. They will find their savings wiped out. The poor will multiply. This time, unlike the 1930s, the state will have tapped into every known source of taxable income. There will be no state-financed "safety net" next time.

Which groups will be ready to offer support by being willing and able to organize and make available charity? Which groups will have prepared their members for the risk-taking and responsibility-bearing that are needed for survival in an economic crisis? Who will be ready to lead?

The churches are just barely getting ready to consider such a shift in responsibility, let alone a shift in authority. If revival comes alongside the economic crises, as I would expect, then church leaders have to be ready to answer the fundamental questions:

- How did the world economy get into such a mess?
- What biblical economic principles were violated?
- How do we return to biblical economic principles?
- Who should finance reconstruction?
- What should I do with my money?
- What should I do if I lose my job?
- How can I afford to tithe?

Pastors and deacons are almost completely unprepared to take leadership today. No one expects them to. They are considered unnecessary by most citizens. After all, the Bible-believing church has had little or nothing to say about economic issues for well over a century. Economics has been considered off-limits to preachers in conservative churches. This will change, and it will change fast, when the crises hit. At that point, those churches that begin to exercise responsibility will position themselves as leaders in the national and perhaps even the worldwide transformation which may lie ahead. Pastors had better begin now to preach God's principles of success, and God's principles of responsible giving. They need lots of practice.

Chapter 19

Civil Covenant

Then Joseph said to the people, "Behold, today I have purchased you and your land for Pharaoh; now, here is seed for you, and you may sow the land. At the harvest you shall give a fifth to Pharaoh, and four-fifths shall be your own for seed of the field and for your food, and for those of your households and as food for your little ones." So they said, "You have saved our lives! Let us find favor in the sight of my lord, and we will be Pharaoh's slaves." Joseph made it a statute concerning the land of Egypt, valid to this day, that Pharaoh was to have the fifth; only the land of the priests did not become Pharaoh's.

Genesis 47:23–26

So Samuel spoke all the words of the Lord *to the people who had asked him for a king. And he said, "This will be the practice of the king who will reign over you: he will take your sons and put them in his chariots for himself and among his horsemen, and they will run before his chariots. He will appoint for himself commanders of thousands and commanders of fifties, and some to do his plowing and to gather in his harvest, and to make his weapons of war and equipment for his chariots. He will also take your daughters and use them as perfumers, cooks, and bakers. He will take the best of your fields, your vineyards, and your olive groves, and give them to his servants. And he will take a tenth of your seed and your vineyards and give it to his high officials and his servants. He will also take your male servants and your female servants, and your best young men, and your donkeys, and use them for his*

> *work. He will take a tenth of your flocks, and you yourselves will become his servants. Then you will cry out on that day because of your king whom you have chosen for yourselves, but the* LORD *will not answer you on that day."*
>
> I SAMUEL 8:10–18

ANALYSIS

Egyptians in Joseph's day believed in a sovereign Pharaoh. They believed that he was the link between heaven and earth. So, God brought a famine, and when it was over, they had sold their lands to this supposed god walking on earth. From that time on, they were taxed one-fifth of their income.

The people of Israel in Samuel's day believed that they needed a king who was comparable to the kings in the covenant-breaking lands around them. God told Samuel to warn them against establishing a king. Biblical law had made a provision for such a king, and had placed him under tight restrictions (Deut. 17). But that was not good enough for the people of Israel. They did not want a restricted king. So, God told Samuel, "Listen to the voice of the people regarding all that they say to you, because they have not rejected you, but they have rejected Me from being King over them" (I Sam. 8:7).

Today, in the nations of the West, total taxation is in the range of 50% of national income. In order for the West to return to the tyranny of Pharaoh's regime, there would have to be a 60% tax cut. In order for them to return to the tyranny is described by Samuel, they would have to have an 80% tax cut. Yet Christians live comfortably in these regimes, and in the case of the United States, they have always had a numerical majority politically. They impose a system of tyrannical taxation that is beyond the wildest dreams of the tyrants of the biblical era, and yet they regard themselves as living in free societies. The extent of the political delusion of modern Christians dwarfs the delusion of the Israelites in the days of Samuel.

How did this happen? It happened because Christians have abandoned any faith in the morally binding nature of Old Testament law or Old Testament history.

A. Smash the Idol

Point one of the biblical covenant is God's transcendence, yet also His presence. This is the biblical concept of God's original sovereignty. It asks: "Who's in charge here?" How does this apply to the state?

The first commandment says: "I am the LORD your God, who brought you out of the land of Egypt, out of the house of slavery. You shall have no other gods before Me" (Ex. 20:2–3). God made it clear that their time in Egypt was a time of slavery. They had lived under the rule of a Pharaoh who was regarded by the people of Egypt as a god. The result was tyranny. God made it clear that to worship another god is a violation of His standards. This was also an implied warning: if they worshiped such a god, they would find themselves back under slavery.

The modern welfare state is a substitute god. No politician refers to the state as divine, but states around the world have created humanist educational systems that deny that God has any relevance in history. They have exiled God from the universe. They have substituted the impersonal God of evolution for the God of the Bible. They have substituted the heat death of the universe, when all life dies, for the final judgment. That will take place tens of billions of years from now. So, God neither begins history nor ends it in judgment. He is therefore irrelevant to history. In the United States, it is illegal to teach anything else in tax-supported schools.

Modern man is surprised when he finds himself under the rule of tyranny. He then redefines tyranny as if it were freedom. This is what teachers in state-run schools told him when he was in high school or college.

B. End State Economic Planning

Point two of the biblical covenant is hierarchical authority. It asks: "To whom do I report?" How does this apply to the state?

Economic planning is an inescapable concept. It is never a question of economic planning versus no economic planning. It is always a question of whose economic plan.

The primary economic agents of planning are individuals who possess assets. God made them responsible as His stewards. This is the heart of the dominion covenant. Their actions in planning for the future are carried out within the framework of trade. They exchange goods and services with each other. The institutions of the market economy have developed in terms of the right of individuals to own property, which means the right of individuals to disown *property*. Individuals' plans are coordinated through the market's pricing system.

The socialists' view is that the state owns all property, and therefore agents of the state should do the economic planning. This is planning by bureaucrats. It is planning without the guidance of free market prices. This system is called socialism. Karl Marx described it as a system in which the means of production are owned by society. He never defined exactly how society would do the planning apart from civil government. He regarded civil government as a temporary way station in between capitalism and communism. But he never did explain how communism would allocate resources. He proposed a religion of revolution, and he justified this religion of revolution in the name of the utopian future that he never described. I wrote about this in my book *Marx's Religion of Revolution*.[1]

There has never been a society in which the government has owned all of the means of production. This is an inconceivable society. Without private property, and without private exchange, there can be no prices. Without prices, central planners have no way of knowing what to produce, in what quantities, or with what quality. They don't know how to distribute economic output. They are flying blind. This was first discussed in detail in a 1920 essay by economist Ludwig von Mises: "Economic Calculation in the Socialist Commonwealth." This article made it clear that socialism is impossible. Even in theory, it could not possibly work. That is because there is no price system to guide the planners. This article was dismissed as irrelevant by socialists and Communists until the Soviet Union finally disappeared on December 25, 1991. Communist economics had been abandoned by China's Deng Xiaoping in 1979. Today, there are few socialists. They finally gave up.

1. Gary North, *Marx's Religion of Revolution: Regeneration Through Chaos* (Moulton, Alabama: Axehead Press, [1968, 1989] 2023).

While full socialist economic planning is now almost universally dismissed, both in theory and practice, virtually all national civil governments and almost all economists still favor partial government economic planning by bureaucrats. The system of economics promoted by John Maynard Keynes and his disciples favors government intervention into the economy whenever there is a recession or a depression. He called for massive national government deficits, which means money borrowed from the private sector or else created out of nothing by the central bank, as the way to raise employment and productivity. He never explained why money owned by investors would not do this in private capital markets, yet somehow it would do this when the government sold government bonds to these investors, and then spent the money.

C. Cut Total Taxation to Under 10%

Point three of the biblical covenant is law. It asks: "What are the rules?" How does this apply to the state?

The Bible is clear that any level of taxation at 10% or above is tyrannical. All Keynesian economists recommend taxes well above 10% for the national government, plus equally large levels of taxation by state and local governments. The level of taxation around the world today is tyrannical. The Bible makes this clear. Yet Christians have voted in favor of government welfare programs and government armaments that require taxes far above those identified in the Bible is tyrannical. Christians have overwhelmingly supported a redefinition of the eighth commandment: "You shall not steal except by majority vote."

Christians no longer take seriously the story of Joseph in Egypt and the story of Samuel and Israel. They believe that these stories have no relevant judicial and economic lessons for people who live in the New Testament era. Nevertheless, prior to the First World War, which began in August 1914, no Western civil government had a level of taxation anywhere near the level promised by Samuel to the rebellious people of Israel. World War I launched the era of tyrannical taxation in the West. The voters in Europe approved of this level of taxation after 1914, and they still do.

Western voters vote for tyranny in the name of economic welfare, yet then they believe fervently that they live in freedom. They have been blinded by their commitment to theft by taxation. They have been blinded by their commitment to the idea of a messianic civil government. They believe that the state can heal. It can make poor people middle-class, and it can make middle-class people upper-middle class. All it takes is government economic planning. All it takes is a level of taxation over twice as high as what Pharaoh imposed on Egypt, and four or five times as high as what Samuel had warned Israel against.

D. Enforce Justice

Point four of the biblical covenant is sanctions. It asks: "What happens if I obey? Disobey?" How does this apply to the state?

The Mosaic law is quite clear as to what constitutes justice: *the rule of law.* "You shall not do injustice in judgment; you shall not show partiality to the poor nor give preference to the great, but you are to judge your neighbor fairly" (Lev. 19:15). A similar law was announced to the people of Israel at the first Passover. "The same law shall apply to the native as to the stranger who resides among you" (Ex. 12:49).

Welfare state economics denies the legitimacy of this principle. The defenders of the welfare state promote what they say is fairness. They promote what they say will produce greater equality. They do not preach equality before the law. They preach *equality of results.* To gain equality of results, it is impossible to have equality before the law. You get your choice: *equality before the law or equality of results.* You cannot get both at the same time. This is because people have different capacities, skills, ethics, and all the other attributes which make for differences in earning power. If the civil government redistributes pre-tax income so as to achieve greater equality of income after taxes, it has to violate the principle of equality before the law. When politicians and bureaucrats interfere with the operations of the free market, they substitute state central planning for individual planning in the market. The price system is not allowed to guide individual planners when they make their plans. Instead, planners have to consider government regulations and government tax policies before they decide what they should produce, in what quantities, and at what price. This system of planning substitutes the coercive power of government bureaucrats, who cannot be fired for incompetence, in favor of planning run by profit-seeking entrepreneurs who will lose money if they fail to predict customer demand accurately. Bureaucrats are not allowed to keep any profits for themselves. They also do not suffer from any losses that their plans produce. In contrast, entrepreneurs, meaning business owners, make money by accurately predicting the future, and they lose money by inaccurately predicting the future. Who is motivated to do a better job of forecasting? It is obvious that private entrepreneurs are, not government-protected bureaucrats who cannot be fired. Each system of sanctions shapes economic performance.

E. Disinherit the Substitute Heir

Point five of the biblical covenant is succession. It asks: "Does this outfit have a future?" How does this apply to the state?

Whenever we see any institution taking over the welfare functions of the family, we also see an institution that will soon claim the right of inheritance of families. *Inheritance is always related to welfare functions.* This is true for the family, true for the state, and true for the church.

Throughout the world, civil governments fund education. They also fund retirement and old-age health expenses. These are functions that for millennia have been performed by families. *These interventions by civil governments are assaults on family authority.* They substitute impersonal written bureaucratic regulations for personal love and responsibility within families. They substitute a compulsory system of income taxed from the general public and then distributed by bureaucrats to special-interest groups rather than a voluntary system of income and savings provided by the heads of households for family members.

The modern welfare state imposes "estate" taxes—death taxes—on the wealthy. These are the people who provide most of the productivity in society. These are also the people who pay the highest estate taxes. Their children are not allowed to inherit all of the wealth accumulated by the parents. Politicians exempt the broad majority of taxpayers from this death tax system. They do not apply the inheritance law to all members of society. Politicians use civil law to discriminate against the wealthy, and they do so in the name of benefitting the average voter.

This is theft. *The modern welfare state is the greatest engine of theft in the history of man.* Christians vote for it. Most Christians are not wealthy, and most Christians do not care anything about the Bible's doctrine of equality before the law. They pay no attention to biblical law. They vote for politicians who promise to redistribute wealth from the rich to the state, officially on behalf of poor people. Christians who live in historically incomparable wealthy societies such as the United States do not acknowledge the legitimacy of this principle of state wealth redistribution when applied to foreign aid: funds sent from their national civil governments to foreign national governments. There is not much foreign aid in any nation's budget, but almost all taxpayers are opposed to it. What they demand that politicians do to the wealthy, they also demand that politicians not do to them in the name of helping foreign populations.

The modern welfare state hopes to become heir to the capital of the wealthy. It is a false hope. Wealthy Americans will not allow this to happen. There has been a loophole ever since the early 1900s. In the United States, they have persuaded politicians to allow them to establish tax-exempt charitable foundations. Then they leave most of their money to these foundations. These foundations pursue the social goals of the rich, and they also have on their boards of trustees the sons and daughters and grandsons and granddaughters of the rich who created the foundations. So, the enormous quantities of money that the tax collectors hope to collect from the rich and the super-rich will wind up in the bank accounts of the tax-exempt foundations that are created by the rich and super-rich in order to escape the confiscation by tax collectors.

Conclusion

According to the standards set forth in the Old Testament, we live in tyrannical societies. The level of taxation that is considered normal by the vast majority of voters in Western nations was identified by the Old

Testament as tyrannical. *No civil government in peacetime should be allowed to collect taxes equal to the 10% collected by the church from tithing members.* Christian voters do not see it this way. Most of them do not tithe to their local congregations. Instead, they hand over far more money to tax collectors. They regard this as liberty.

Christians have refused to take seriously the specific warnings about taxation that are provided in the Genesis account of Egypt and the account of the creation of the first monarchy in Israel. Christians enjoy these stories as historical narratives, but they do not regard them as judicially binding today. Christians dismiss biblical law and biblical narratives as having been annulled by the New Covenant. Then they find themselves operating under secular messianic states whose politicians and bureaucrats claim the ability to plan the economy, as if they were God. They are not God. Neither was Pharaoh. Neither was King Saul.

We know where this is heading. We have seen it before.

> And King Rehoboam consulted with the elders who had served his father Solomon while he was still alive, saying, "How do you advise me to answer this people?" Then they spoke to him, saying, "If you will be a servant to this people today, and will serve them and grant them their request, and speak pleasant words to them, then they will be your servants always." But he ignored the advice of the elders which they had given him, and consulted with the young men who had grown up with him and served him. He said to them, "What advice do you give, so that we may answer this people who have spoken to me, saying, 'Lighten the yoke which your father put on us'?" And the young men who had grown up with him spoke to him, saying, "This is what you should say to this people who spoke to you, saying: 'Your father made our yoke heavy, now you make it lighter for us!' You should speak this way to them: 'My little finger is thicker than my father's waist! Now then, my father loaded you with a heavy yoke; yet I will add to your yoke. My father disciplined you with whips, but I will discipline you with scorpions!'" (I Kings 12:6–11)

In response, Jeroboam began a tax revolt. The kingdom of Israel was divided. Rehoboam kept only one other tribe along with Judah: Benjamin. The other ten tribes went with Jeroboam. Jeroboam was a bad king theologically, but when it came to taxation, he was a better king than Rehoboam.

Today, Christians live under the rule of humanistic Rehoboams. The counselors of these kings are very much like the counselors of Rehoboam. They imagine that there are no biblical limits to taxation and central planning. They imagine that they can use scorpions to afflict the citizenry. But the citizenry has the right to vote, and the citizenry is willing to accept these levels of taxation only because they believe in this maxim: "Don't tax you. Don't tax me. Tax the guy behind the tree." At some point, the public will finally figure out that they, collectively speaking, are the guys behind the tree. But until that time, they will not resist politically the level of taxation that they suffer under today.

Ideas have consequences. Bad ideas have bad consequences. Immoral ideas have bad consequences. This is a very bad idea: "You shall not steal except by majority vote."

I hope you will take a stand intellectually against this idea. I hope you will organize locally to prevent this idea from being applied to your community. At some point, the national governments will run out of money to pay the obligations of the modern welfare state. At that point, there is going to be a great default, and there is going to be a great transformation of the political order across Western civilization. Let us hope that Christians will finally learn not to trust the modern welfare state, which is messianic to the core.

Conclusion to Part IV

I do not expect any of my suggestions in these four chapters to be taken seriously by most pastors and most laymen in American congregations unless there is a huge economic crisis. The tradition of American Christians' political support for the welfare state goes back to the mid-1930s: President Franklin Roosevelt's New Deal. Theological support goes back to the late nineteenth century, when the social gospel was first introduced to Northern Protestant congregations.

If this book is read by large numbers of Bible-believing Christians in the Third World, these ideas may be accepted more readily. But Christians do not have political power in the Third World. They are voices crying in the wilderness. I hope that they will attempt to implement some of my recommendations in Part IV with respect to individual, family, and church covenants. It is better to start now than later. It is better to start small than not at all. But with respect to civil government, Third World Christians must bide their time. They must build up their churches, families, and capital. They must do what they can locally to gain experience in Christian service.

American Christian voters are not ready to hear fundamental criticisms of the modern welfare state. They really do believe in social salvation (healing) through legislation. So, why did I write Chapter 19 on civil government? First, because I think that my position is true. I have a moral imperative to write what I think is true. Second, there is going to be a monumental economic crisis which will extend into all of Western politics when the world's welfare states go bankrupt. They will not be able to meet the promises made to generations of voters. Tens of millions of retired people will find their promised incomes from the civil government cut off. They will have to go to their children for support, as parents have since Adam's generation. Today, they believe they have voted scarcity out of their lives. They have not. They will learn the hard way that political promises are not safely trusted.

This massive default on inter-generational payments will take place in all Western welfare states. It will bring into complete disrepute the whole idea of the welfare state. Hundreds of millions of Western voters will ask the leaders of the generation of the great default this question: "Why didn't you tell us?" The answer is obvious: because the politicians who sounded a warning would not have been re-elected. The public does not wish to hear the truth.

The great default will force a rethinking of the political structures and presuppositions of the humanistic West. There will be a search for explanations for how this happened. Many explanations will be offered by fringe groups as well as disillusioned political insiders. There will be a growing receptivity for the ideas that I have presented in this book. I want this book to serve as a clear-cut statement to the generation of the great default that somebody with an understanding of Christian economics sounded the alarm before Western politicians admitted publicly that there was a problem.

There are built-in negative sanctions in every covenant-breaking institution, trend, or movement. Their arrival may be delayed. They are always denied by leaders in these institutions and movements. But they always come.

It is imperative for future Christian leaders that a remnant within the churches sounds the alarm now. It will be crucial that during the crisis, critics of the welfare state be in a position to say: "We told you so. We also told you why. You did not listen. You had better listen now."

Most people will not listen until the crisis is upon them. But they deserve a warning.

Conclusion

You have now read my book. It took me about a hundred hours to write it and 57 years to research it. I began in 1960 with a question: "I wonder what the Bible has to say about economics?" I was 18 years old.

I hope you have understood the book. Most of all, I hope you understand the biblical covenant structure. I hope you also understand that this structure is basic to a correct understanding of the entire Bible. If you do not understand it, you will miss important aspects of God's requirements for His people in history. The five points of the biblical covenant are far more than just a handy way to understand economic theory.

Here is the number-one message of this book. *God requires covenant-keeping societies to establish laws enforced by the civil government that defend the private ownership of property.* God mandates civil laws against theft. Theft was man's original sin. But covenantal economic theory goes deeper than this. The dominion covenant has built-in economic sanctions that God enforces even when a society does not. First, God's law defending private property means that all forms of socialism are morally wrong. Second, socialism comes under God's negative sanctions. This is why all forms of socialism fail. I extend this analysis to the welfare state. The welfare state is morally wrong, and this is why it is going to fail in full public view.

The free market society recommended by Adam Smith and a long line of economists after Smith is closer to biblical economic theory than the writings of socialists such as Karl Marx and his followers. This is why free market societies prosper. This is why Communism failed in Red China and the Soviet Union. Free market societies did not self-consciously adopt the principle of private ownership in response to Christian economic theory. Smith was a deist, not a Trinitarian. His rhetorical invisible hand was not God's invisible hand. God blesses outward obedience. He curses outward disobedience. His common grace has blessed humanistic free market societies, and His common curse has cursed humanistic socialist societies.

My approach to economic theory is based on the biblical covenant, which means it is based on the concept of ethics: point three of the biblical covenant. My approach categorically denies the idea that economic science is morally neutral. This represents a fundamental break with free market economics as it has been taught by the vast majority of free market economists, beginning around 1880. Adam Smith was a moral philosopher, and economics was a subset of moral philosophy. It became more secularized in the nineteenth century, when it was called political economy. Today, it is entirely secularized. I am doing my best to de-secularize economics.

This brings me to the free market's accounting concept known as the bottom line.

> But prove yourselves doers of the word, and not just hearers who deceive themselves. For if anyone is a hearer of the word and not a doer, he is like a man who looks at his natural face in a mirror; for once he has looked at himself and gone away, he has immediately forgotten what kind of person he was. But one who has looked intently at the perfect law, the law of freedom, and has continued in it, not having become a forgetful hearer but an active doer, this person will be blessed in what he does. (James 1:22–25)

You now have more information about Christian economics than the vast majority of pastors possess today or in the past. You have a better understanding of economic cause-and-effect than the vast majority of citizens who have voted for the politicians who constructed and defended the welfare state. You are in a position of greater responsibility than your peers because you possess this information. What are you going to do about it? With knowledge comes responsibility.

I hope you will commit to spreading the message in this book. I hope you will become a teacher. I'm going to do what I can to help you become a teacher.

A few of you are going to become leaders. An even smaller group will become scholars who will be in a position to defend Christian economics to other scholars. This will take you a few years, but if you're young enough, you have plenty of time. I did not write this book for old people.

There is an old political rule: *you can't beat something with nothing.* With respect to the looming failure of the welfare state, nothing is better than something. But I'm not proposing nothing. I am proposing a reconstruction of economic thought, which in turn will lead to a reconstruction of the economy of the whole world. The gospel of Jesus Christ challenges every institution and every institutional arrangement of the covenant-breaking world. This certainly includes economics.

This book is written for students. There is a follow-up volume written for teachers. I plan to write a large edition for scholars. There is a volume on activism. This will take several years. But this book is sufficient to get you started.

It is not good enough to know the truth. You must also apply the truth. You must gain experience as a doer of the word. Dominion is a long-term process. It began on the sixth day of creation, and it will extend beyond the grave in the new heaven and the new earth. It is time to get started. Remember, I got started in 1960. These things take time.

Scripture Index

In any printed book on *The Christian View of [Whatever]*, go to the Scripture index. See how long it is. If it is either short or nonexistent, you may safely conclude one of the following: (1) the author is lazy; (2) there are no scripture passages in the text, indicating either (a) there is nothing explicitly biblical about the book, or (b) the author understands the Bible, but does not integrate actual Bible passages into his text. All are bad signs.

If there is an index, look for passages that appear on several page numbers. These will be passages that are central to the book's themes. Then go to these pages. See how he explains the passages. This will help you assess the reliability of the author as an applied theologian.

Boldface entries indicate a passage has been quoted or discussed at length.

Old Testament

New Testament

About Gary North

Gary North (1942–2022) was one of the most influential and prolific Christian writers, thinkers, and strategists of the last generation. He was the author of approximately 80 books on a wide array of subjects from economics, history, and social issues to ethics, theology, and ecclesiology. His 31-volume economic commentary on the Bible and his 4-volume introduction to Christian economics are veritable modern classics. After receiving his PhD in History from the University of California, Riverside, he served on the staffs of the Foundation for Economic Education, the Chalcedon Foundation, and Congressman Ron Paul. He went on to establish, with his wife Sharon, the Institute for Christian Economics, Dominion Press, *Remnant Review*, Free Christian Educational Resources, and GaryNorth.com. Thousands of his essays, articles, and columns have been published in *The Wall Street Journal*, *National Review*, *The American Spectator*, *The Freeman*, and a host of other publications. He was the intellectual mentor to an entire generation of Christians concerned about the cultural disarray of Western Civilization in general and the United States in particular.

Made in United States
Orlando, FL
05 November 2026

90231085R00157